Developing Women Leaders in the Academy through Enhanced Communication Strategies

Communicating Gender

Series Editors: Diana Bartelli Carlin, Saint Louis University; Nichola D. Gutgold, Pennsylvania State University; and Theodore F. Sheckels, Randolph-Macon College

Communicating Gender features original research examining the role gender plays in communication. It encompasses a wide variety of approaches and methodologies to explore theoretically relevant topics pertaining to the interrelation of gender and communication both in the United States and worldwide. This series examines gender issues broadly, ranging from masculine hegemony and gender issues in political culture to media portrayals of women and men and the work/life balance.

Recent Titles in This Series

Developing Women Leaders in the Academy through Enhanced Communication Strategies, edited by Jayne Cubbage

Empowering Women: Global Voices of Rhetorical Influence, by Julia Spiker

Technofeminist Storiographies: Women, Information Technology, and Cultural Representation, by Kristine Blair

Women of the 2016 Election: Voices, Views, and Values, edited by Jennifer Schenk Sacco

Adolescence, Girlhood, and Media Migration: US Teens' Use of Social Media to Negotiate Offline Struggles, by Aimee Rickman

Consuming Agency and Desire in Romance: Stories of Love, Laughter, and Empowerment, by Jenni M. Simon

Michelle Obama: First Lady, American Rhetor, edited by Elizabeth Natalle and Jenni M. Simon

Women in the Academy: Learning From Our Diverse Career Pathways, edited by Nichola D. Gutgold and Angela R. Linse

Communication and the Work-Life Balancing Act: Intersections across Identities, Genders, and Cultures, edited by Elizabeth Fish Hatfield

The Global Status of Women and Girls: A Multidisciplinary Approach, edited by Lori Underwood and Dawn Hutchinson

Developing Women Leaders in the Academy through Enhanced Communication Strategies

Edited by
Jayne Cubbage

LEXINGTON BOOKS
Lanham • Boulder • New York • London

Published by Lexington Books
An imprint of The Rowman & Littlefield Publishing Group, Inc.
4501 Forbes Boulevard, Suite 200, Lanham, Maryland 20706
www.rowman.com

6 Tinworth Street, London SE11 5AL, United Kingdom

Copyright © 2020 The Rowman & Littlefield Publishing Group, Inc.

All rights reserved. No part of this book may be reproduced in any form or by any electronic or mechanical means, including information storage and retrieval systems, without written permission from the publisher, except by a reviewer who may quote passages in a review.

British Library Cataloguing in Publication Information Available

The hardback edition of this book was previously catalogued by the Library of Congress as follows:

Library of Congress Cataloging-in-Publication Data Available

ISBN 978-1-4985-9531-5 (cloth)
ISBN 978-1-4985-9533-9 (pbk.)
ISBN 978-1-4985-9532-2 (electronic)

Contents

Acknowledgments — vii

Introduction — 1

1. At Long Last: Women Presidents Communicating Leadership at HBCUs — 9
   Jayne Cubbage

2. "You Ain't Neva Lied!": Isolation and the Meaning of Friendship for Two Sistahs in Leadership at HBCUs — 37
   Nicole Files-Thompson and L. Simone Byrd

3. Black Diamonds: African American Women Executives Embody Transformational Leadership at Community Colleges — 53
   Karima A. Haynes

4. The Impact of Maternity Leave Advice within the Academy on Work-Life Balance of Women Faculty and Administrators — 75
   Pavitra Kavya and Michael W. Kramer

5. When External Networks Bolster Internal Prestige: Establishing and Sustaining Support Systems for Black Women in the Academy — 103
   Sheryl Kennedy Haydel and Shearon D. Roberts

6. Cultivating Feminist Reflexivity and Resilience in Leadership Communication — 131
   Stephanie Norander

7	Communicating Lead(her)ship in the Academy: Navigating a Sea of Organizational Patriarchy *Laura C. Prividera and John W. Howard III*	151
8	No Gentlemen's Agreement Here: Higher Education Reflections on Being Womanist and the Dialectics Present in an African American Woman's Administrative Journey *Jeanetta D. Sims*	175
9	Enacting a Feminist Ecological Ethos of Leadership at a Christian Liberal Arts College *Sarah Stone Watt*	191
10	Contemplating Leadership: Struggles, Transformation, and Transcendence *Mary E. Wildner-Bassett*	217

Index	239
About the Editor	243
About the Contributors	245

Acknowledgments

I am profoundly grateful and delighted to have served as editor of this volume, which brings together the work and insights of several accomplished scholars. To the volume's contributors, I thank you each resoundingly for your research, willingness to contribute to this necessary and timely work—and most importantly, thank you for your diligence and perseverance. *We DID it!* Cheers to each one of you for an outstanding accomplishment and a job *WELL DONE!*

Thank you to Bowie State University for the ongoing support and encouragement of my development as a scholar and leader in my own right. I thank also my department colleagues for their encouragement. To my department chair, Dr. Otis Thomas, and Dean of the College of Arts and Sciences, Dr. George Acquaah, for their exemplary leadership and support. I would like to send a special word of thanks to President Aminta H. Breaux, the first woman appointed to lead Bowie State University, for serving as the source of inspiration for my chapter on women presidents at HBCUs (Historically Black Colleges and Universities).

To Dr. Ronald L. Jackson, II for his brotherly support and scholarly insights into my work and career, in general. You are greatly appreciated. To Dr. Loren Saxton Coleman for her sisterly support and your review, "after the bell rang." Thank you to all of my friends near and far who have lent themselves to me at any time to ensure that I would make it through and get the job done.

To my "ride share" colleagues and friends, Dr. Kimberly Moffitt, Dr. Clover Baker Brown, Dr. Heather Harris, and specifically to Dr. Leanne Bell McMannis for the opportunity to present, I hope to see each of you at the next conference. Also to Dr. Jannette Dates, Dean Emerita of the Cathy Hughes School of Communication at Howard University, I thank you for everything.

Quite literally, so many of us stand on your shoulders and we have your example of dedication, vision, and leadership to uphold on our own academic journeys.

I would also like to send a special "shout out" to my sister circle and JOMC "conference call colleagues" for our Monday chats and support sessions—*may we all be upheld.*

To Nicolette Amstutz and Jessica Tepper along with the entire editorial team at Lexington Books, I send a special word of thanks and gratitude. Thank you for your insight, diligence, and patience. Most importantly, I thank you for the opportunity to publish my work with you. *This journey has been most delightful.*

To the participants of the survey on women presidents at HBCUs, I owe a special word of thanks and gratitude—not only to the presidents themselves for their keen insights and willingness to participate and share their leadership experiences, but also to their wonderful executive assistants and administrators who helped to ensure that the interviews were scheduled and that the online surveys were completed. And yes, I will name and thank each of you here: to Dr. Brenda A. Allen, President of Lincoln University of Pennsylvania and to Ms. Vicki Reeves, Dr. Heidi M. Anderson, president of the University of Maryland Eastern Shore along with Ms. Priscilla A. London—to you, I send a REALLY BIG thank you!! I also thank Dr. Paulette Dillard, President of Shaw University along with fellow Howard University alumna Dr. Kandace Harris for that *diligence and follow-through.* I send a particularly fond word of thanks to Marion Fedrick, President of Albany State University for her gracious participation and candor and to Ms. Janet Puckett for arranging the interview. I also send a very warm and heartfelt thank you to Dr. Beverly W. Hogan, President Emerita of Tougaloo College along with best wishes for your next chapter and greetings to Ms. Vicki Clanton. An especial word of thanks to Dr. Martha G. Lavender, President of Gadsden State Technical and Community College along with Jackie Edmondson of Public Relations, Dr. Lily D. McNair, President of Tuskegee University along with Ms. Chandra Chambliss and Ms. Verna Little, Dr. Lisa Mims-Devezin, President of Southern University at New Orleans and Ms. Julia Johnson, along with Dr. Valerie Montgomery Rice, President and Dean of the Morehouse School of Medicine, and also to Dr. Adena Williams Loston, President of St. Phillips College and to her outstanding assistant Ms. Christina Butler and to Ms. Marsha P. Hall—*you are all greatly appreciated and remembered fondly.*

Finally to my family—countless as you are, I thank you for your support, encouragement, for your shoulders to cry on along with the laughs and hugs. Thank you for the guidance, direction, reminders, the legacy, and the LOVE! Most importantly, I thank Yahuah for the blessings and grace to make it all possible.

Introduction

Compiling and editing this volume has been a venture in leadership and communication, itself. The idea of this book stems from an involved and fortuitous process that began with a trip to a national communication convention in the fall of 2017. Upon landing in the city of the conference, I'd realized that a number of my colleagues had also flown in on the same flight. As we meandered over to baggage claim all the while exchanging warm and friendly hellos, hugs, and introductions, we gave one another that sisterly acknowledgment as we retrieved our "too large for the overhead bin" suitcases from the luggage carousel. Once again, we had all over packed—*we needed wardrobe options,* we rationalized. *Yeah, that's it*! After that proclamation was firmly established, we agreed to take a rideshare service together to the conference hotel, where for this year's conference we all happened to be staying. As we walked to the curbside to hail our ride, we bumped into none other than the illustrious, esteemed and dean emerita of the school of communications where all but one of us had attended and earned our doctorates from. The dean, who was also attending the conference that year, had astutely packed light and with a compact and smartly styled carry-on in tow, she skipped baggage claim and headed straight to the rideshare pickup location and was waiting for her own ride. Well, now we couldn't allow *THE DEAN* to ride alone—she must come with us, *and sit upfront*!! After all, we were riding in a very large vehicle with room to spare—even with all of our oversized bags in the back—*and no we weren't riding in a bus.*

During the ride to the hotel, we started updating one another on our latest accomplishments. After listening to the others, I jumped in and began to relate my latest goings-on, a recent trip to the Middle East for a media literacy conference for faculty and students, which culminated with my

1

giving a (near impromptu) ninety-minute presentation and discussion on media literacy and so-called Black women in the United States to an international audience, an upcoming edited volume on media literacy in higher education and more, everyone in the ride exclaimed "wow, that's wonderful, you're doing so much." The dean who was seated in front of me turned and proudly exclaimed—"I am so excited to hear about your accomplishments!" Of course, I thanked her for her kind words (blushing). The next day of the conference, I ran into one of my colleagues from the ride the day earlier who I had just met. As it turned out—she was listening closely to my "share" also and was serving as first vice president and organizer for an upcoming regional communication conference to be held during the first quarter of the following year and needed spaces filled on several panels. She asked me to submit a couple of proposals for panels and urged me to register for the conference. I told her I would do so. Of course, given my high teaching load and many other duties along with the tendency toward overwork—I didn't propose or submit any proposals, let alone register before the deadline had passed. When I finally thought about my failed promise, I emailed her and explained that I had gotten overwhelmed with work and her invitation slipped my mind—*it had*. She reassured me that everything was fine and she recommended two panels that she would like me to participate on and she informed me of the topics one, which covered mindfulness and communication and the other, women and leadership communication. Of course, I cleaned up my act, registered for the conference, and completed both presentations.

As it turns out, once the conference program had been set and posted online, an editorial representative at Lexington Books contacted me and asked about my presentation on women and leadership. A meeting was arranged and *voilà*—in a roundabout manner and after discussion on the merits of a solo work or an edited volume, a call for chapters and much labor—*here we are*—with said work, published and in hand. Though it wasn't an easy process, I recognized the importance of this assignment and opportunity. Upon hearing of the topic, I as an instructor in organizational communications and having taught courses in organizational leadership fully comprehend the gendered differences in approach to leadership and that these approaches however divergent they may sometimes be, still lead to excellence. In fact, I understood the importance, the salience and the necessity of this work and other similarly situated volumes on this subject for both women and men in the academy and beyond. Additionally, the manner in which women communicate leadership and exude leadership in their everyday lives, even when they believe no one is watching or when they think no one cares, can often determine one's next steps in life and career. Each person has leadership qualities within themselves and someone somewhere is always watching—*or listening*.

Accordingly, this work stands among a list of other edited volumes and solo works, which highlight the importance of delving more deeply into the topic of communication and leadership for women and it serves as a reminder of its timeliness. This compilation along with other similarly situated research also establishes the importance of exploring and hearing the voices of those with common experiences, of any nature, both positive and negative. These experiences serve as a reminder that we are not alone on our journey and that hope, progress along with personal and professional fulfillment are all attainable attributes of the profession. Hearing the stories of other women in the academy not only serve as a source of comfort, but those experiences, when synthesized with other pertinent information gathered from various sources, serve as a point of strategy for women navigating the complexities of a patriarchal academic realm.

The chapters in this volume represent a culmination of the lived experiences of women who are among the ranks of leadership within the academy. Not necessarily all women who hold leadership positions today, but those who are leaders—potentially every woman. One of the most poignant statements I took from writing the first chapter on women presidents at HBCUs (Historically Black Colleges and Universities) came from an interview I conducted with a president of a college in the South who was retiring after seventeen years at her post. She adeptly noted that leadership does not require a title and that it is about what you do when you are going about your everyday life, working your everyday job, showing up on time, keeping your word, getting along well with others and collaboration. "That is leadership," she said during our telephone interview. Her statements along with those from other college and university presidents about communication and its importance for women are profound. Women are urged to understand the finer points of self-expression as it relates to power and leadership from speaking up about their leadership desires, defining their own communication approach and style, communicating in a direct and clear manner along with developing the ability to listen effectively and "read the room" to determine the power play, were particularly salient highlights gleaned from writing this chapter.

As such, this work covers such themes as they intersect with the genre of leadership communication and women and meld nicely with the title of this work, *Developing Women Leaders in the Academy through Enhanced Communication Strategies*, which presumes that as women lead in their current roles and seek higher levels of office and rank in academe, they are often left to navigate in a world they are not familiar and have only relative—rather than practical knowledge of. To change the current situation—and bring to equity the number of women who are in leadership positions commiserate to the numbers of women who enroll and go on to graduate from colleges and universities in the nation each year (now at 60 percent of all graduates), the themes in several chapters within the volume call on women to become strategists. It should be noted that nothing *will* be changed, if it is *not* changed. Lack of knowledge is not an excuse—but rather an invitation to become more knowledgeable—and more strategic in the approach to leadership and communication for women at all levels of academic service.

As noted earlier, chapter 1 "At Long Last: Women Presidents Communicating Leadership at HBCUs" is born of a small research study ($N = 10$) that surveyed women presidents of HBCUs to determine the manner in which each president communicated leadership as head of her institution. Via online surveys and telephone interviews, the study's respondents convey powerful insights and revealed salient information the manner in which women presidents perceive themselves as leaders and the unique strengths they bring to their roles. Among the findings, women were able to ascend to higher levels of leadership with mentoring, they also established mentoring relationships to help others along, they spoke of the double standard among male and women leaders, and also the joys of seeing their students succeed and go on to be contributing members of society.

In chapter 2 "'You Ain't Neva Lied!': Isolation and the Meaning of Friendship for Two Sistahs in Leadership at HBCUs," Nicole Files-Thompson and L. Simone Byrd relate their experiences as department chairs at two HBCUs. One in a Mid-Atlantic State and the other situated in the Deep South. What the two chairs have in common is they formerly held faculty positions in their departments and were appointed to leadership roles after administrative shifts. Although they each state that they were not seeking leadership roles, they did what many of women do when they are tapped for leadership—they answered the call and accepted the challenge. While they have challenges, which they share through a new supportive friendship, they each allowed this experience to serve as an avenue of growth as they renewed their strength to persevere through challenging conditions.

Karima A. Haynes writes chapter 3 titled, "Black Diamonds: African American Women Executives Embody Transformational Leadership at Community Colleges," where she provides highlights of a leadership program at an HBCU which trains future leaders, mostly women of color to assume leadership positions at community colleges. These leadership roles at schools that serve students from all walks of life in various institutions have led to the increase in number of college presidents who are women today.

In chapter 4, authors Pavitra Kavya and Michael Kramer detail the results of a study which polled forty ($N = 40$) academic women at various stages of their career on the experiences with institutional maternity leave polices, titled "The Impact of Maternity Leave Advice within the Academy on Work-Life Balance of Women Faculty and Administrators." They reveal the labyrinth of advice women faculty are given by university leaders and administrators, which were labeled by women faculty members themselves as "phantom" or "cryptic" in nature. The authors establish the link between the existing mandates and the ability of institutional leadership to communicate those stated policies in order to ensure adherence to the federally mandated Family Medical Leave Act, or FMLA Act, and other internally established leave polices. Both the authors use their own experiences with these processes to inform their work, and the study will serve as a blueprint for women who also experience similar circumstances at their own institutions.

Sheryl Kennedy Haydel and Shearon Roberts detail in chapter 5 the necessity of shared narratives and sustained networks of support for Black women in the academy who typically operate within the margins of many academic institutions. The chapter titled, "When External Networks Bolster Internal Prestige: Establishing and Sustaining Support Systems for Black Women in the Academy" provides numerous examples that provide insights into the ways in which Black women gird themselves against the various challenges, often racial in nature, that they will ultimately face while serving as faculty at institutions in the United States.

In chapter 6, "Cultivating Feminist Reflexivity and Resilience in Leadership Communication," author Stephanie Norander writes on the development and sustenance of leadership pathways employing both a feminist and organizational communication approach and by drawing upon auto-ethnographic experiences of leadership. In this chapter, Norander offers suggestions for women to assist with the process of navigation of the complex academic arena through the development of both "reflexivity and resilience" via "stronger, supportive pipelines for emerging women leaders."

Laura C. Prividera and John W. Howard III both authored chapter 7, "Communicating Lead(her)ship in the Academy: Navigating a Sea of Organizational Patriarchy," which examines "the experiences, perceptions, and communication practices of women in leadership positions in the academy." In this work, the authors use grounded theory to establish the patriarchal tradition in institutions of higher learning. They also posit that women leaders experience their leadership in an environment rife with double-bindedness, which leads to phenomena such as "horizontal matriarchy," "laboring communication," and "eternal work." Prividera and Kramer also engage in a subsequent discussion of the implications for women leaders in the academy who are communicating leader(her)ship at the end of the chapter.

In chapter 8, titled "No Gentlemen's Agreement Here: Higher Education Reflections on Being Womanist and the Dialectics Present in an African American Woman's Administrative Journey," author Jeanetta D. Sims, who is both the first woman and the first African American woman to serve a dean of the college of graduate studies at her university, shares the experiences of her own journey as she details under the frame of womanist theory and a combined dialectic approach to offer suggestions on leadership strategies and other insights for female academicians.

Sarah Stone Watt, in chapter 9, "Enacting a Feminist Ecological Ethos of Leadership at a Christian Liberal Arts College," details through the establishment of a Committee on Women Faculty on her campus and the impact of such a committee held on women and their ascension to leadership roles as a matter of reinforcing the institutional mission, which reflects Christian values that serve as a representative example for faculty, students, and staff. Using feminist ecological ethē as a theoretical frame, Stone Watt posits that the newly formed committee has broadened the ability of women to connect more easily with university stakeholders at all levels through the firm establishment of "dwelling place" for women at the university.

In chapter 10, titled "Contemplating Leadership: Struggles, Transformations, and Transcendence," author Mary E. Wildner-Bassett uses an autoethnographic narrative to reveal ways that wisdom is gained through various leadership experiences that have evolved over the course of the lives of women. She notes that when women are able to share their "lived" experiences they are able to transform their lives as they provide an example to other women. Accordingly and in addition to her own story, she fuses the stories of other women and their experiences in a variety of leadership positions both in and outside of the academy. Through this work, Wildner-Bassett chronicles her thirty-three-year career by incorporating the metaphors of "heart, head, and hands" to illustrate the ways in which "women's lives and leadership can evolve."

As you explore each chapter and imagine the experiences shared within this volume, my hope is that you walk away empowered, enriched and enlivened to enhance your own leadership experiences and those of others. Also, that by reading this work, we can each be a part of the circle which advances the lore, the lexicon, and the literature of women's leadership and communication.

Jayne Cubbage, PhD
Editor

BIBLIOGRAPHY

Baldoni, John. *Great Communication Secrets of Great Leaders*. New York, NY: McGraw-Hill, 2003.

Bower, Beverly L., and Mimi Wolverton. *Answering the Call: African American Women in Higher Education Leadership*. Sterling, VA: Stylus, 2009.

Cunningham, Carolyn M., Heather M. Crandall, and Alexa M. Dare, Editors. *Gender, Communication, and the Leadership Gap*. Charlotte, NC: Information Age, 2017.

Johnson, Heather L. *Pipelines, Pathways, and Institutional Leadership: An Update on the Status of Women in Higher Education*. Washington, DC: American Council on Education, 2017.

Longman, Karen A., and Susan R. Madsen, Editors. *Women & Leadership in Higher Education*. Charlotte, NC: Information Age, 2014.

Chapter 1

At Long Last

Women Presidents Communicating Leadership at HBCUs

Jayne Cubbage

INTRODUCTION

This chapter seeks to explore the leadership and communication strategies of women presidents who lead historically Black colleges and universities. The number of women presidents at predominately White Institutions has stood at 30 percent for a number of years. Alternatively, the number of women who serve as president or chancellor of an HBCU has only recently entered parity with other institutions (non-HBCUs) and now stands at 30 out of the existing 102 HBCUs in the United States today. Now that women are advancing through the ranks and attaining the presidency at HBCUs, how is their leadership impacted by their style of communication? This study interviewed via online survey and telephone interviews ten ($N = 10$) presidents at HBCUs both large and small to gain insights into how these women are applying various communication strategies to enhance their leadership style.

Using upper echelon theory,[1] (also referred to and used interchangeably in this work as upper echelons theory), which incorporates personal perspectives and experiences that leaders bring to their positions to frame the study, the results of this study revealed that women presidents at HBCUs bring a unique perspective to their positions, while at the same time they have a keen understanding that as change is occurring within the academy, institutions of higher learning are still largely patriarchal in nature, despite the fact that the majority of college students and graduates today are women.[2] This study stands on foundational research that has well established that the way women lead is in fact different—yet those differences are not considered deficient when researchers control for personal leadership deficits.[3] Also, while operating in a largely male domain, women are noted by several studies to possess a unique temperament and approach to leadership, which affords them the ability to be both agentic and collaborative, although these two skills sets are often considered as diametrically opposed.[4] Women presidents at HBCUs belie this concept by employing both constructs in their leadership style.[5]

In order to determine how women leaders at HBCUs communicate leadership in their roles as president or chancellor of their institution, most of the respondents in the study spoke of their perspective on communication and leadership and they overwhelmingly related that the two are intertwined concepts. Many also openly discussed the unresolved issue of continued double standards for women leaders. This concept is recognized by researchers as double-bindedness, whereby in highly patriarchal cultures and organizations such as the academy, women are seen to have unrealized potential, which is limited due to patriarchy, contradiction in presentation, behavior, treatment, and accommodation.[6] When women are placed in such situations, it is argued that they are prevented from performing their best at their jobs.[7] Other studies also speak to the additional threats women of color tend to face to their credibility when they assume leadership positions.[8]

Despite the known challenges they encounter, respondents speak of the joys and rewards of leadership, such as mentoring colleagues, developing strong and prepared students, and making a difference in their work and for their respective communities—today and for years to come. Yet, women presidents at HBCUs who were polled for this study also detailed a frightening trend, which if not abated will further stall the process of bringing to equity the number of women college and university presidents to the office of the president or chancellor at all categories of universities. In aggregate, this trend includes phenomena such as the lack of awareness of leadership opportunities, the tendency of women to "play it safe" and avoid leadership positions, also their failure to speak up and articulate their desire to seek leadership positions, the lack of mentoring among existing leaders—both male and female, and self-doubt, which has been documented by Margaret Madden as the concept of "internalized oppression."[9]

Some of the respondents to this study stated that there is also a lack of awareness of training programs or too little access and information about existing programs, which is also established by the work of other scholars on this topic.[10] Of these phenomena, one president who responded to this study stated:

> We don't have nearly as many females in the pipelines for leadership opportunities. I think some of that is the old adage that they're not prepared—not ready for that. I think, females we do not speak up for ourselves as a male would. We do not go at it seriously. Whether that is "hey I want this next role, help me prepare for the next role." "I think I deserve the next role even if I don't know what it is—*I can learn it.*" We do not speak like that. We do not believe like that. We

don't ask those kinds of questions. We don't seriously challenge the status quo. I would say that is female and that is being African American.[11]

Several of the women, particularly those who were interviewed via telephone interview spoke in bold and confident tones and many of their answers were akin to the concept of *telling it like it is*. Of the failure of women to ascend to the highest institutional office at colleges and universities more often, one such president emphatically stated that regarding the dearth of women in the academic leadership pipeline in higher education, women

> tend to sit around and think something is going to happen to us. That is not the case—*we must make it happen*.[12]

Continuing, she added that women who seek leadership positions must demonstrate that they are ready to take on such roles by showing such skills in their current job with an emphasis on serving with purpose.[13] Yet another president, who responded to the study online, added that although women comprise a significant percentage of the professorate at many colleges and universities, the "pipeline to the presidency does not reflect these numbers." She also stated that mentoring opportunities are lacking for women who seek to become president of a college or university.[14]

LITERATURE REVIEW

The literature, which frames this study, provides a broad overview of themes and circumstances that situate the experiences of women in academic leadership at many institutions, particularly HBCUs. First, regarding HBCUs, in marking this historic milestone, it should be noted that upon their establishment, most if not all institutions, including HBCUs were run by White men—as was common for institutions of higher learning at the founding of the United States. Black males were increasingly selected to lead HBCUs with Martin Henry Freeman selected to run the former Avery College near Pittsburgh, Pennsylvania, and Bishop Daniel Payne leading Wilberforce University in Wilberforce, Ohio, in 1863.[15] After a series of appointments of Black men to HBCUs and PWIs alike, the first Black woman to lead a college or university of any kind did not occur until 1987 when Johnnetta B. Cole was appointed to lead Spelman College in Atlanta, Georgia.[16] Three years later in 1990, Marguerite Ross Barnett is selected a President of the University of Houston[17] and in 1995, Ruth J. Simmons is appointed as president of Smith College before going on to become the first Black woman to lead an Ivy League institution as president of Brown University in 2001.[18] Subsequently, in 2007 Julianne Malveaux was selected to lead Bennett College for Women, whereby Johnnetta B. Cole was also appointed as president in 2002 before going on to serve as the director of the Smithsonian Institute National Museum of African Art.[19] Today, there are scores of women of all walks of life who are successfully leading institutions of higher learning while at the same time advancing the legacy of their predecessors—*both male and female.*

HBCUs Today

For the purposes of this study, the focus will be trained onto HBCUs due to their established historical and current day significance.[20] For a number of years, HBCUs graduated more males than females. In the 1960s, the number began to shift as with the general population and today most HBCUs, though they are favored heavily by Black males, are often unbalanced with regard to gender ratios with women in some cases outnumbering enrolled men on various campuses at alarmingly large margins.[21] This imbalance however disturbing bodes that women who attend HBCUs earn the bulk of diplomas from these institutions. These datasets for HBCUs are reflective of earned degrees for all colleges and universities in the United States today.[22]

Yet despite these encouraging strides toward equity in the number of women presidents in leadership, all is not well with HBCUs. Several scholars or studies point to a host of challenges that create obstacles for students who need support the most when seeking higher education, such as first generation, Pell Grant eligible students from low-income families.[23] Both Rushing Daniel and Carolyn O. Wilson discuss a variety of other "challenges" HBCUs have faced in recent years such as decreased enrollment, stagnant endowments, fiscal challenges, and students who are graduating with staggering amounts of debt with few real employment prospects and the opportunity to pay off their student loans, various scandals, or the ongoing "crisis of Black colleges."[24]

Conversely, Wilson Mbajekwe, in her work *The Future of Historically Black Colleges and Universities: Ten Presidents Speak Out*,[25] notes that while HBCUs constitute 3 percent of all colleges and universities in the United States, they boast of very diverse student populations, and that collectively, they carry the primary responsibility of educating students from underrepresented groups. They also produce 28 percent of all bachelor's degrees, 15 percent of all master's degrees, and 17 percent of all "first-professional degrees" earned by African Americans. She also mentions notable successes in STEM and ROTC programs at HBCUs.[26] In one of the featured interviews of the work, Carolynn Reid-Wallace, President Emerita of Fisk University succinctly noted that HBCUs are "doing some remarkable things, but nobody knows about it."[27]

Sandra Edmonds Crew echoes this sentiment in a published work titled, "Education with Intent: The HBCU Experience" as she writes of the good HBCUs engage in, such as racial uplift and racial advocacy, empowerment, and improving the quality of life for African Americans. These institutions are open to all groups regardless of racial background, with a unique mission of serving as intellectual centers for knowledge which are designed in turn to strengthen the Black community. HBCUs are able to graduate world-class professionals with far fewer resources than their PWI (Predominately White Institution) counterparts. She goes on to argue that their relevance, debated today, is preposterous.[28]

Tiffany Mfume writes in *What Works at Historically Black Colleges and Universities: Nine Strategies for Increasing Retention and Graduation Rates*, about the primary mission for HBCUs, which is ensuring student success. In this work, Mfume stresses the notion that HBCUs are "only as good as their leaders."[29] She also notes that HBCU presidents must develop and maintain a gift for raising money for a university, while at the same time maintaining a "traditional connection to faculty and students." She writes further, citing the work of Hayes, that HBCU presidents must keep "their finger on the pulse of the university's lifeline of recruitment, retention and graduation rates, as well as changing technology, including online education."[30]

Also, according to Charles V. Willie, Richard J. Reddick, and Ronald Brown authors of *The Black College Mystique*, HBCUs possess many outstanding qualities including the care of students, diversity of the faculty, accommodation of students from all walks of life, individual enhancement along with advancement of the community imbedded within its mission.[31] And they write that, despite their ongoing "marginalization" by academe at large, they are still part of the larger dialogue on the future of education. While HBCUs are not always viewed in a favorable light, they suggested that increased efforts in explaining their mission and educational goals can go a long way in terms of reshaping the image of these institutions.[32] The authors also write on the manner in which HBCUs import the mandate of "the archetype of an educated person," as one who is able to combine academic achievement with professional success, personal integrity, and social concern to their graduates.[33] They also note that challenges notwithstanding, at the end of the day, HBCUs are multimillion dollar educational enterprises and are often a major source of Black employment in many communities.[34]

Willie et al. also discuss the imbalanced trend in male leadership at HBCUs and they posit that women often enter the presidency at HBCUs after long and illustrious careers in public service, government, and other industries. They bring with them a demonstrated excellence in the public arena and from other leadership posts at previous institutions.[35] More importantly, they write that women presidents can serve as role models to students both male and female.

No matter the state in which they find themselves today, HBCUs are undergoing a reckoning of sorts regarding the relevance and future of such institutions, which calls for dynamic and visionary leadership in the twenty-first century. Women presidents along with their male counterparts have accepted the challenge to right their respective institutions. The nuanced leadership of women is especially salient here as noted in an article by Eryn Mathewson on the impact of women leaders at HBCUs, who have in recent years overcome numerous fiscal and administrative challenges, and yet, managed to keep their respective institutions afloat.[36] Yet, in order for institutions, particularly HBCUs, to experience this brand of leadership, women must reach the upper echelons of the institutional helm—*Office of the President.*

Leadership and Opportunity–Striking While the Iron Is Hot

With a number of existing male HBCU college presidents, either entering retirement or who are nearing the end of their contractual obligations, a new era of women leaders are poised to accept the challenge of leadership in the highest form at HBCUs. For all institutions, when there is a change at the leadership level, an opportunity arises for women to assume positions previously held by men.

As part of a global trend, women have increasingly taken on the positions of president and chancellor at numerous universities. These women represent various ethnic and racial backgrounds and they hail from diverse environments prior to their ascent to the leadership post at their respective institutions. At the same time leaders from every walk of life in every kind of institution must engage in leadership communication. The work of John Baldoni serves as the foundation for the concept of leadership in this study. In his work he writes that communication leadership encompasses three main areas: developing the leadership message which is a leader stating what they want to say and do; communicating the leadership message, which is manifest by delivery of said message "verbally, mentally and metaphorically," and by sustaining the leadership message by "keeping the message alive, fresh and meaningful."[37] Baldoni reinforces these concepts by suggesting that leadership success is directly related to successful communication of the leader in an organization.

Intersections of Leadership, Gender, and Race

In addition to the work of Baldoni, other scholars discuss the barrier to effective leadership roles for women that prevent them from communicating their vision and leadership approach. Often there is a gender bias and a host of stereotypes that women must break through to even start the process. Dana E. Christman and Rhonda H. McClellan in their article, "Discovering Middle Space: Distinctions of Sex and Gender in Resilient Leadership" write on the concept of male and female leadership traits and characteristics and "markers," which they say foster workplace trends of categorization of male and female leadership styles and outcomes. They also discuss the manner in which women leaders can shape their own leadership styles, which are divergent to the gendered imperatives of society at large by undoing such harmful practices, adopting a more fluid concept of gender, and using resilience as a coping strategy to reaffirm women's leadership practices.[38]

Other authors offer salient points on the values related to women leaders and their divergent approach to gender normative rules. In a chapter titled "Narrating Gendered Leadership," Jill Mattuck Tarule, Jane Henry Applegate, and Penelope M. Earley stated that leadership between men and women can be both different and similar at the same time. They also noted that since historically men have held leadership positions, the characterization of leadership skills, traits, and the very mannerisms of leaders are often perceived as skewed toward being labeled as masculine traits.[39]

Caroline Sotello Viernes and Janelle Kappos in their work "Preparing Women of Color for Leadership," citing Walton and McDade, found that women in senior leadership positions at all universities and colleges lag considerably behind men despite the fact that women constitute a majority of students enrolled. This phenomenon persists due to continuing and pervasive racist and sexist attitudes that limit leadership training opportunities for women of color. They write citing the work of Allen et al. that, "Women from underrepresented populations face barriers because of historical, cultural, and social factors that have shaped their experience and development in American society." Further, they add that "The number of women of color administrators pales in comparison with the rising number of underrepresented students entering higher education."[40] Yolanda Moses, in her work titled, "Advice from the Field: Guiding Women of Color to Academic Leadership" echoed this sentiment noting the continued dominance of White males in leadership despite changing enrollment demographics.[41]

Regarding women of color, specifically African American women who ascend to the presidency of a college or university, Sandra Jackson and Sandra Harris conducted a survey titled, "African American Female College and University Presidents: Experiences and Perceptions to the Presidency." The coauthors write of the deeply entrenched institutional barriers for such women who seek and are appointed to leadership positions, citing the work of Quinta et al. They name those persistent and pervasive roadblocks such as systemic power among males, specifically White males, skewed and unfair hiring and promotion practices, few opportunities for professional development for women, and the tendency to track women in stereotypical and less desirable areas, along with the lack of available information about leadership roles, family "issues," and the "old boy network." Citing Vaughn, they also establish that women are taken less seriously when it comes to the male aspects of the job such as "fiscal management of the physical plant" and that they are more likely to be criticized and more harshly if they adopted a masculine form of leadership. Jackson and Harris also encourage women leaders to stand strong and to develop a "work ethic, sense of self worth, self confidence and their own leadership style."[42]

Dorine L. Lawrence-Hughes in her work titled, "She Just Doesn't Seem Like a Leader: African American College Women Presidents and Rhetorical Leadership" examines the inaugural speeches of three women leaders who are presidents at PWIs to determine the components of leadership, specifically the words and phrases that directly impact leadership and communication throughout her term as president. She stated that the presidential inaugural speech is the most listened to speech of a new president's tenure at the helm of a college or university. Lawrence-Hughes also addresses the notion of difference in leadership styles, such as "strength, self-efficacy, control, and authority—which are commonly associated with good leadership and therefore reinforce masculine models of leadership."[43] She also states that "women of color must be encouraged to develop communication competency in public address. Developing a language of leadership requires a deliberate effort to understand how language can be powerful and influential for women of color who seek leadership positions by helping them find their own voice in order to be authentic leaders."

Similar sentiments are reflected in the work of other scholars, who speak about the vast challenges encountered by women and people of color in the academy who have accepted leadership roles including unconscious bias, the missing presumption of competence generously afforded to White males, along with the idea that they must work harder to achieve similar results as men.[44]

The work of Joris Lammers and Anne Gast also offers a cautionary tale.[45] Addressing the backlash faced by women as they advance to leadership roles, they debunk the concept of a burgeoning "male minority," which is based on the opposition presented when women seek leadership and they added that as sexism persists, women will require ongoing support in order to lead effectively. They also write that women speak of not being listened to and not being taken as seriously as male colleagues and that women of color are particularly likely to report having their competence and credentials questioned. They note that this phenomenon can be costly, for an unpopular decision in an unforgiving environment can waylay a career, and fearing that they will be more harshly judged, women tend to shy away from risks. They also internalize prevailing stereotypes and discount their own leadership potential. The authors add that a lack of confidence and fear of failure can keep women from even aspiring to top positions.

In her work "Gender Stereotypes of Leaders: Do They Influence Leadership in Higher Education?" Margaret Madden offers a comprehensive viewpoint on women and leadership in the academy from the perspective of gender norms. She discusses the "think manager-think male" model, which predominates the research lexicon and frames much of the work and studies on this topic. Furthermore, she also establishes the true link between "agentic and communal" work and leadership styles that are predominant among women in leadership positions. Concomitantly, these styles are actually ascribed characteristics of women leaders. She also speaks to stereotypes and the devastating role they play on the careers of both would-be and actual leaders who are women.

Madden also notes that when stereotypes are pervasive, as they are today, women often internalize those stereotypes, which in turn reinforces society's downcast view of women and their leadership potential and capabilities—rather than the reality of their own capabilities.[46] As such women don't assume leadership positions or even think that they can. This phenomenon is termed *internalized oppression*.[47] Madden's findings are also reaffirmed in the work of Eyrich[48] who notes that women presidents are often held to a double standard in the workplace when they are leaders.

Similar themes are found in the research of Kelly Lynch McKenzie and Tammy J. Halstead who elaborate on the kinds of overt and covert gender-based *microaggressions,* which are typically defined as subtle, demeaning or sexist and/or racist behavior that women leaders experience in the form of *microassaults*, intentional or unintentional nonverbal or verbal messages, which communicate inferiority or non-belonging, *microinsults*, unintentional insults about women, which evoke benevolent sexism and ideas of how "wonderful women are"—in service to patriarchal customs and norms and *microinvalidatons,* forms of gaslighting which invalidate the feelings and experiences of women, thereby allowing the worldview, perceptions and experiences they face to remain unsupported because they are "too sensitive" or are seen as "making things up." These covert insults and slights, when practiced collectively and over time, serve to place women off-center and reinforce and maintain the male dominant status quo. The authors offer tips to women in these circumstances to overcome these challenges through the use of the following practices: *assertive accommodation*, the communication and assertion of a strong self-concept, by naming the discriminatory act along with an expression of unwillingness to tolerate said behavior, ultimately bringing it to a halt, *assertive communication*, which is used to combat and end microaggressions as they are occurring, thereby providing a "quick and direct way" to bring attention to offensive acts, *humor*, is often used in unfavorable and discriminatory circumstances as a way to diffuse microaggressive behavior without the escalation of conflict, while at the same time alerting the offender of the receiver's awareness and discomfort of the offense, *bystander interpersonal communication*, is another strategy which allows a bystander, male or female, who has witnessed inappropriate behavior to intercede interpersonally with the receiver after the fact to assist in naming and situating the sender's behavior as a microaggression with the intention to devalue one's worth, *collaborative communication* occurs when victims of microaggression band together to collectively fight discrimination and to lend voice to expression and plan of action absent of the fear of retaliation, and *inclusive communication strategies*, which involve members of dominant groups who do not face discrimination and yet are empathetic to the concerns of marginalized groups, to join in the fight to end all forms of abuse under the guise of a fair and equitable work environment for everyone.[49]

Halstead and McKenzie further state that the notion of male dominance is often dismissed and not thoroughly addressed in research. This process belies the fact that gender constructs are deeply imbedded into the fabric of many organizations and that gender is highly instrumental in maintaining the gendered status quo. They also cite the work of Bornstein who writes that women presidents must work twice as hard to prove themselves in the quest for legitimacy,[50] and they also noted that masculine environments are particularly entrenched in universities with Division-I athletic programs and medical schools.[51]

The addition of racial and ethnic bias further exacerbates the existing state of affairs when it comes to leadership and gender within the academy as women of color have been found to suffer more acutely in their roles as leaders and they are seldom given the benefit of the doubt and are often afforded no margin of error. Bornstein adds that when women of color make mistakes, they are not given a second chance. This sentiment is echoed in the work of Crystal deGregory who discusses the double standard among male board of trustees who offer no grace for women who misstep in their positions even when they are still learning the job, yet provide countless instances of "cover" for similarly situated male presidents—even some who have made severe mistakes.[52]

While commemorating the leadership achievement of women leaders at HBCUs and other institutions today, the implication of such leadership is often called into question. This notion, as noted previously, is an unfortunate by-product of slowly shifting mindsets (among both men and women and those among fellow HBCUs led by males). In order to overcome and combat these schisms, an understanding of the differences in communication styles among men and women is critical to fostering collaborative workplace engagement.[53]

Of this phenomenon, one survey respondent stated that she found it especially hurtful when disparaged by other male HBCU presidents and she stated "We're basically in the same boat." She also noted that in some cases many Black male HBCU presidents were the victims of overt forms of racism and discrimination and yet they are incredulous when they see women who have endured some different and more covert forms of racism develop the formidability to overcome barriers, become leaders of educational institutions, and still retain a firm sense and air of femininity. On this topic and reflecting the research of Jackson and Harris, who speak directly to this phenomenon in their work,[54] she stated the following during a telephone interview:

> I think when you look at it from a perspective of from a pure aesthetic point of view, you now have a female that is running everything from the grounds, to the law enforcement, to athletics to the academics ... it's like you're running a small city—or a large city and you look around you and how many female mayors do you have? How many female governors do you have? All of it fits right in the same realm. There's no way you could be well versed enough, strong enough, resilient person to be in those roles. So that's that male counterpart coming to the table and not wanting to accept that reality. And we've seen that forever.[55]

While leadership qualifications are scrutinized more closely in women leaders more often than they are among male leaders, women continue to answer "the question" about their leadership quotient or aptitude in the affirmative—*they can lead, they are prepared to lead, and YES, they are dynamic and capable leaders.*

Furthermore, while differences in leadership effectiveness and overall quality and impact are known to be identical among effective leaders both male and female, it is also well known that communication style is different and it not only varies, but it is often misperceived or misinterpreted when women are in leadership positions when compared to their male counterparts. One of the respondents to the study noted that:

> Strong communication skills are essential for women. Every word is weighed and judged more stringently than the words of a male president. Women are highly scrutinized but if competent, generally respected for our holistic approach.[56]

Yet, another respondent emphatically added that leadership and communication are inseparable and are "at the core of what you do as a leader."[57]

Accordingly, in order to learn more about the phenomenon of communication style among women leaders, this chapter surveyed female presidents of HBCUs, in order to determine their style of communicating leadership at their respective institutions and the manner in which their unique leadership qualities are able to transform their institutions where they serve.

THEORETICAL OVERVIEW

As stated previously, the theoretical frame for this study is the upper echelons theory as defined in the work of Jeff Seaton, which offers a working definition of the concept and defines it as the influencing power of the demographic composition of the top management team (TMT) and its impact on the decision-making style of that team as a form of "bounded rationality."[58] The term bounded reality is defined by researchers to connote behavior, which fails to conform to an idealized form of rationality, yet that still fosters success as the end goal. This concept is germane to the study herein as it is reflective of the results of previous studies, which firmly establish that through a gendered and masculinized lens, the ways women operate as academic leaders are deemed irrational and are thus devalued. Conversely, while the practices of such leaders are construed to seem counterintuitive, in essence they are simply *alternative*. If the result yielded is successful, and when it is, the process is valueless. Seaton further states that strategy factors high in this process, which fosters a visionary focus with an eye to the future over the day-to-day operations.[59] He also establishes that leaders show competencies that reveal the strategic direction, exploit and maintain core competencies, develop human capital, sustain an effective corporate culture, emphasize ethical practices, and establish strategic controls.

These findings are also supported in the work of Milan Franki and Sharon Roberts who offer a similar, yet more nuanced definition of upper echelon theory (UET), which fosters the allowance of self-manifestation of leadership within healthcare management systems. They define UET, an aggregate of practices, which establish that "the executive's experiences, values, and personalities significantly influence their interpretations of situations they face, and in turn, affect their decision-making process."[60] Also, Donald Hambrick offers a definition of what he terms "upper echelons theory" whereby he posits that executives base their decisions on a set of experiences, values, and personalities and they influence their interpretation of situations they face. He stated that in order to "understand why organizations do the things they do" or why they perform in the manner that they do, the biases and dispositions of their most "powerful actor"—their top executive(s), must be considered.[61] These processes are apt when examining leadership communication among women presidents at HBCUs.

METHODOLOGICAL APPROACH

As such, this study polled ten respondents ($N = 10$) about their own approach to leadership communication at their respective institutions. Geographically speaking, the numbers of women who are leaders at HBCUs today are clustered in southern U.S. states. For example, Alabama has four institutions that are led by women, Georgia has five, Maryland, North Carolina, and Texas each has three, while Tennessee and Virginia have two each. These results are reflective of the states, which have the largest concentrations of HBCUs and offer greater opportunities for women to assume leadership roles.

The method for this study was a qualitative survey, which is used by researchers to secure information about sociological phenomena.[62] The surveys were administered online and via telephone based on respondent preference. As it relates to the ongoing quest to bring or to make equitable the number of women who achieve the presidency at institutions of higher learning or at colleges and universities in the United States—of any kind, this study, as noted previously, seeks to gain more information into the insights, particularly the mind-set, level of preparation, barriers, and leadership communication styles of such leaders at HBCUs. The study employed the use of the following research questions:

> RQ1: How do women leaders at HBCUs communicate leadership at their institutions?
>
> RQ2: What barriers to communication and leadership do women leaders at HBCUs experience?
>
> RQ3: What uniqueness and quality of experiences do women leaders at HBCUs gain from their positions?

The Instrument

The online survey consisted of seventeen questions, with five Likert-scale questions about their preparedness for the job and overall job satisfaction with their current position. A total of five open-ended questions at the end of the instrument, which focused on the individual thoughts of each leader and their own personal experiences and perspective in their role as a women leader at their respective institution. Demographic questions were posed at the end of the survey, which asked for respondent name, age bracket, and the number of years in their current position. The researcher obtained IRB approval from her institution to conduct this study and provided respondents with an informed consent form.

Also, a list of study participants and their respective colleges and universities is listed in the Appendix of this chapter.

While the bulk of respondents were more than happy to provide answers to what some may deem questions, which are sensitive in nature, only one respondent requested anonymity. As a matter of courtesy due to the sensitive nature of the office of the presidency, respondent quotations and institution are omitted from the chapter. Each respondent has been numbered by order of interview completion, from one to ten. The responses have been edited for brevity.

Four respondents preferred to be interviewed via phone or paper survey and their questions were then tallied by the researcher, electronically. Answers provided via telephone were more detailed as respondents had the opportunity to offer more loquacious and detailed responses. During telephone interviews, respondents were also able to ask for additional clarification to some of the questions and provide anecdotal evidence for many of their answers.

RESULTS

As polled in the survey "Are you the first woman to serve as permanent leader of your institution?" Three respondents indicated that they were the first woman to serve as permanent head of their institution, while seven stated that they were not. Question #15 asked respondents about the number of years served in their current position with seven indicating that they held their posts between zero and five years, one respondent who held her post for 5–10 years, and two who were in their positions for ten years or more. Question #16 asks about previous leadership experiences as a university president or chancellor prior to their current appointment. Only one respondent indicated that she had previous experience as a university president prior to her current position, the other nine respondents indicated that this was their first appointment as university president or chancellor.

The other demographic question at the end of the survey asked for respondent's age, which was distributed into three groups, 45–54 with three respondents, 55–64 with five respondents, and 65–74 with two respondents in each group, respectively. These responses are a reflection of the data sets, which suggest that women wait longer to assume leadership roles and therefore trend higher in age.[63] Demographic responses also suggest that most seated presidents are in their first role as president, though they may have held previous leadership posts in other industries or as mid-range leaders in academic institutions.

For research question #1 (RQ1), which asked how do women leaders at HBCUs communicate leadership at their institutions? The following survey questions addressed this question.

Question #2: "When first appointed, how prepared did you/do you feel you were to fulfill the duties of your position?" Four respondents reported that they felt "very prepared" when they assumed their roles as president or chancellor, while five respondents indicated that they felt they were "prepared" and one respondent indicating that she was "neither prepared nor unprepared" when she assumed the role as president or chancellor at her institution. These answers most likely reflect participation in leadership programs, which highlight the importance of developing communication skills for leadership positions. It is also a mainstay of mentoring programs and mentoring relationships, which would explain the number of responses indicating that women presidents felt they were at least prepared and mostly "very prepared" to assume their leadership roles when they were appointed.

Question #3 asked respondents to rate "How satisfied are you with your ability to communicate leadership?" "very satisfied" netted seven responses and "somewhat satisfied" garnered three responses.

Question #4: "Women who are president or chancellor at HBCUs bring unique strengths and aptitudes to their roles." Nine respondents indicated that they strongly agree with this statement and one respondent stated that she agreed with this statement.

Question #8: "Describe how you believe communication and leadership intersect to impact women who are appointed as president or chancellor at an HBCU." Selected responses below include:

> The communication style of women can be both a barrier and a catalyst to a woman who is seeking a path to presidency. It is critical for women to be able to understand the power play in the room of the audience she is engaged with, which determines which style could be used at that time. Where women get diminished is when they provide too much explanation (asking for permission) as to why they arrived at a decision, versus being decisive and concluding with "the why as the required solution."[64]

Another respondent wrote that women should be clear in their ability to "articulate vision, mission strategic direction" and other decision points as president. She added that a woman's "tone and tenor" can be challenging and it is a hurdle men don't have to be concerned about.[65] Another stated that the manner in which women communicate is often evaluated along with their leadership abilities and that women must be mindful of being too "soft spoken" or "evasive" when communicating. She also pointed out the double standard of women being judged negatively for being "commanding and confident," which is an expectation for men.[66] Another added that strong communication skills were necessary in order to "be perceived as powerful, credible and self-confident."[67]

One president wrote that clarity in communication is also important, particularly when giving directions to others and gathering information. She also stated that it is helpful to provide feedback to others especially when they are "veering off from the mission."[68]

Yet, another president added:

> Communication is a greater part of being accepted as a leader. Communication is more than spoken word, it is a presence, a command, how you are able to interact from the standpoint of faculty alumni, from the donors. When you walk

into the room you are communicating a message that says I am comfortable in my skin, I can do this job, I am comfortable with all of the things that are going to come to me. That's confidence *and* you have to have self-control. You are going to get rattled a lot. You have to have self-control or you're going to lose control. It's different for men. They can have outbursts.[69]

She added that women cannot use profanity the way men in leadership can, yet she noted that "we as women can be firm, fair and friendly."[70]

Question #9 asked respondents to "describe your leadership style(s): *visionary*, leading a team toward a common goal, *coaching*, which focuses on the development of people, *affiliative*, prioritizes teamwork and collaboration, *democratic*, places an emphasis on hearing the voice of all involved parties, *pacesetting*, involves setting a high bar for standards of performance, while a *commanding* leadership style entails a leader who controls and subordinates who follow."[71] This question elicited feedback from each respondent on how they present their leadership styles at their respective institutions. The most commonly selected responses were visionary with four mentions, democratic with three selections, pacesetting with three mentions, along with affiliative and commanding with two selections each. Respondents were able to select more than one choice, and most respondents favored between one and two styles with a tally of sixteen responses in total. The most common styles, "visionary", "democratic", and "pacesetting", trend along the lines of research that state women are often more collaborative in their approach to leadership.

Question #10: "Describe your personal use of social media or social networking sites in your role as institutional leader and how you use such tools to reflect your leadership style." Selected responses below outline various personal and institutional approaches to social media.[72] Many stated that while they are wary of social media for personal reasons and prefer to keep a lower profile in their own online presence, they recognize the necessity of its use as an institutional tool and a manner to highlight the good that their school is doing through its use.

This question was posed with a frame of leadership and communication because previous research states that while many college and university presidents refrain from using social media to communicate leadership or campus initiatives or other news events, presidents at HBCUs were even less likely to engage in the practice or use of social media.[73] Among the respondents of this study, several stated that they use social media personally, while some indicated that they were working to incorporate social media more effectively, yet there were others who stated that they left those duties to the public relations or university communications office. Some even indicated that they allowed posts to be sent with their approval or allowed members of their staff to follow them around on their campus travails and post about happenings as they occurred. Some stated that they use social media very sparingly while others are enthusiastic users of the most popular platforms—even stating that while they use it, they plan on becoming more adept in incorporation of SNS into their leadership repertoire. One president indicated that she and her students actually communicate via social media and that she uses postings as teachable moments and offers suggestions to some students about their personal use of social networking sites.

Research question #2 (RQ2)—What barriers to communication and leadership do women leaders at HBCUs experience?—correlated to several survey questions including #7, which asked, "In what way, from your perspective, does communication, as it relates to leadership, impact the numbers of women who seek to become presidents or chancellors at HBCUs? In your answer please address known concerns such as a leadership pipeline for women, training programs, mentoring opportunities, and personal aspirations of potential candidates."

As noted previously several respondents spoke candidly of the notion that women are not speaking up or out often enough about their desire to assume leadership positions within the academy. This reticence can carry over to leadership positions, even when women are appointed to such positions. Respondents offered similar sentiments to question #11 which asked, "What communication challenges or barriers, if any, do you face in your current position?" and directly informs research question #2 (RQ2) as it asks respondents to discuss challenges to communication in their role as president of an HBCU. Some responses are as follows:

> I think all presidents are challenged with "being heard" when we share a message. Cascading communication and repeated messages are necessary to ensure the message is sent.[74]

Still others wrote or spoke of the challenges and barriers such as determining the amount information, how little or how much to share with an audience, or the challenge of not having enough time to meet with all stakeholders. Others stated that they had no communication barriers and enjoyed harmonious relationships with all stakeholders on their campus. Some also said that they viewed communication challenges as an opportunity for growth for themselves and all leaders.

For research question #3 (RQ3): What uniqueness and quality of experiences do women leaders at HBCUs gain from their positions? Responses to this question were procured from question #6, which asked respondents to rate their response to the statement "Mentoring is an important part of the leadership communication in my current role as president or chancellor at my institution." For this question, a Likert-scale question respondents answered that they "strongly agreed" with seven selections and three respondents who stated that they "agreed" with the statement.

Additionally, question #7, as noted previously, asked presidents to discuss how women communicate their intention or desire to seek leadership positions as president at HBCUs. When it comes to mentoring, when described as something a president or chancellor seeks or loves to do, the majority of respondents indicated that they not only benefited from mentoring in their ascent to leadership, but that they also wholeheartedly encourage and facilitate its practice in their own institutions stating in some instances that they would not be where they are today without mentoring.

The next set of responses correspond to the notion addressed in question #5 of the survey, which asked presidents to respond to the following statement: "Women presidents and chancellors at HBCUs face unique challenges in their role when compared to their male counterparts at other HBCUs and other kinds of institutions such as PWIs and HSIs (Hispanic serving institutions)." Four respondents indicated that they "strongly agree" with this statement, five stated that they "agreed" with statement, while one "strongly disagreed" with the statement. The respondents also discussed their experiences of living and existing in a "fish bowl" environment and the near constant stage like presence associated with the job of college or university president, which could be construed as one aspect of a "unique challenge." One president stated:

> It is all encompassing—all inclusive, I mean my family is part of this job. My extended family has to be a part of this job. *You're all in.* And that's what I would say for any president, is I wasn't as prepared for this aspect of the job. How you are always on. How you are always a public figure—sometimes, in certain situations, you can dive out of the way—*nope*, not when you're college president. Wherever you go you're always on—somebody will more likely than not, know who you are. Even when you are incognito, *they know who you are.*[75]

Yet another president echoed those sentiments:

> Presidents become the face of an institution. If I am out shopping, people always see you as the face of the institution, when I'm just trying to see if this lettuce is right, or whether I am attending church or with my grandchildren. No matter where you are, I stop and talk to them. I stop and talk to them even when I am on my personal time.[76]

Another president stated that she is working diligently to acculturate her campus community on proper protocols and procedures related to the chain of command. She added that complaints are a chief concern, which she prevents from becoming a larger communication challenge.[77]

Finally, question #12 asked respondents to, "Describe the biggest joys and benefits you have found in your role as leader of your institution." Respondent answers reflect the primary tenet of educational leadership which is to foster student success. Many presidents surveyed said they feel as though they were called to be "cheerleader in chief" to celebrate the successes of their students, faculty, and staff. Women who are presidents at HBCUs named seeing students excel, changing lives, and improving futures, particularly among students who enter their institutions as first-generation learners and those who have overcome so many odds to achieve, as highlights of their positions. They emphatically related:

> I lead an institution with an incredible history and it brings a great deal of joy to share the story of the resilience that has allowed the university to exist for over 153 years. The greatest benefit is the opportunity to participate in the transformative process of an HBCU education on the students who enter and leave the institution.[78]

Another stated her raison d'etre:

> Graduating my students. Student success is why we're here. When we see students who have jobs or that they are on their way to graduate or professional school, we know that we've prepared them for that. That's what's important.[79]

PRACTICAL APPLICATION AND STRATEGIES

As indicated from the responses from participants in the study, and as these women presidents at HBCUs have articulated in their own words, they are experiencing the impact of gendered ascriptions to their roles as they work to navigate around the constrictions of a male-dominated arena. By engaging in and incorporating the tenets of upper echelon theory, they recognize the need to chart their own definition of leadership as they forge ahead with competence, clarity, and communication. They are moving beyond internalized oppression and divisive interpretation of their leadership skills and ability. Women leaders of HBCUs understand the need for vision and they possess a keen awareness of the factors that may foster their success in their roles or lead to failure. Yet, despite the odds, these presidents take on all of the responsibilities, duties of the position with cheer and good will, as they understand they are shaping future generations.

The implications of women in leadership at HBCUs are clear. When women lead, they make a difference. While the presidency or chancellorship at an HBCU is a position which requires focus on matters both large and small, women respondents to this study indicate that they've clearly learned and incorporated ways to manage the macro and the micro aspect of their positions to foster a holistic approach to the twenty-first-century president.

As the women presidents who responded to this study reflect, leadership is not accidental. Women who are aspiring leaders may follow varying paths to positions of power within the academy, yet there are several mainstays, which may foster success.

Mfume recommends that HBCU leaders focus on student success by improving retention and graduation rates. She also suggests leaders excel at fundraising and budgeting, navigating board politics, strengthening academic programs, engaging with faculty and alumni along with making tough and necessary decisions and personal sacrifices, when necessary.[80] Jackson and Harris state that women leaders must be curious scholars who are current on world affairs as well as state, local, and community affairs. They add that effective leaders have expert listening skills and are open and receptive to the ideas of others, that they are open to everyone, respect everyone, and maintain a sense of humor to relieve pressure.[81] Lammers and Gast suggest that women present themselves as relentlessly pleasant, collaborative, and authoritative with a combination of masculine and feminine styles and that they should choose their battles carefully.[82] Madden suggests along with Jackson and Harris that women promote gender-neutral environments when possible as leaders. She urges women to define their own leadership style and approach, and reminds them to be ever aware of gender stereotypes that lead to a state of double-bindedness from the impact of sexism and racism as they navigate the terrain of academic leadership.[83] Also women of color are encouraged to form collaborative and supportive networks to offset institutionalized biases.[84]

One respondent to the study offered the suggestion that women who aspire to leadership begin to prepare for leadership roles accordingly:

> All women seeking the path to presidency should undergo media training and have an executive coach to provide insight and feedback. Women must develop a voice that will be heard in multiple settings. This only occurs with practice, which will include some failure.[85]

Finally, it is strongly recommended that women who are seeking to enter the ranks of leadership speak up and articulate their desire to lead. They must also learn to advocate for themselves and actively seek leadership opportunities which they must prepare for by seeking training and mentoring relationships and by grooming and mentoring others once they have ascended to roles in key leadership positions. Finally, women leaders are further encouraged to do all they can to positively influence workplace culture to make it more favorable for other women who are seeking to advance to leadership roles in the future.

As reflected in the study responses and in the literature, despite the enormous challenges facing some HBCUs today, women presidents, in many cases, are uniquely poised to step into leadership roles at their respective institutions and to get the job done—*at long last*.

NOTES

1. Milan Franki and Sharon Roberts. "Female Executives in Healthcare Management in the Context of Upper Echelon Theory." *Journal of Business Diversity*, 18, no. 2 (2018): 98; Donald C. Hambrick. "Upper Echelons Theory: An Update." *Academy of Management Review*, 32, no. 2 (2007): 334; Jeff L. Seaton. "The Relationship of Confucian Dynamism and the Strategic Leader: An Upper Echelon Theory Perspective." *International Journal of the Academic Business World*, 12, no. 18 (2018): 113.

2. Heather Johnson. *Pipelines, Pathways, and Institutional Leadership: An Update on the Status of Women in Higher Education* (Washington, DC: American Council on Education, 2017).

3. Ashleigh Shelby Rosette, and Leigh Plunkett Tost. "Agentic Women and Communal Leadership: How Role Prescriptions Confer Advantage to Top Women Leaders." *Journal of Applied Psychology*, 95, no. 2 (2010): 221–235. doi: 10.1037/a0018204.

4. Louise Morley. "The Rules of the Game: Women and the Leaderist Turn in Higher Education." *Gender and Education*, 25, no. 1 (2013): 116, 118.

5. Beverly Bower, and Mimi Wolverton. *Answering the Call: African-American Woman in Higher Education Leadership* (Sterling, VA: Stylus, 2009).

6. Kimiko Akito. "A Female Teacher and Sexual Harassment in a Japanese Women's Junior College: A Case Study." *Women and Language*, 24 no. 2 (2002): 10–11; Walter S. Gershon. "Double Binds, Ab-uses and a Hopeless Hope: Epistemological Questions and Sensual Possibilities for Spivak's *Introductory Framing of an Esthetic Education in the Era of Globalization*." *Critical Literacy Theories and Practices*, 9, no. 15 (2015): 2–4; Lotte S. Luscher, Marianne Lewis, and Amy Ingram. "The Social Construction of Organizational Change Paradoxes." *Journal of Organizational Change Management*, 19, no. 4 (2006): 493–498.

7. Akito, 10–11; Gershon, 2–4; Luscher et al., 493–498.

8. Sandra Jackson, and Sandra Harris. "African-American College and University Presidents: Experiences and Perceptions to the Presidency." *Journal of Women in Educational Leadership*, 5, no. 2 (2007): 123.

9. Margaret Madden. "Gender Stereotypes of Leaders: Do They Influence Leadership in Higher Education?" *Wagadu*, 9, no. 1 (2011): 59.

10. Felecia Commodore, Sydney Freemen, Jr., Marybeth Gasman, and Courtney M. Carter. "'How It's Done': The Role of Mentoring and Advice in Preparing the Next Generation of Historically Black College and University Presidents." *Education Sciences*, 6, no. 19 (2016): 1–4.

11. Respondent #9. Of the ten respondents to this study presidents are named anonymously by order in which they completed the survey either online or via telephone interview.
12. Respondent #7.
13. Ibid.
14. Respondent #1.
15. *The Journal of Blacks in Higher Education.* "Key Events in Black Higher Education." Last Modified on June 5, 2019. https://www.jbhe.com/chronology/.
16. Ibid.
17. Ibid.
18. Ibid.
19. Ibid.
20. Charles V. Willie, Richard J. Reddick, and Ronald Brown. *The Black College Mystique* (Lanham, MD: Rowman & Littlefield, 2006).
21. Marybeth Gasman. *The Changing Face of Historically Black Colleges and Universities.* The PENN Center for Minority Serving Institutions, 2013. https://www.gse.upenn.edu/pdf/cmsi/Changing_Face_HBCUs.pdf.
22. Johnson. *Pipelines, Pathways, and Institutional Leadership.*
23. Gasman. *The Changing Face of Historically Black Colleges and Universities.*
24. James Rushing Daniel. "Crisis at the HBCU." *Composition Studies*, 44, no. 2 (2016): 159–160.
25. Carolyn O. Wilson Mbajekwe. *The Future of Historically Black Colleges and Universities: Ten Presidents Speak Out* (Jefferson, NC: McFarland & Company, 2006).
26. Mbajekwe. *The Future of Historically Black Colleges and Universities*, 30–31.
27. Ibid.
28. Sandra Edmonds Crew. "Education with Intent: The HBCU Experience." *Journal of Human Behavior in the Social Environment*, 27, no. 1 (2017): 363.
29. Tiffany Beth Mfume. *What Works at Historically Black Colleges and Universities: Nine Strategies for Increasing Retention and Graduation Rates* (Lanham, MD: Rowman & Littlefield, 2016), 17.
30. Mfume. *What Works at Historically Black Colleges and Universities*, 1.
31. Charles V. Willie, Richard J. Reddick, and Ronald Brown. *The Black College Mystique* (Lanham, MD: Rowman & Littlefield, 2006).
32. Willie, Reddick, and Brown. *The Black College Mystique*, 4.
33. Ibid., 22.
34. Ibid., 13.
35. Ibid., 81.
36. Eryn Mathewson. "Female Presidents Are Playing Critical Roles in the Survival of HBCUs." *Theundefeated.com*, November 9, 2017. https://theundefeated.com/features/female-presidents-are-playing-critical-roles-in-the-survival-of-hbcus/.
37. John Baldoni. *Great Communication Secrets of Great Leaders* (New York, NY: McGraw-Hill, 2003), iv.
38. Dana E. Christman, and Rhonda H. McClellan. "Discovering Middle Space: Distinctions of Sex and Gender in Resilient Leadership." *The Journal of Higher Education*, 83, no. 5 (2012): 648–670.

39. Jill Mattuck Tarule, Jane Henry Applegate, Penelope M. Early, and Peggy J. Blackwell. "Narrating Gendered Leadership," In Diane R. Dean, Susan J. Bracken, and Jeanie K. Allen, eds. *Women in Academic Leadership: Professional Strategies, Personal Choices* (Sterling, VA: Stylus, 2009), 48–49.

40. Caroline Sotello Viernes Turner, and Janell Kappes. "Preparing Women of Color For Leadership," In Diane R. Dean, Susan J. Bracken, and Jeanie K. Allen, eds. *Women in Academic Leadership: Professional Strategies, Personal Choices* (Sterling, VA: Stylus, 2009), 149–151.

41. Yolanda Moses. "Advice From the Field: Guiding Women of Color to Academic Leadership," In Diane R. Dean, Susan J. Bracken, and Jeanie K. Allen, eds. *Women in Academic Leadership: Professional Strategies, Personal Choices* (Sterling, VA: Stylus, 2009), 183.

42. Sandra Jackson and Sandra Harris. "African American Female College and University Presidents: Experiences and Perceptions to the Presidency." *Journal of Women in Educational Leadership*, 5, no. 2 (2007): 119–137. https://digitalcommons.unl.edu/cgi/viewcontent.cgi?article=1000&context=jwel, 123.

43. Dorine L. Lawrence-Hughes. "She Just Doesn't Seem Like a Leader: African American College Women Presidents and Rhetorical Leadership." In Carolyn M. Cunningham, Heather M. Crandall, and Alexa M. Dare, eds. *Gender, Communication, and the Leadership Gap* (Charlotte, NC: Information Age, 2017), 233–238.

44. Lynn M. Gangone, and Tiffani Lennon. "Benchmarking Women's Leadership in Academia and Beyond." In Karen A. Longman, and Susan R. Madsen, eds. *Women & Leadership in Higher Education* (Charlotte, NC: Information Age, 2014), 10–13; Barbara Kellerman and Deborah L. Rhode. "Women at the Top: The Pipeline Reconsidered." In Karen A. Longman, and Susan R. Madsen, eds. *Women & Leadership in Higher Education* (Charlotte, NC: Information Age, 2014), 27.

45. Joris Lammers and Anne Gast. "Stressing the Advantages of Female Leadership Can Place Women at a Disadvantage." *Social Psychology*, 48, no. 1 (2017): 28–39. doi: 10.1027/1864-9335/a000292.

46. Madden. "Gender Stereotypes of Leaders," 61.

47. Ibid., 59.

48. Tess Eyrich. "Female Presidents Are Held to Higher Standards Than Males." *University of California Riverside News*. February 19, 2019. https://news.ucr.edu/articles/2019/02/19/female-presidents-are-held-higher-standards-males.

49. Kelly Lynch McKenzie, and Tammy J. Halstead. "Narrowing the Leadership Gap: Communication Strategies to Combat Microagressions." In Carolyn M. Cunningham, Heather M. Crandall, and Alexa M. Dare, eds. *Gender, Communication and the Leadership Gap* (Charlotte, NC: Information Age Publishing, 2017), 37–41.

50. McKenzie and Halstead. "Narrowing the Leadership Gap: Communication Strategies to Combat Microagressions," 66; Rita Bornstein. "Presidents and the Big Picture." *The Chronicle of Higher Education*, 54, no. 40 (2008). http://eds.b.ebscohost.com.proxy-bs.researchport.umd.edu/eds/detail/detail?vid=4&sid=90edd522-b3df-469d-bbf0-1d5e7b7ca437%40sessionmgr102&bdata=JnNpdGU9ZWRzLWxpdmU%3d#AN=edsgcl.179980375&db=edsgbc.

51. McKenzie and Halstead. "Narrowing the Leadership Gap: Communication Strategies to Combat Microagressions," 69.

52. Crystal deGregory. "Where Have All of the Black Woman HBCU Presidents Gone?" *HBCU Digest*, November 28, 2016. https://hbcudigest.com/where-have-all-the-black-women-hbcu-presidents-gone/.

53. Stephanie K. Johnson, Susan Elaine Murphy, Selamawit Zewdie, and Rebecca J. Reichard. "The Strong Sensitive Type: Effects of Gender Stereotypes and Leadership Prototypes on the Evaluation of Male and Female Leaders." *Organizational Behavior and Human Decision Processes*, 106, no. 1 (2008): 39–60. doi: 10.1016/j.obhdp.2007.12.002.; Uta Klein. "Gender Equality and Diversity Politics in Higher Education: Conflicts, Challenges and Requirements for Collaboration." *Women's Studies International Forum*, 54, no. 1 (2016): 147–156. http://dx.doi.org/10.1016/j.wsif.2015.06.017.

54. Jackson and Harris. "African American Female College and University Presidents," 123.

55. Respondent #9.

56. Respondent #3.

57. Respondent #5.

58. Seaton. "The Relationship of Confucian Dynamism and the Strategic Leader," 113.

59. Ibid., 113–114.

60. Franki and Roberts. "Female Executives in Healthcare Management in the Context of Upper Echelon Theory," 98.

61. Hambrick. "Upper Echelons Theory: An Update," 334.

62. John W. Creswell and J. David Creswell. *Research Design: Qualitative, Quantitative and Mixed Methods Approaches* (Los Angeles, CA: Sage, 2018); Carol A. B. Warren and Tracy X. Karner. *Discovering Qualitative Methods, Field Research, Interviews and Analysis* (Los Angeles, CA: Roxbury Publishing, 2015).

63. Rita Borenstein. "Women and the Quest for Presidential Legitimacy," In Diane R. Dean, Susan J. Bracken, and Jeanie K. Allen, eds. *Women in Academic Leadership: Professional Strategies, Personal Choices* (Sterling, VA: Stylus, 2009), 209.

64. Respondent #1.

65. Respondent #5.

66. Respondent #7.

67. Respondent #3.

68. Respondent #6.

69. Respondent #7.

70. Ibid.

71. Daniel Coleman, Richard Boyatzis, and Anne McKee. *Primal Leadership* (Boston, MA: Harvard Business Review Press, 2013), 53–54.

72. Gasman. *The Changing Face of Historically Black Colleges and Universities*.

73. Evelyn H. Thrasher. "The Links of LinkedIn: Impression Management," In Carolyn M. Cunningham, Heather M. Crandall, and Alexa M. Dare, eds. *Gender, Communication and the Leadership Gap* (Charlotte, NC: Information Age Publishing, 2017), 312.

74. Respondent #6.

75. Respondent #9.

76. Respondent #7.
77. Respondent #10.
78. Respondent #4.
79. Respondent #6.
80. Mfume. *What Works at Historically Black Colleges and Universities*, 7.
81. Jackson and Harris. "African American Female College and University Presidents," 124–125.
82. Lammers and Gast. "Stressing the Advantages of Female Leadership Can Place Women at a Disadvantage," 30–31.
83. Madden. "Gender Stereotypes of Leaders," 70–71.
84. Ibid., 77–78.
85. Respondent #1.

BIBLIOGRAPHY

Akito, Kimiko. "A Female Teacher and Sexual Harassment in a Japanese Women's Junior College: A Case Study." *Women and Language*, 24, no. 2 (2002): 8–13. https://search-proquest-com.proxy-bs.researchport.umd.edu/openview/bf09d243c87b097424b89214b6353d2a/1?cbl=31040&pq-origsite=gscholar.

Baldoni, John. *Great Communication Secrets of Great Leaders*. New York, NY: McGraw-Hill, 2003.

Bornstein, Rita. "Presidents and the Big Picture." *The Chronicle of Higher Education*, 54, no. 40 (2008). http://eds.b.ebscohost.com.proxy-bs.researchport.umd.edu/eds/detail/detail?vid=4&sid=90edd522-b3df-469d-bbf0-1d5e7b7ca437%40sessionmgr102&bdata=JnNpdGU9ZWRzLWxpdmU%3d#AN=edsgcl.179980375&db=edsgbc.

Borenstein, Rita. "Women and the Quest for Presidential Legitimacy." In *Women in Academic Leadership: Professional Strategies, Personal Choices*, edited by Diane R. Dean, Susan J. Bracken, and Jeanie K. Allen, 208–237. Sterling, VA: Stylus, 2009.

Bower, Beverly L., and Mimi Wolverton. *Answering the Call: African American Women in Higher Education Leadership*. Sterling, VA: Stylus, 2009.

Christman, Dana E., and Rhonda H. McClellan. "Discovering Middle Space: Distinctions of Sex and Gender in Resilient Leadership." *The Journal of Higher Education*, 83, no. 5 (2012): 648–670.

Coleman, Daniel, Richard Boyatzis, and Anne McKee. *Primal Leadership*. Boston, MA: Harvard Business Review Press, 2013, 53–54.

Creswell, John W., and J. David Creswell. *Research Design: Qualitative, Quantitative and Mixed Methods Approaches*. Los Angeles, CA: Sage, 2018.

Cunningham, Carolyn M., Heather M. Crandall, and Alexa M. Dare, eds. *Gender, Communication, and the Leadership Gap*. Charlotte, NC: Information Age, 2017.

deGregory, Crystal. "Where Have All of the Black Woman HBCU Presidents Gone?" *HBCU Digest*, November 28, 2016. https://hbcudigest.com/where-have-all-the-black-women-hbcu-presidents-gone/.

Eyrich, Tess. "Female Presidents Are Held to Higher Standards Than Males." *University of California Riverside News*. February 19, 2019. https://news.ucr.edu/articles/2019/02/19/female-presidents-are-held-higher-standards-males.

Gangone, Lynn M., and Tiffani Lennon. "Benchmarking Women's Leadership in Academia and Beyond." In *Women & Leadership in Higher Education*, edited by Karen A. Longman, and Susan R. Madsen, 3–22. Charlotte, NC: Information Age, 2014.

Gasman, Marybeth. *The Changing Face of Historically Black Colleges and Universities*. The PENN Center for Minority Serving Institutions, 2013. Retrieved from: https://www.gse.upenn.edu/pdf/cmsi/Changing_Face_HBCUs.pdf.

Gershon, Walter S. "Double Binds, Abuses and a Hopeless Hope: Epistemological Questions and Sensual Possibilities for Spivak's *Introductory Framing of an Esthetic Education in the Era of Globalization*." *Critical Literacy Theories and Practices*, 9, no. 15 (2015): 4–16. https://www.academia.edu/11672375/Double-binds_Ab-uses_and_a_Hopeless_Hope_Epistemological_Possibilities_and_Sensual_Questions_for_Spivaks_Introductory_Framing_of_An_Aesthetic_Education_in_the_Era_of_Globalization.

Higginbotham, Elizabeth. "Re-framing the Discussion: How White Male Supremacy Continues to Obscure the Reality of Gender in Higher Education." In *The "Woman Question" and Higher Education: Perspectives on Gender and Knowledge Production in America*, edited by Ann Mari May, 119–131. Northampton, MA: Edward Elgar Publishing, 2008.

Hodges, Carolyn R., and Olga M. Welch. *Truth Without Tears: African-American Women Share Lessons in Leadership*. Cambridge, MA: Harvard Education Press, 2018.

Jackson, Sandra, and Sandra Harris. "African American Female College and University Presidents: Experiences and Perceptions to the Presidency." *Journal of Women in Educational Leadership*, 5, no. 2 (2007): 119–137. https://digitalcommons.unl.edu/cgi/viewcontent.cgi?article=1000&context=jwel

Johnson, Heather L. *Pipelines, Pathways, and Institutional Leadership: An Update on the Status of Women in Higher Education*. Washington, DC: American Council on Education, 2017.

Johnson, Stephanie K., Susan Elaine Murphy, Selamawit Zewdie, and Rebecca J. Reichard. "The Strong Sensitive Type: Effects of Gender Stereotypes and Leadership Prototypes on the Evaluation of Male and Female Leaders." *Organizational Behavior and Human Decision Processes*, 106, no. 1 (2008): 39–60. doi: 10.1016/j.obhdp.2007.12.002.

Kellerman, Barbara, and Deborah L. Rhode "Women at the Top: The Pipeline Reconsidered." In *Women & Leadership in Higher Education*, edited by Karen A. Longman, and Susan R. Madsen, 23–40. Charlotte, NC: Information Age.

Klein, Uta. "Gender Equality and Diversity Politics in Higher Education: Conflicts, Challenges and Requirements for Collaboration." *Women's Studies International Forum*, 54, no. 1 (2016): 147–156. http://dx.doi.org/10.1016/j.wsif.2015.06.017.

Lammers, Joris, and Anne Gast. "Stressing the Advantages of Female Leadership Can Place Women at a Disadvantage." *Social Psychology*, 48, no. 1 (2017): 28–39. doi: 10.1027/1864-9335/a000292.

Longman, Karen A., and Susan R. Madsen, Editors. *Women & Leadership in Higher Education*. Charlotte, NC: Information Age, 2014.

Luscher, Lotte S., Marianne Lewis, and Amy Ingram. "The Social Construction of Organizational Change Paradoxes." *Journal of Organizational Change Management*, 19, no. 4 (2006): 491–502. doi: 10.1108/09534810610676680.

Lynch McKenzie, Kelly and Tammy J. Halstead. "Narrowing the Leadership Gap: Communication Strategies to Combat Microagressions." In *Gender, Communication and the Leadership Gap*, edited by Carolyn M. Cunningham, Heather M. Crandall, and Alexa M. Dare, 37–41. Charlotte, NC: Information Age Publishing, 2017.

Madden, Margaret. "Gender Stereotypes of Leaders: Do They Influence Leadership in Higher Education?" *Wagadu*, 9, no. 1 (2011): 55–88. http://sites.cortland.edu/wagadu/wp-content/uploads/sites/3/2014/02/genderStereotypes.pdf.

Mathewson, Eryn. "Female Presidents Are Playing Critical Roles in the Survival of HBCUs." *Theundefeated.com*, November 9, 2017. https://theundefeated.com/features/female-presidents-are-playing-critical-roles-in-the-survival-of-hbcus/.

Mattuck Tarule, Jill, Jane Henry Applegate, Penelope M. Early, and Peggy J. Blackwell. "Narrating Gendered Leadership." In *Women in Academic Leadership: Professional Strategies, Personal Choices*, edited by Diane R. Dean, Susan J. Bracken, and Jeanie K. Allen, 31–49. Sterling, VA: Stylus, 2009.

Morley, Louise. "The Rules of the Game: Women and the Leaderist Turn in Higher Education." *Gender and Education*, 25, no. 1 (2013): 116–131. http://dx.doi.org/10.1080/09540253.2012.740888.

Moses, Yolanda. "Advice From the Field: Guiding Women of Color to Academic Leadership," In *Women in Academic Leadership: Professional Strategies, Personal Choices*, edited by Diane R. Dean, Susan J. Bracken, and Jeanie K. Allen, 181–207. Sterling, VA: Stylus.

Shelby Rosette, Ashleigh, and Leigh Plunkett Tost. "Agentic Women and Communal Leadership: How Role Prescriptions Confer Advantage to Top Women Leaders." *Journal of Applied Psychology*, 95, no. 2 (2010): 221–235. doi: 10.1037/a0018204.

Sotello Viernes Turner, Caroline, and Janell Kappes. "Preparing Women of Color for Leadership." In *Women in Academic Leadership: Professional Strategies, Personal Choices*, edited by Diane R. Dean, Susan J. Bracken, and Jeanie K. Allen, 149–170. Sterling, VA: Stylus, 2009.

Thrasher, Evelyn H. "The Links of LinkedIn: Impression Management." In *Gender, Communication and the Leadership Gap*, edited by Carolyn M. Cunningham, Heather M. Crandall, and Alexa M. Dare, 311–326. Charlotte, NC: Information Age Publishing, 2017.

Warren, Carol A. B., and Tracy X. Karner. *Discovering Qualitative Methods, Field Research, Interviews and Analysis*. Los Angeles, CA: Roxbury Publishing, 2015.

APPENDIX A

Survey Respondents And Institution

President/Chancellor	Institution	Location
Brenda A. Allen	Lincoln University (Pennsylvania)	Lincoln University, PA
Heidi M. Anderson	University of Maryland Eastern Shore	Princess Anne, MD
Paulette R. Dillard	Shaw University	Raleigh, NC
Marion Fedrick	Albany State University	Albany, GA
Beverly W. Hogan, *President Emerita*	Tougaloo College	Tougaloo/Jackson, MS
Martha G. Lavender	Gadsden State Community College	Gadsden, AL
Lily D. McNair	Tuskegee University	Tuskegee, AL
Lisa Mims-Devezin	Southern University at New Orleans	New Orleans, LA
Valerie Montgomery Rice	Morehouse School of Medicine	Atlanta, GA
Adena Williams Loston	St. Phillips College	San Antonio, TX

Chapter 2

"You Ain't Neva Lied!"
Isolation and the Meaning of Friendship for Two Sistahs in Leadership at HBCUs

Nicole Files-Thompson and L. Simone Byrd

INTRODUCTION: HARD DAYS MAKE FAST FRIENDS

Our former professor from the HBCU (Historically Black College and University) that we had both attended for graduate school, at different times, brought us together. Ever in need of her mentorship, serendipitously, we had both arranged to lunch with her while attending an academic conference. She insisted that the two of us, the young Black female associate professors serving as department chairs at HBCUs calling on her, meet. Perhaps because of her own experiences in departmental leadership at an HBCU, she sensed that the two of us would find in each other what we were not finding at our institutions. The introduction proved invaluable. From our first conversation, we found solace in that we were not alone in our experiences of isolation, disillusionment, and stress. We quickly bonded, chatting several times a week via text message, and having long phone calls biweekly after the conference.

We both chair communication departments at public HBCUs, however, our institutional characteristics are very different. One is a small liberal arts university in a mid-Atlantic state, with a department of six full-time faculty offering two concentrations serving fewer than 200 students. The other is a small regional comprehensive university in the Deep South, with a department of nine full-time faculty offering six concentrations serving more than 300 students. Despite these differences, whenever one of us would reach out to talk about something that happened that day, it was as if we were on the same campus, living the same life. In the regularity in which we share our experiences with one another, we exercise solidarity. We also exercise understanding. "In the comfort of daily conversations, through serious conversation and humor, African American women as sisters and friends affirm one another's humanity, specialness, and right to exist."[1]

There is substantive meaning-making even when our response to the other's text message is a simple "emphasis reaction," emoji, or graphics interchange format (GIFs). This type of quick response explicitly affirms the sender's message while simultaneously affirming the realities of the high demands of our time that comes with serving at an HBCU. In every exchange, there exists a dynamic of mutual support and growing relational kinship. Therefore, the purpose of this essay is to encourage *friendship* as an enhanced communication strategy for women in academic leadership. In this context, we explore the themes that emerged from an informal interview developed as a means to articulate our lived experiences as young Black women navigating the role of department chair. "When African-American women use dialogues in assessing knowledge claims, we might be invoking ways of knowing that are also more likely to be used by women."[2] Situated in Black feminist epistemology, then, we offer reflections about the communication dynamics that have challenged us in solidarity.

Where we have experienced the isolation of leadership at the intersections of age, race, and gender, through analysis of our experiences we find meaning in our friendship. Different from formal and even informal mentoring relationships, *friendship*—purely having someone to talk to, having someone that "gets it"—within the same peer group and leadership role at similar institutions, has been key in our developing leadership in the academy. As such, we uphold the epistemological significance dialogue in both our friendship and the exercise of writing this essay. Friendship among young Black women in the academy is an inherent threat to the status quo. Entering scholarship *friend*-authors instead of coauthors is a decided act of resistance.

The peculiarity of academia rests at the intersections of knowledge production, gatekeeping, and capital fosters a competitive and guarded culture of insecurity. Situating our personal narratives as scholarly work affirms the methodological breadth of Black feminism yet makes us vulnerable.[3] As a feminist practice, the "narrativizing process involves analysis, self-reflexivity, and making judgment, it becomes an important means through which to reveal and illuminate complexities of our actions, complexities which are often ignored as women of color."[4] We embrace our vulnerability in the communicative act of resistance of telling the reality of our lived experience as "'trustworthy, valid, and useful knowledge.'"[5]

TRIAL BY FIRE: THE TRANSITION TO CHAIR

Women in leadership positions benefit greatly from mentoring, and women with marginalized identities benefit at an even greater level from career guidance.[6] Although we came to departmental leadership at different points in our careers, neither of us became department chairs at the time because it was planned or intentional. Additionally, neither of us really received formal career guidance or mentorship. Furthermore, as often happens at HBCUs, there was an absence of leadership, due to personnel factors such as retirements and resignations which, as a result, created a need. When no one else would step up, external mentors encouraged us to apply for these positions. However, we did so with an immense feeling of trepidation. This is because, for example, in our observations as faculty members prior to assuming these administrative roles, there were perceived downsides which included lack of departmental funds, and more importantly, dealing with faculty personnel and collegiality issues. (The chapter authors will hereafter be referred to as Nicole Files-Thompson [NFT] and L. Simone Byrd [LSB].)

NFT: I had just finished my third year as an assistant professor at the university, and I had only been in academia for four years. . . . At that point, I would say I was both willing and reluctant when the opportunity to become chair presented itself. I had done a lot of admin work building a new department, which made me go ahead and think about if I could be chair. So in that respect, I was willing to put my name in the ring. I was reluctant because I was not tenured and you know a department chair definitely should be tenured. I knew that I didn't have the power that was necessary. After talking to my external mentor about me putting my hat in the ring, it meant I was going to have to go up for tenure two years early to be able to get things done. . . . I saw a lot of work ahead of me. *Laughs*.

LSB: The situation that *slight sigh* emerged for me to be able to become department chair was an internal search after the retirement of the previous department chair who had been in the position for at least twenty years. I was an associate professor for four years already but I was very reluctant. I think that I saw the position from the lens of working in a department that wasn't exactly *overly* collegial through the years. So, yeah that type of behavior turned me all the way off. I definitely did *not* want the position. I really fought it tooth and nail and the other thing that sort of emerged for me was I also didn't want to give up the freedom that I had as a faculty member because I sort of knew that becoming a department chair meant longer hours, I had to be on campus more, etc. However, I did begin to embrace things; especially when I saw the positive things I could do for students beyond my previous role.

We anticipated an increased workload, but we underestimated the amount of work we would have to do just to figure out everything we had to do as chairs. Specifically, we struggled to find resources that gave us the full list of responsibilities and duties at department chairs. Moreover, we didn't have our former department chairs to rely on, and our universities offered no formal training or mentoring.

NFT: When I was appointed I asked, *chuckle,* specifically the administrator who gave me the position, "Oh, is there a handbook or something for being chair?" and they were like "No, um . . . you can look in the CBA," which is our collective bargaining agreement. It had short one paragraph about chair responsibilities. *laughs* So, everything was very much, I have to find out, figure it out. I had to ask a million questions. I had to ask for meetings with administrators so that I could ask questions.

LSB: It was absolutely on the job training and trial by fire; there was nothing. They throw you in the deep end of the pool and it is sink or swim. It was all let me figure it out, and no one willing to say let me make this—let me tell you these five things that are important for you to know. *Nothing* like that! I have always heard that young men were intentionally groomed; being sent to administrative meetings on the chair's behalf . . . you know . . . exposure. I wasn't afforded any of those opportunities. I was handed a stack of folders and told to handle the fires that needed to be put out. *That was my first day.* Information was there, but I had to search for it. I decided to just ask questions. The department's administrator was great; she helped to fill in a lot of the gaps, but as far as someone over me and anchored in the department, there was no one to say, "Well you should make sure you do these things," or "These are the things that are written," or "This is a calendar to go by," Nothing like that. *Laughs*

During that first year, we did figure enough of it out. Thankfully, we both had external mentors who had held a variety of leadership positions to call when we were at a loss, or particularly challenged. However, we largely worked in the same way that other women of color in leadership tend toward self-reliance and personal diligence.[7] That we needed to learn the rules so that we could play the game was intuitive. "African American women learned to identify how the internal politics operated and developed strategies to decipher the organizational bureaucracy. By learning how to play the game skillfully, these women learned how to become politically savvy and navigate around potential organizational landmines."[8] Adaptability and acuity emerged as salient features of navigating the first year with a lack of institutional support.

The isolation that comes with moving from peer to supervisor was a particular challenge that left us both feeling alone. We were in some cases, blindsided, and unprepared for the shift in our interpersonal relationships with colleagues that we once had positive and supportive relationships with.

NFT: When I became chair, I thought that it (working as a team) would be very much continued, like "let's help each other out," and that was my attitude. Like, the things that we had difficulties with, now that I am in the position to ask about and make changes . . . my strategy was "I want to make things better for everyone," but then I felt like my colleagues were very much like, *short pause* "You're trying to do too much" or didn't feel like I was the authority

... or that I should continue to bounce everything off of them, or get their permission for everything. I guess like we were before ... but, that's because we didn't have leadership and we were just making it work with no structure! So now, I didn't need to get permission for or check in about, or give a report of everything I did and every conversation I had with administration ... and I had way more on my plate and I didn't think that they understood.

LSB: That first year was just so stressful and tough. I didn't like it at all; I think I let some people intimidate me. There were at least two bullies I had to deal with often. I was disappointed that I let them get to me like that! I found myself thinking about how much I missed my privacy and solitude. I'm an introvert at heart, so I didn't need all that external stimulation. I just missed what I had before I transitioned into the chair position. Of course, things weren't all negative, but I did feel extremely isolated and I felt like people who I was close to when I was only in the faculty role and friendly with; now they were just acting strange with me ... like, they had no idea who I was. *Sigh* I was just being treated with a long-handled spoon. All of a sudden, I had to establish friendships outside of the department. I'd already done that, but now the shift was palpable. I watch people's behaviors and ... you can tell who is going to give you attitude and who is going to really help and support you. I learned those lessons and paid close attention to those actions far before I became a chair. Then, it was crazy because some of these same people, who were acting funny, now wanted "favors" from me. Some of them also would only speak to me on certain days or if it benefited them. Again, the whole *favor* thing. I just felt used. It made me not trust certain people.

Our experiences aren't unique as these dynamics also function in non-academic settings. For example, researchers found that African American women executives, in general, are often placed in positions where they are the only one like them; both in terms of race and gender, thus adding the layer of isolation, which reveals itself through a series of limited and distanced interpersonal communications.[9]

SILENCED AND DISMISSED: LEADING AT THE INTERSECTIONS OF AGE AND RACE

Marginalized identities such as class, gender, age, sexuality, and nationality often emerge as more salient features of marginalization on an HBCU campus, where most of the population is Black. Moreover, patriarchal hegemony is maintained in African American communities, broadly.[10] "In their goal of dispelling the myths about African American women and making Black women acceptable to wider society, some historically Black colleges may also foster Black women's subordination."[11]

NFT: Among faculty, men speak and women listen, for example at faculty meetings and in committees. . . . And a lot of this is because the higher ranks are dominated by men . . . men are very much the people with voices that always want to be heard and always want to speak . . . they're the one's always championing, or, you know, disrupting ideas . . . they're the ones that speak the loudest, they're the ones that dominate conversations . . . and I feel like woman are silenced, particularly junior faculty . . . they have no voice, they're intimidated, I'd even say bullied in some instances I've witnessed.

LSB: It's still super male-dominated although there are women; some deans, other chairs, uh . . . but it's . . . it's very rooted . . . well . . . wait a second; it's *significantly* rooted in. "*Southerness*," so it's very, very . . . in a way the undercurrent is very patriarchal and in some ways a bit sexist. I am not born nor raised in the South, so . . . yeah, there are definitely norms that are very different from how my parents raised me. So . . . yeah, here at the "top," a lot of the top decision-makers are men and it sometimes effects my ability to lead because I get questioned about decisions sometimes which is super irritating. It's hard not to talk back, but I choose my battles. Also, if I try to share with someone my experience or something I may notice in terms of gender bias or discrimination I am sort of written off or I'm sort of just dismissed or minimized. I am told, "Sexism at an HBCU? *Really*? Nah, that can't be," or "Oh, you know I don't think that really exists; it's just all in your head," so that can become a bit annoying because I think there's this idea that because it is a historically Black college or university that there's no sexism on campus which is absolutely . . . uh, untrue. Yeah, a *major* misconception!

As Black women on campus, we are acutely aware of sexism that is normalized, politicized, and communicated in subtle and not so subtle ways as those "isms" are reinforced and therefore, create the space for those conditions to be not only amplified but also contextualized within the institutional culture. For example, "Black women, including faculty and administrators on historically Black campuses, experience and must deal with not only the effects of racism, but also those of sexism. Racism and sexism may be so fused in a given situation that it is difficult to tell which is which."[12]

Thus, as department chairs, the necessity to navigate the power dynamics at play heightens our awareness and interactions with gendered micropolitics that "act as a demonstration micropolitics"[13] of how patriarchal power is practiced not just possessed."[14]

LSB: It was said that "I was the best female boss that they ever had." At first, I was like . . . in my head, "*Wait. What?*" Next, I vividly remember texting another girlfriend in higher ed later that day and she responded, "SMH"; shaking my head. I responded, "Right. Like, who actually forms their lips to say that?" I also sent the straight face emoji and the emoji with the woman with her hand on her forehead as if to say, "Good grief!" Overall, I just, you know . . . walked away feeling a bit odd about that because why couldn't I be one of the best leaders you ever worked with or have been supervised by? Why did my gender need to be mentioned at all? Would you say to a man, "Hey, Bob, you're the best male boss I've ever had?" Probably not. That was very disconcerting for me and it actually said a lot to me about the attitude, disposition of the person who said it.

NFT: Male colleagues speak about other female colleagues in gendered ways like "what about their family? What about their kids?" . . . there are situations where I feel like they are speaking to me in the way that they are because I am a woman. . . . I had a conversation with another department chair, who is male, about another woman who was (long pause) ambitious and wanted to have leadership roles on campus and he was saying "she's not doing it in the right steps" and "when you have kids you want to slow down." And, this same person has been very supportive of me, so I had to say "well you didn't say those things in terms of what my steps should be, or what first things first are, or I should do this before I do that, or I shouldn't strive to do certain things." So in general, I think that the implicit boundaries are that woman can work, but should not focus too much on climbing administrative ladders from faculty positions. Now we have a lot of women in leadership, but it's largely in nonacademic units. But in terms of faculty and climbing, men are typically in the leadership roles, we do not have women who are full professors.

Scholarly communities often reify racialized gender politics. Ideologically, even academic settings are prone to uphold a racialized gender hierarchy. Furthermore, even institutions such as an HBCU can and should work to "maintain its credibility as defined by the larger population in which it is situated and from which it draws its basic, taken-for-granted knowledge. For instance, if scholarly communities stray too far from widely held beliefs about Black womanhood, they run the risk of being discredited."[15]

The microaggressions we have experienced can be seen as tactics that silence women on campus, and keep them marginalized and "in their place." In our leadership roles, age has also represented a site where we should be subordinated.

NFT: Because I am young, and a woman, I definitely see that there are patterns, more so with other women in my experience. From older faculty within the department, but older administrators. An administrator has told me I was "incredulous" that, and other instances have made me feel like their attitude was "little girl sit down." I definitely see ageism. The lack of respect, or that I'm not expected to know what I am doing . . . and it's not just that I am young, it's that I am a young woman. I don't feel that people will speak to me or say the things that they say to me if I was a young man among the faculty in my department, I often get that same sense of "they are older and wiser," and they kind of speak to me in ways that are like instruction, or offer unsolicited advice on actions I should take, even though they are untenured, and I have more overall experience than them, have been at the university longer.... It's really just blatant, because even when I try to give faculty development advice, it's like I can't tell them anything. They can be very dismissive. That's a feeling I get from administrators as well. It's a stark contrast to the faculty who are the same age as me or younger—they always make me feel appreciated and respected. They think that I am qualified—they respect my leadership. They respect my intellect. They respect my research. They get my work ethic.

LSB: So, for me; being young and a woman, for the faculty that we are in the same age range and have generational similarities, the vibe is different; more respectful. They outwardly go out of their way to show support and offer a kind word to let you know they appreciate you. While older faculty and administrators are blatantly disrespectful, it's an undercurrent. It's like if you are a younger woman, I would say, less than 50 or 40 that you're looked at a little bit differently, or you know you are not necessarily expected to speak your mind or be direct with them. Even if it's another female in leadership, they may treat you very differently and make smart remarks to you in administrative meetings. It's a thorny issue at my institution.

These lived experiences are not isolated. In a study which examined Black female school principals and how their age impacted their ability to earn respect and lead, some respondents expressed that they were both scrutinized and challenged based on their image and in the way they carried themselves; both through blatant and more subtle communication. In fact, irrelevant and petty conversations surrounding fashion choices and questions related to these individuals' personal lives outside of work were prevalent. Particularly, one respondent noted that "her superiors and colleagues had increased attention around her personal life. More questions were posed about her marital/dating status."[16]

THE EXPECTATIONS AND REALITIES OF INTERNAL SUPPORT

Black women are constantly faced with undue surveillance. Within the disciplinary domain of power, sanctioning and discipline through bureaucratic control, whether in middle management, prisons, on social media, or in the academy is "ensured by keeping Black women as a mutually policing subordinate population under surveillance."[17] Additionally, some Black women in leadership believe they have to alter who they are to maintain the position.

Oftentimes, this results in the adoption and embodiment of a masculine leadership style as a means to be perceived as competent leads to not embracing women incorporating a feminist mode of empowerment. However, the danger in trying to adopt a masculine approach to leadership can be detrimental to women. For instance, women are "expected to present themselves in a more modest way and are more effective in male-dominated groups when they demonstrate hedging and self-doubt in their speech and are self-effacing in their behavior."[18]

NFT: A female administrator has never said anything outright praising me, or even really a "good job!," "you're doing great!" "I think that idea is great!" *chuckles* and now that I'm thinking about it that's a pretty interesting dynamic . . . I rarely, hell if ever feel from them that my authority on something is automatic . . . I also think they make me do more busy work, for example writing formal reports for any and everything I request . . . I feel like I've been asked to do tasks that they wouldn't ask a male to do. There have also been instances where I felt my intellectual property was stolen in that I've been asked my opinion, or to do something for someone without getting credit for it, and I feel like that's because I am a woman. Because I'm young. I mostly felt unheard, and yeah, I also have been yelled at by an administrator in a completely inappropriate way for no reason, in front of my peers . . . I was surprised when I first got here, even somewhat devastated, at the lack of "I wanna reach out and mentor you, make sure doing good sis, give you the tools you need to advocate" by Black women who are in leadership or more senior than me on campus. I just have not found that, even though administrators have largely been women. I have yet to have a woman that was above me, who I felt that because I was a woman or because I was young Black woman and doing the best that I can every day that they wanted to reach out and help me. I have felt like I have had to fight for every single thing I have gotten for my department or myself. It's exhausting. It's made me fear career burnout. And even post-tenure, the feeling of imposter syndrome, and insecurity persists.

LSB: One of the consistent themes that I notice is I will often receive these passive aggressive emails from some of the male faculty members. These messages are frequently demanding and downright rude. I've even had an experience where I received what I like to call, *"low-key shade."* Specifically, I was asked to make time in my schedule to meet with this particular faculty member. In the same message—and this is where the "low-key shade" comes in—the faculty member tried to accuse me of giving a student some incorrect information. The accusatory tone really annoyed me. It's the same thing with this person every time. Then, there was another faculty member who posted something about me on social media; I didn't see it directly, but someone else saw it, took a screenshot and texted it to me. While the person didn't specifically reference me by name, it doesn't take a rocket scientist to determine who the individual was referring to in their angry post. Among my circle of support, I like to joke and call these folks *"keyboard gangsters"*; and the reason I call them that is because they are emboldened and have courage to lash out, but would never say it to you in-person. These interactions leave me feeling annoyed and angry.

Although all forms of support within academic institutions are critically important and necessary for women, support, or lack thereof, from other women can be impactful. This is especially significant for Black women, who epistemologically acknowledge that mentoring other Black women is important, yet, there is a lack of leadership preparation involved in these relationships.[19]

Many African American women have not been exposed to or been shown how to effectively engage in networking activities. However, "African American women who aspire to become leaders must be willing to step outside their comfort zones to establish a network of people who are different from them and who hold higher rank or positions. Establishing strategic relationships in the academy is a valuable tool for African American women to gain access to higher-level promotions and career opportunities."[20] Support and mentorship are only pieces of the puzzle. Sponsorship includes guidance, professional mentorship, and investment in our upward career mobility.[21]. "Mentoring and sponsorship by males was prominent in the experiences of African American women as they recognized that sponsorship was vital to their career advancement and provided support in their professional growth and development. Sponsorship from unexpected individuals was heralded as a key element of the success that these women attained."[22] Similar to other African American women in leadership, we found support from men in leadership positions. Moreover, we found a willingness to be advocates, and provide sponsorship.

NFT: Men have been more helpful to me on campus honestly. Just generally more forthcoming, when, especially Black women in leadership positions have not been forthcoming with information or assistance that I need to lead my department. In that way, I have worked to build male allies . . . I know they have information, they can help me stay in the loop. They are more receptive and more helpful to me. But also, they praise my leadership and my action in ways I haven't gotten from senior female colleagues. Whereas male senior faculty and in leadership positions have told me things like "you're the future of this university!" I guess this affirmation makes it easier to communicate "I need your mentorship, I need your advice, I need your leadership" which is absolutely true, when I'm talking to anybody more seasoned than me . . . I do think my age and my gender shapes how they talk to me and how I talk to them too. Being "womanly" it's a you know, balancing act . . . for lack of a less cliché way to say it. Things like deferring or yielding to male colleagues in personal conversations and smiling a lot.

LSB: I haven't really sensed anything as far as from the top down and perhaps that's probably because I have a very good relationship working relationship with my dean . . . he's very supportive and I can ask critical questions. But terms of boundaries, if you have a good support system and somebody who really is an advocate for you I don't really think that . . . that necessarily matters so long as you show promise of progressive leadership; things such as contributing selflessly to the organization in a way that highlights others and their talents, doing the right thing when no one is looking, being open and transparent, holding the self and others accountable, etc. While I definitely have a few people in close proximity who I can call any time with questions, concerns, I do notice the absence of other women, mostly older on the academic side who are willing to be a mentor. *Full* professors. They talk down to women who are less experienced than they are. They don't seem very eager or, let's say, interested in being approached. It's an "I got mine; you better get yours" mindset. I am very big on watching people and how they treat others to determine if they're even the type of person that I would consider a good mentor.

In learning to make it work, we had to find those willing to be contributors to our success. Still we both yearn for the Black women that are in positions we may aspire to, see the potential, and actively nurture the potential. To be seen by them, because it is valuable. "By paying it forward, the experiences of African American women senior leaders could provide a roadmap for African American women aspiring to advance to senior leadership roles in academia."[23] But we are not quite there. And it is problematic. We both find this phenomenon a challenge to our leadership and our ability to communicate our leadership. We acknowledge that some of this dynamic is born of self-preservation among older faculty members who may also be troubled by the paranoia that exists within the academy which creates the perception that there is not enough space for all of us—the myth of scarcity. It is in this toxicity where we become threatening to one another. "There are senior people who resent a young person who is a rising star. She may remind them of what they will never be. These senior people may even be unconscious about what they're doing."[24] For all of the ways that our HBCUs foster a culture that feels like family, the spirit of wanting better for your children has been lost in translation.

"FRIENDSHIP—THE GAME CHANGER"

There is more work to be done at our institutions to engage and develop the talent of young, African American women to assume leadership roles at HBCUs. Pipelines and opportunities must be created and integrated as part of the organization's overall strategy for long-term sustainability. As "increasing formal and informal mentorship connections between younger and older Black women principals may have a positive impact on the leadership practices for both generations, and the schools, students, and communities they serve,"[25] the same can be true at HBCUs. By creating more internal opportunities among Black women to create mentoring and sponsorship relationships, the long-term benefits are far-reaching beyond the confines of the institution. Some of these activities include in-depth conversations and acknowledging the elements that shape Black women's experience in leadership roles. Poignantly articulated

> engaging in deep and sustained dialogue with Black women leaders is key to understanding our realities, experiences, culture, and leadership—and to inform your own as well. I often describe our stories about identity and personhood as gifts. So if we understand that what Black women leaders are doing, and what meaning we are making of what we are doing, then we will understand that when we offer a glimpse into our pain, dreams, hopes, whatever, it might be received with open hands: Gently and honorably, treasured for the gift that it is. Otherwise, Black women risk continued silence for the sake of self-preservation and those around us do not receive the benefit of the legacy of wisdom and brilliance that we are.[26]

Until more strategic effort is placed on this type of faculty development, women will continue to deliberately seek and engage in informal networks where they feel accepted and welcomed to discuss their experiences without fear of judgment. This is precisely what happened to us.

Despite our geographical distance from one another, we feel more connected to each other as we navigate this unpredictable landscape of pursing the attainment of leadership goals and experiences at our respective HBCUs. Furthermore, while we engage in both mediated communication through our smartphones and traditional phone calls, it is the frequent text messages that provide the enduring relief and support. This is because even if there is a day (or days) where we do not communicate, we can easily scroll through and retrieve the previous messages and find the humorous comments, emojis, GIFs. Literally, by doing so, this is sometimes how we are able to make it through the day; by continually uplifting and supporting one another. We need women to engage in this behavior at all levels. As one former department head explained that in facing her own discriminatory experiences in her path to becoming a university president, "this moment should be a call to action for women who wield power in higher education. We should be more forceful advocates for redress of the discriminatory conditions that women still face—women that include our own students, graduates and quite possibly, our own colleagues. We must do more to promote women to positions of authority throughout our own institutions."[27] As we wait for this systemic change, we take shelter in our friendship.

We are passionately invested in and doing the best job possible in our current leadership roles. Equally, we hold ourselves accountable and do what we can to ensure that our students succeed and that our institutions are sustainable in the long-term. However, accountability requires a village of support. A support network not only to assist you as you navigate unknown territory but to also act as organizational advocates. We know and understand the difficulty that is required to turn the mirror on ourselves and establish an understanding of the cultural and systematic influences that have helped to shape the culture and character of HBCUs. And, while we laud and proudly uphold the advances that African American women have made at our institutions and elsewhere, we recommend friendship as a healthy starting point. Regardless of what formal and informal policies are enacted, that cultivating the bonds of friendship and solidarity is intentional, selfless, and deep-rooted. And it is through these traits that we offer our approach as viable and enduring communication strategies for Black women seeking entry into or who are already situated in leadership positions at HBCUs.

Foremost, this approach can help younger Black women who have been unexpectedly catapulted into a leadership role by developing the very necessary, but highly impactful support system that is needed; even when a formal structure does not exist on the campus. Secondly, having "sister friends" is a hallmark of Black womanhood and becomes even more important within the confines of the academy. Historically, it has always been a fact that Black women have often congregated away from mainstream society to air grievances, share experiences, be a network and support to one another and generally, vent about issues they're currently facing through traditional avenues such as church and sorority membership. In our experience, we have found that, through these informal networks, we have created a safe space—one that is necessary in the preservation of our well-being and support as our careers advance. Simply put, friendship in this context equates to a form of self-care.

We did not endeavor upon our initial project about our experiences in leadership with the goal of taking stock of our friendship. Analyzing our experiences led us to take stock of how we manage the isolation we experience. Ultimately we concluded that since we've been friends, it has been a lot less lonely. In having a sister friend who has days that look a lot like yours, who also deals with the same frustrations and challenges, we each find that a burden has been lifted. As we work tirelessly to navigate the landscape of academia and to build strategic relationships, we have come to see that our friendship constitutes one of those strategic relationships.

There is incredible power in having your experiences affirmed with a "Girl! You ain't neva lied!" at the end of particularly difficult and trying day, or at the end of a meeting. The ability to converse knowing that there are no strings attached, no expectations, no deliverables, no pressure, our friendship represents a site of empowerment. Having a *friend* that is similarly situated in academic leadership is an *enhanced communication strategy*. Thus, we offer this advice—find a sister friend! Introduce women in similar institutional contexts to someone for the purpose of friendship. Introduce yourself, or ask your mentors to introduce you to someone in a similar institutional context to be *friends* with. Be a help to another sister instead of a hindrance. For example, check on each other if long periods of time go by with little to no communication. Make a genuine attempt to learn what the other's research interests are and develop innovative ways to engage and contribute to your respective disciplines through scholarly projects. Write letters of support/ recommendation for each other when it becomes necessary. Review each other's tenure and promotion materials and provide honest, yet constructive feedback. Additionally, invite other, like-minded young women into the fold and be a friend and mentor. Finally, remember to, as you advance through your career, reflect on where the gaps were in terms of sister friend support and be committed to not repeating that legacy for the women who will succeed you.

NOTES

1. Patricia Hill Collins, *Black Feminist Thought: Knowledge, Consciousness and the Politics of Empowerment* (New York, NY: Taylor and Francis Group, 2002), 102.
2. Collins, *Black Feminist Thought*, 262
3. bell hooks, and Tanya McKinnon, "Sisterhood: Beyond Public and Private." *Signs 21* (1996): 824.
4. Kyoko Kishimoto and Mwangi Mumbi, "Critiquing the Rhetoric of 'Safety' in Feminist Pedagogy: Women of Color Offering an Account of Ourselves." *Feminist Teacher*, 19, no. 2 (2009): 87–102.
5. Kishimoto and Mumbi, "Critiquing the Rhetoric of 'Safety' in Feminist Pedagogy," 88.
6. Jenny Bimrose, Mary McMahon, and Mark Watson, "Career Trajectories of Older Women: Implications for Career Guidance." *British Journal of Guidance and Counseling*, 41, no. 5 (2013): 587–601.
7. Niki T. Dickerson, "We Are a Force to be Reckoned With: Black and Latina Women's Leadership in the Contemporary U.S. Labor Movement." *Working USA*, 9, no. 3 (2006): 293–313.
8. Deanna Davis and Cecilia R. Maldanado, "Shattering the Glass Ceiling: The Leadership Development of African American Women in Higher Education." *Advancing Women in Leadership*, 35 (2015): 59.
9. LaSharnda Beckwith, Danon Carter, and Tara Peters, "The Underrepresentation of African American Women in Executive Leadership: What's Getting in the Way?" *Journal of Business Studies Quarterly,* 7, no. 4 (2016): 123.
10. Collins, *Black Feminist Thought*.

11. Collins, *Black Feminist Thought*, 87.

12. Gaetane Jean-Marie, "Standing on the Promises: The Experience of Black Women Administrators in Historically Black Institutions." *Advancing Women in Leadership Online Journal*, 19 (2005).

13. Yolanda T. Moses, "Black Women in Academe: Issues and Strategies," in the *Black Women in the Academy: Promises and Perils*, ed. Lois Benjamin (Gainesville, FL: University Press of Florida, 1997), 22–38.

14. Linley Anne Lord and Alison Preston, "Understanding Leadership Experiences: The need for Story Sharing and Feminist Literature as a Survival Manual for Leadership." *Journal of Gender and Education*, 21, no. 6 (2009): 774.

15. Collins, *Black Feminist Thought*, 253.

16. Latish Cherie Reed, "The Intersection of Race and Gender in School Leadership for Three Black Female Principals." *International Journal of Qualitative Studies in Education*, 25, no. 1 (2012): 51.

17. Collins, *Black Feminist Thought*, 281.

18. Asha N. Gipson, Danielle L. Pfaff, Danielle, David B. Mendelsohn, Lauren T. Catenacci, and Warner W. Burke, "Women and Leadership: Selection, Development, Leadership Style, and Performance." *The Journal of Applied Behavioral Science*, 53, no. 1 (2017): 32–65.

19. Adrien Katherine Wing, "Lessons From a Portrait: Keep Calm and Carry On," in *Presumed Incompetent: The Intersections of Race and Class for Women in Academia*, ed. Gabriella Gutierrez Muhs, Yolanda Flores Niemann, Carmen G. Gonzalez and Angela P. Harris (Logan, UT: University of Utah Press, 2012), 356–370.

20. Davis and Maldanado, "Shattering the Glass Ceiling," 60.

21. Davis and Maldanado, "Shattering the Glass Ceiling."

22. Davis and Maldanado, "Shattering the Glass Ceiling," 58.

23. Davis and Maldanado, "Shattering the Glass Ceiling," 60.

24. Wing, "Lessons From a Portrait," 366.

25. Reed, "The Intersection of Race," 56.

26. Cynthia B. Dillard, "To Address Suffering That the Majority Can't See: Lessons from Black Women's Leadership in the Workplace." *New Directions for Adult & Continuing Education*, 152 (2016): 34.

27. Patricia McGuire, "President's Use Your Voice," Last modified March 25, 2019, https://www.chronicle.com/interactives/the-awakening.

BIBLIOGRAPHY

Beckwith, LaSharnda, Danon Carter, and Tara Peters. "The Underrepresentation of African American Women in Executive Leadership: What's Getting in the Way?" *Journal of Business Studies Quarterly*, 7, no. 4 (2016), 115–134.

Bimrose, Jenny, Mary McMahon, and Mark Watson. "Career Trajectories of Older Women: Implications for Career Guidance." *British Journal of Guidance and Counseling*, 41, no. 5 (2013), 587–601. https://doi.org/10.1080/03069885.2013.779639.

Collins, Patricia Hill. *Black Feminist Thought: Knowledge, Consciousness and the Politics of Empowerment.* New York, NY: Taylor and Francis Group, 2002. https://doi.org/10.4324/9780203900055.

Davis, Deanna and Cecilia R. Maldanado. "Shattering the Glass Ceiling: The Leadership Development of African American Women in Higher Education." *Advancing Women in Leadership,* 35 (2015), 59. http://www.advancingwomen.com/awl/Vol35_2015/Davis_Shattering_the_Glass_Ceiling.pdf.

Dickerson, Niki T. "We are a Force to be Reckoned With: Black and Latina Women's Leadership in the Contemporary U.S. Labor Movement." *Working USA,* 9, no. 3 (2006), 293–313. https://doi.org/10.1111/j.1743-4580.2006.00114.x.

Dillard, Cynthia B. "To Address Suffering That the Majority Can't See: Lessons from Black Women's Leadership in the Workplace." *New Directions for Adult & Continuing Education,* 152 (2016), 29–38. https://doi.org/10.1002/ace.20210.

Gipson, Asha N., Danielle L. Pfaff, Danielle, David B. Mendelsohn, Lauren T. Catenacci, and Warner W. Burke. "Women and Leadership: Selection, Development, Leadership Style, and Performance." *The Journal of Applied Behavioral Science,* 53, no. 1 (2017), 32–65. https://doi.org/10.1177/2F0021886316687247.

hooks, bell and Tanya McKinnon. "Sisterhood: Beyond Public and Private." *Signs,* 21 (1996), 814–829. https://doi.org/10.1086/495122.

Jean-Marie, Gaetane, "Standing on the Promises: The Experience of Black Women Administrators in Historically Black Institutions." *Advancing Women in Leadership Online Journal,* 19 (2005). https://doi.org/10.18738/awl.v19i0.193.

Kishimoto, Kyoko and Mwangi Mumbi. "Critiquing the Rhetoric of 'Safety' in Feminist Pedagogy: Women of Color Offering an Account of Ourselves." *Feminist Teacher,* 19, no. 2 (2009), 87–102, 88. https://doi.org/10.1353/ftr.0.0044.

Lord, Linley Anne and Alison Preston. "Understanding Leadership Experiences: The need for Story Sharing and Feminist Literature as a Survival Manual for Leadership." *Journal of Gender and Education,* 21, no. 6 (2009), 769–777. https://doi.org/10.1080/09540250903119153.

McGuire, Patricia. "President's, Use Your Voice!" in *The Awakening: Women and Power in the Academy,* The Chronicle of Higher Education. Last modified March 25, 2019. https://www.chronicle.com/interactives/the-awakening.

Moses, Yolanda T. "Black Women in Academe: Issues and Strategies," in *Black Women in the Academy: Promises and Perils*, edited by Lois Benjamin. Gainesville, FL: University Press of Florida, 22–38, 1997.

Reed, Latish Cherie. "The Intersection of Race and Gender in School Leadership for Three Black Female Principals." *International Journal of Qualitative Studies in Education,* 25, no. 1 (2012), 39–58. https://doi.org/10.1080/09518398.2011.647723.

Wing, Adrien Katherine. "Lessons From a Portrait: Keep Calm and Carry On," in *Presumed Incompetent: The Intersections of Race and Class for Women in Academia*, edited by Gabriella Gutierrez Muhs, Yolanda Flores Niemann, Carmen G. Gonzalez and Angela P. Harris, Logan, UT: University of Utah Press, 356–370, 2012.

Chapter 3

Black Diamonds

African American Women Executives Embody Transformational Leadership at Community Colleges

Karima A. Haynes

Thirty years ago, African American women with ambition and determination began to take their seats in the executive suites at colleges and universities in the United States. Although the percentage of college and university presidents of color has slowly increased in the past three decades, African American women are the most underrepresented in presidential positions. The purpose of this literary analysis is to explore transformational leadership theory, industrial-organizational psychology, womanist theory, barriers and biases around executive leadership, transformational executive leadership at community colleges, African American women transformational leaders at community colleges, and pathways to developing the leader within. It is imperative that African American women who are seeking leadership roles develop a transformational leadership style that embraces their cultural disposition toward caring, empathy, encouragement, motivation, positive reinforcement, ethics, integrity, trustworthiness, pride, and risk-taking.

African American women began to occupy presidential suites at colleges and universities across the United States nearly three decades ago. Although the percentage of college and university presidents of color has increased slightly since the 1980s, African American women remain the most underrepresented demographic in presidential positions.[1] A 2016 nationwide survey of more than 1,500 college and university presidents indicated that African American women were vastly underrepresented in the college presidency and they were more likely than other college presidents to be serving in their first presidency.[2]

The profile of the typical college or university president in the United States is a White male in his sixties with a doctoral degree who has served in his current position for seven years, a reflection of a dearth in the number of women of color who have ascended to the executive suites in higher education.[3] Still, some progress is being made, according to the study, which indicated that the number of college presidents who were members of racial minority groups rose by 4 percentage points from 13 percent in 2011 to 17 percent in 2016, 36 percent of presidents of color are serving in top positions at two-year institutions, and 5 percent of college presidents are women of color.[4]

African American women executives must endure the challenges on many fronts before they can become chief executive officers at institutions of higher learning. Those challenges include race, ethnicity, gender, and age discrimination; a lack of effective networks and mentors; caregiving responsibilities; and stereotypes and biases. Eight of thirty-four African American women community college presidents bore witness to these challenges in a 2009 research study in which they provided detailed responses to the following research questions: (1) What is the typical career preparation of African American women presidents of community colleges? (2) What are the common strategies that African American women presidents of community colleges use to negotiate their careers? and (3) What were the salient factors that affected or shaped their career paths?[5]

Five major themes emerged in the qualitative research study: (1) striving and succeeding through extensive preparation, (2) constructing a well-developed personal image, (3) taking risks for learning and professional advancement, (4) enduring race and gender discrimination, and (5) having the support of their community. The five themes that arose in the study were indicators that the eight African American women community college presidents were engaged in transformational leadership that was reflected in their verbal and nonverbal communication styles at their respective institutions of higher learning.[6]

Today's African American women academics are attempting to lead the nation's community colleges at a time when major shifts in the American economy, globalization, and an ever-increasing need for a technologically sophisticated and well-educated domestic labor force are placing significantly more pressure on the nation's 1,103 community colleges to produce graduates prepared for the twenty-first-century workplace.[7] Community colleges are being asked to engage on multiple fronts, including engaging in workforce development, serving as a gateway to higher education, and addressing equity and diversity social mandates.[8] It is imperative that community colleges' boards of trustees and executive leadership teams mutually focus on recruiting and retaining community college presidents who reflect the school's diverse student populations, especially in urban areas, to maintain institutional stability and viability.[9]

With increased pressure on two-year institutions to produce graduates ready to enter a complex workplace, community college presidents must have the support of members of their boards of trustees that is sometimes lacking. The report, "Executive Leadership Transitioning at Community Colleges," found that trustees at community colleges assumed that that their work was completed as soon as a new chief executive officer took the reins at the institution. To ensure a smooth transition of leadership, the report recommended that trustees continue their work in support of both the outgoing and incoming presidents to improve executive continuity.[10]

Women academics desiring to ascend to the executive ranks at institutions of higher learning must clear barriers and overcome bias before they can lead institutions successfully.[11] The American Association of University Women addressed these challenges and provided a path forward in its report, "Barriers and Bias: The Status of Women in Leadership."[12] The report focused on four essential questions: (1) What is the gender leadership gap? (2) What explains it? (3) What strategies have already helped narrow the leadership gap? and (4) What can we do about it now?[13] The report also incorporated the intersections of race, ethnicity, socioeconomic status, disability status, sexual orientation, gender identity, and age as variables that have an effect on a woman's ability to achieve executive leadership roles in academia.[14]

The purpose of this literary analysis is to explore transformational leadership theory, industrial-organizational psychology, womanist theory, barriers and biases around executive leadership, transformational executive leadership at community colleges, African American women transformational leaders at community colleges, and pathways to developing the leader within. Relevant works were selected based on a systematic search of EBSCO, ERIC, Google Scholar, and websites of leading academic associations for relevant material. Search words and phrases included: transformational leadership, transformational theory, organizational psychology, African American women community college presidents, womanism, womanist, and higher education, among other terms and keywords.

Moreover, this analysis includes detailed accounts from African American community college presidents who candidly discussed issues of race and gender bias that they experienced both before and after taking the helm at their institutions. The literary analysis further explores the creation of a doctoral program founded and expanded by African American women academicians at a historically Black university in Maryland that has created opportunities for Black women to break through at the executive level. The chapter concludes with suggestions for future research culled from the current literature and by the author.

TRANSFORMATIONAL LEADERSHIP THEORY

Transformational leadership is a term used broadly to describe a leadership approach that "creates valuable and positive change in the followers with the end goal of developing followers into leaders."[15] The end goal of transformational leadership is to enhance motivation, morale, and performance among followers. Transformational leaders connect their followers' sense of self to an organization's mission, serve as an inspirational role model for their followers, challenge their followers to take greater ownership of their work, and possess an understanding of their followers' strengths and weakness so that they can assign their followers to tasks that optimize their performance.[16]

James MacGregor Burns, a Pulitzer Prize-winning presidential biographer and pioneer in the study of leadership, first introduced the concept of transforming leadership in 1978 in his descriptive research on political leaders.[17] His book, *Leadership*, published in 1978, is still considered the seminal work in the field of leadership studies. His theory of transactional and transformational leadership has been the basis of more than 400 doctoral dissertations.[18] In presenting his theoretical perspective, Burns drew a distinction between management and leadership, claiming that the difference is in characteristics and behaviors.[19]

Burns established two concepts: "transforming leadership" and "transactional leadership."[20] The transforming approach changes the lives of people, and the organizations in which they work, by redesigning employees' perceptions and values and changing employees' expectations and aspirations. This approach is set apart from transactional leadership that is based on a "give and take" relationship. Furthermore, Burns theorized that transforming and transactional leadership were mutually exclusive styles, positing, "transactional leaders usually do not strive for cultural change in the organization, but they work in the existing culture while transformational leaders can try to change organizational culture."[21]

Nearly a decade later, researcher Bernard M. Bass expanded on Burns' work by exploring the psychological foundations that undergird transformational and transactional leadership styles as well as how transformational leadership could be measured.[22] Bass surmised that transformational leaders engender trust, admiration, loyalty, and respect from their followers because as leaders they are willing to work harder than their followers expect; transformational leaders offer followers a sense that they are working for more than just self-gain; transformational leaders provide their followers with an inspiring mission and vision that give them an identity; transformational leaders transform and motivate their followers through his or her personal charisma, intellectual stimulation and individual consideration, and transformational leaders encourage their followers to challenge the status quo and to change the environment to support success.[23] However, unlike Burns, Bass proposed that transformational and transactional leadership are not mutually exclusive and can be successfully displayed simultaneously.[24]

In extending the work of his predecessor, Bass identified four elements of transformational leadership: The first element is individualized consideration which occurs when the leader pays attention to followers' needs, acts as a mentor or coach to followers, and listens to followers' concerns and needs. The leader is empathetic and supportive, keeps the lines of communication open, and challenges followers to excel. This element also holds the expectation that leaders will respect and celebrate followers' individual contributions and makes them feel like part of the team. In addition, followers will aspire toward self-improvement and develop intrinsic motivation for their tasks.[25]

Second, intellectual stimulation is the degree to which the leader challenges assumptions, takes risks, and solicits followers' ideas. Under this style of leadership, leaders stimulate and encourage creativity in their followers and nurture and develop employees who think independently. Leaders value learning and view unexpected situations as opportunities to learn. Moreover, they encourage their followers to ask questions, think deeply, and figure out better ways to perform their tasks.[26]

Third, inspirational motivation is the degree to which the leader articulates a vision that is appealing and inspiring to followers. Transformational leaders with inspirational motivation challenge their employees with high standards, communicate optimism about future goals, and provide meaning for the task at hand. An outcome of this leadership style is that followers invest more effort in their tasks, are encouraged and optimistic about the future, and believe in their abilities.[27]

Lastly, idealized influence is the degree to which a transformational leader serves as a role model for high ethical behavior, instills pride, and gains respect and trust from his or her followers.[28]

INDUSTRIAL-ORGANIZATIONAL PSYCHOLOGY

Although the concept of transformational leadership was first introduced by Burns in relationship to political leaders, today the term has been broadened to include industrial-organizational psychology. The specialty of industrial-organizational psychology is characterized by the "scientific study of human behavior in organizations and the workplace."[29] The discipline focuses on deriving principles of individual, group, and organizational behavior and applying this knowledge to find solutions to problems within the workplace.[30]

Industrial-organizational psychology requires an in-depth knowledge of organizational development, attitudes, career development, decision theory, human performance and human factors, small group theory and process, job and task analysis, and individual assessment, among other specialized knowledge and training.[31] In addition, industrial-organizational psychology requires knowledge of ethical considerations as well as statutory, administrative, and case law and executive orders as related to workplace activities.[32] Furthermore, industrial-organizational psychology addresses recruitment, selection and placement, training and development, performance measurement, workplace motivation and rewards systems, quality of work life, structure of work and human factors, organizational development, and consumer behavior.[33]

WOMANIST THEORY

In her volume of essays, *In Search of Our Mothers' Gardens: Womanist Prose*, Alice Walker introduced the term "womanist."[34] There are four meanings for the term womanist: (1) a Black feminist or other non-White feminist, (2) someone who is committed to the survival and wholeness of males and females, (3) someone who loves herself, and (4) an analogy of womanism as being to feminism as purple is to lavender.[35] Walker explained her rationale for using the term "womanist," stating that she did not choose the term because it was "better" than feminism. Rather she said the term captured the spirit of women's rights activists and suffragists and Walker's desire to introduce a new word into the American lexicon "when the old word it is using fails to describe behavior and change that only a new word can help it more fully to see."[36] In introducing the term, Walker cited the phrase "acting womanish," which was said to a child who "acted serious, courageous, and grown-up rather than girlish."[37] The adoption of the term "womanist" signified an expansion of the Women's Liberation Movement of the 1970s from its primary focus on the concerns and problems of middle-class White women to include race and class issues in feminism.[38]

Because womanism seeks to explain the experiences, thoughts, and behaviors of African American women, it is critical that their thoughts and actions are examined within the context of their cultural and historical legacies.[39] Womanists, and specifically, womanist educators, often exhibit three common characteristics: (1) an embrace of the maternal, (2) political clarity, and (3) an ethic of risk.[40]

Regarding an embrace of the maternal characteristic, women in the academy demonstrate a tendency toward a maternal sensibility. This is visible in the pedagogy of African American women educators.[41]

Political clarity is defined as the recognition by educators that there is a relationship between schools and society that has a direct effect on the success or failure of students.[42] Womanist educators see racism and other systemic injustices as social and educational problems, and as a result, they demonstrate an awareness of their power and responsibility as adults to challenge stereotypes forced on their students.[43]

Lastly, African American womanist educators exemplify an ethic of risk in that they are willing to step out of their individual comfort zones for the collective good to educate students as a means of uplifting the greater community. Thus, informed by an ethic of risk, womanist caring encourages educators to see their action as a humble, yet essential, contribution to an extensive, collaborative, and enduring project of social change.[44]

Although seemingly unrelated, transformational leadership, industrial-organizational theory, and womanist theory all work together in the leadership and communication styles of successful African American women community college presidents. In addition, a review of the literature showed a strong work ethic, collaborative disposition, and a desire to mentor and encourage others are common characteristics among effective African American women community college presidents.

TRANSFORMATIONAL EXECUTIVE LEADERSHIP AT COMMUNITY COLLEGES

For nearly nine decades, the definition of leadership has been at the epicenter of scholarly and popular debate, yet no mutually agreed-upon definition has arisen.[45] A leader is one who possesses position, personality, moral authority, power, or by intellectual contributions.[46] Similarly, individuals at any level within an organization, including people without formal authority as well as top executives, can exercise leadership.[47]

In the report, "Barriers and Bias: The Status of Women in Leadership," American Association of University Women researchers focused on "positional leadership," which was defined as "people who occupy positions of power and are recognized and rewarded in observable ways."[48]

Although leadership has been viewed through the stereotypical masculine lens, leadership is not inherently masculine. Given that White men have dominated leadership positions in politics, business, medicine, law, religion, education, among other disciplines, stereotypical masculine traits such as aggression, decisiveness, willingness to engage in conflict and strength, and other attributes have been associated with leadership.[49]

However, these traits are not the exclusive purview of White men nor are they inherent in all men. On the contrary, researchers who have investigated the essential ingredients of leadership found no gender differences in leadership effectiveness.[50] Moreover, researchers found that women tend to adopt a transformational leadership style, which motivates followers through charisma, intellectual stimulation, and consideration of the individual.[51]

Race and ethnicity, among other factors, affect African American women's leadership opportunities. Women of color experience race and ethnic discrimination that White women do not face, they also experience racial bias differently than men in their same racial or ethnic group.[52]

In higher education, African American women have served as faculty, administrators, and presidents at historically Black colleges and universities, but their numbers remain small at traditionally White institutions of higher learning.[53] Overall, women of color made up 17 percent of college presidents in 2011; represented 8 percent of all faculty in 2011 (11 percent of instructors, 11 percent of assistant professors, and 4 percent of full professors); accounted for 13 percent of private boards of trustees in 2010, and consisted of 23 percent of public board members in 2010.[54]

Women of all racial and ethnic backgrounds lag behind their male counterparts in top academic leadership, where they are underrepresented among tenured faculty and full professors who have the power to hire and tenure colleagues as well as direct research initiatives. Without tenure or the rank of full professor, women's opportunities to advance to formal leadership positions at colleges and universities are severely curtailed.[55]

A LABYRINTH, NOT A GLASS CEILING

The shortage of women in executive leadership positions has been described as a glass ceiling through which women in middle-management positions can see the upper echelons, but are unable to break through invisible barriers to get there. In recent years, the barrier to women's advancement has been likened to a labyrinth where women's attempts at upward mobility have been thwarted at various points throughout their journey.[56] Women are not denied executive leadership positions at the end of their careers, rather they are denied opportunities, or opportunities vanish, as they progress through their careers.[57]

Researchers have identified five factors contributing to this situation: (1) the pipeline problem, (2) persistent sex discrimination, (3) caregiving and women's "choices," (4) lack of effective networks and mentors, and (5) stereotypes and bias.[58]

Regarding the pipeline problem, researchers have found that the notion is essentially a myth. With women now earning most university degrees at every level, with the exception of professional degrees, and possessing many years of professional experience in the workforce, "qualified and ambitious women are not in short supply."[59]

Pervasive and persistent sex discrimination in the workplace continues to impede women's advancement into executive suites. In academia, the "gendered realities of alcohol consumption, date rape, and sexual harassment at U.S. universities . . . can work to depress women's autonomy" and reinforce the different roles for men and women in college and influence the choices men and women make.[60]

Balancing work and family responsibilities is one of the most daunting barriers for women seeking to move into executive positions. Women must make choices about working after childbirth, taking family leave, leaving a position, returning to the workforce, living on a single income, maintaining a dual income, and managing child care issues all within the context of "cultural expectations, gender socialization, and financial constraints."[61]

A lack of effective networks and mentors also hamper women's efforts to move up the executive leadership ladder.[62] This situation is particularly exasperating for women of color aspiring to executive leadership because they have "limited access to social networks that can provide information about jobs, promotions, professional advice, resources, and expertise."[63]

Moreover, the lives of women of color are less likely to intersect with that of powerful White male managers outside of the workplace because they live in different neighborhoods, send their children to different schools, hold memberships in different organizations, and attend different houses of worship, which does not necessarily hold true for their White male and female colleagues.[64] Stereotypes and biases, sometimes subtle and other times overt, are major hindrances for women seeking executive leadership positions.[65]

Researchers have identified four types of stereotypes and biases: (1) stereotype threat, (2) stereotypes about leadership, (3) stereotypes about race and ethnicity, and (4) implicit bias.[66]

Stereotype threats occur when people are made aware that they are negatively stereotyped in their present role or activity. This threat affects their performance in areas in which they are negatively stereotyped.[67]

Leadership stereotypes that are typically ascribed to males include competitiveness, rationality, independence, dominance, objectivity, and aggression. These are all expectations that can affect women's self-perceptions regarding their executive leadership capabilities.[68]

Racial and ethnic stereotypes involve complex relationships among race, gender, and leadership style.[69] For example, most of the research on the pushback on women's leadership has focused mainly on White women, leaving an open question as to how African American women fare when their leadership styles run counter to prevailing gender stereotypes.[70]

Implicit bias, or unconscious bias, occurs when a person on a conscious level rejects stereotypes, but unconsciously judges others based on those same disavowed stereotypes. Women in the workplace may consciously support women in executive leadership positions; however, research has found that women harbor implicit bias against female bosses.[71]

When women leaders are expected to be kind and cooperative as women, yet assertive and competitive as leaders, they are placed in the untenable position that researchers call "role incongruity" that leaves them vulnerable to criticism and resistance from subordinates and colleagues and discouraged from actively seeking executive leadership opportunities.[72]

While the issue of narrowing the gender leadership gap is not new, there are several strategies that appear to be working to vault more women into executive leadership positions. Diversity training, implicit association testing, employment practice reforms, role models, gender quotas, and hiring goals are some of the efforts identified as a means to transform talented, ambitious, experienced, and educated women into chief executives.[73]

Diversity training workshops have shown some progress in narrowing the gender leadership gap. For instance, college faculty who participated in an interactive, bias-reduction intervention workshop were more likely to monitor their personal attitudes and behaviors about gender equity. Researchers at Harvard University pioneered "Project Implicit" in 1998, which is a series of tests that use word association to detect implicit bias with the idea that once people are made aware of the biases, they are more likely to be responsible for their attitude and behaviors.[74]

In the United States, gender quotas and hiring goals have had mixed results.[75] The downside is that women who have been hired or promoted as a result of a quota program are often stereotyped as less-qualified and self-assessment of competence may suffer. On the positive side, top technology companies such as Apple, Intel, and Google have made public internal hiring data to shine light on their hiring and promotion practices involving ethnicity, gender, and race. To ensure meaningful progress in the hiring and promotion of women of color, reforms in employments must hold managers accountable for their employment practices.[76]

Objective performance-based promotion practices are critical to women's success and job descriptions using gender-neutral language have been shown to have made a positive difference in hiring.[77] Lastly, recurrent, positive exposure to successful female role models has improved college women's self-assessment of their leadership capacities and career ambitions.[78]

GETTING INTO THE DRIVER'S SEAT

The American Association of Community Colleges strongly recommends that boards of trustees have a presidential transition plan in place well before the process begins. The presidential succession and transition process should delineate the entire process from presidential search to installation of the new chief executive officer and include the following milestones along the way: transition and management protocols; a comprehensive communication strategy; and maintaining access to data and facts in real time through an electronic dashboard.[79]

The presidential search and transition plan should be part of an overall strategic plan that sets forth in explicit terms the board of trustees' strategic priorities for the community college that it expects the incoming president to address and the skill set and leadership traits the new executive must possess to realize the vision.[80]

Following a successful search for a new chief executive officer at the community college, it is important for the outgoing president to serve as a mentor, sounding board, and wise counselor for the incoming president who attempts to establish their own leadership style. Moreover, it is imperative that the institution's board of trustees, departing president, and the incoming president "exhibit high levels of emotional intelligence" throughout the transition process by staying focused on the community college's needs and not their own "pride or sense of self-sufficiency."[81]

As the new chief executive assumes the presidency at a community college, there are three parties that play a critical role during the transition process: the board of trustees, the board liaison, and the incoming president. While all three entities are equally important in a successful presidential transition, the incoming president must possess the following: a due-diligence strategy; access to accurate information and data; support of the outgoing president and management team; and an understanding of the institution's "core functions, drivers, and enablers."[82]

Two community college presidents offered insights into the presidential onboarding process. One community college president interviewed for the report stated the following: "You never find out where all the skeletons are from the inside. I often get more insights into the culture and politics of an organization by talking to [external stakeholders]."[83]

Another community college chief executive with more than two decades of community college presidential leadership discussed some of the obstacles that can impede a smooth transition. The former executive noted that it was unfortunate that in some instances new presidents experience difficulty within the first months of their presidencies due to the lack of a reliable leadership system. Additionally, new presidents need coaching during their first six to nine months to launch a successful tenure in office.[84]

Community college presidential transitions have failed miserably due to several factors: breakdowns in communication between the incoming president and the board of trustees; a lack of clarity in terms of the college's mission, value, and standing when compared to peer institutions; cliquishness;

weak boards with insufficient knowledge of peak performance for itself and its institution; failure to embrace aspirational standards; resistant to adopt data analytics, assessments, or evaluations as a means to measure progress toward goals; a lack of discretion regarding internal matters and discussions; and a "daunting hubris that betrayed their individual and collective insecurity."[85] The responsibility for a smooth, orderly, sustainable, and effective presidential transition sits squarely on the shoulders of the board of trustees with support from the outgoing chief executive and his or her successor.[86]

While the percentage of college presidents who are persons of color has increased slowly in the last three decades, women of color are the most underrepresented in the presidency, according to the American Council on Education's "American College President Study 2017." The report is the leading and most comprehensive study of the college presidency and the higher education leadership pipeline from public and private and two- and four-year institutions.[87]

African American women are underrepresented in higher education leadership roles.[88] Although there are qualified, interested, and capable African American women in the education field, few African American women actually hold the position of college president.[89] Moreover, a disparity exists even in the lack of available research regarding African American females in higher education leadership positions.[90]

TALES FROM THE FRONTLINES

Challenges of race, ethnicity, gender, and age discrimination; a lack of effective networks and mentors; caregiving responsibilities; and stereotypes and biases notwithstanding, African American women have assumed the positions as leaders of institutions of higher learning. In the research study, "Rising to the Top: A National Study of Black Women Community College Presidents," eight of thirty-four African American women community college presidents serving at the time the study was conducted provided responses to the following questions: (1) What is the typical career preparation of African American women presidents of community colleges? (2) What are the common strategies that African American women presidents of community colleges use to negotiate their careers? and (3) What were the salient factors that affected or shaped their career paths?

Five major themes emerged in the qualitative research study: (1) striving and succeeding through extensive preparation, (2) constructing a well-developed personal image, (3) taking risks for learning and professional advancement, (4) race and gender discrimination, and (5) supported by their village community.[91] The themes indicated that the eight African American women community college presidents were engaged in transformational leadership at their institutions of higher learning.[92]

Regarding the theme "striving and succeeding through extensive preparation," each of the college presidents held a terminal degree, attended leadership training programs, and engaged in formal or informal mentoring experiences.[93] However, at least four of the executives' preparation went above and beyond the standard credentials and fell under a subtheme of "over credentialing," in which they describe extensive experience in administration at the community college district level, statewide education policy, and higher education consulting.[94]

This motivation to outperform expectations is indicative of the transformational leadership element of inspirational motivation in which leaders challenge followers with high standards, communicate optimism about future goals, and provide meaning for the task at hand.[95] In summary, the African American women college presidents asserted that the "Black woman has to be 'over-prepared' . . . to achieve 'validity' at a level that would meet or exceed that of other women and men."[96]

Findings also showed that all of the Black women community college presidents were engaged in "sustaining beneficial mentoring relationships," which was a subtheme of the larger theme of "striving and succeeding through extensive preparation." The executives stated that they were both mentored and served as mentors in their capacity as community college presidents.[97]

As mentors and/or mentees, the executives were exhibiting the transformational leadership element of individualized consideration in which the leader attends to each follower's needs, acts as a mentor or coach to the follower, and listens to the follower's concerns and needs.[98] In addition, the leader provides support, empathy, keeps the lines of communications open, and challenges the mentee.[99] Idealized consideration also means that the mentor has a desire to bring out the very best efforts in her follower to develop the follower's leadership potential.[100]

With respect to the theme "constructing a well-developed professional image," African American community college presidents stated that this attribute included personal appearance and interpersonal skills.[101] While on the surface, personal appearance involved clothing, hair, makeup, manicures, and the overall outer appearance of the body, several of the respondents suggested that "a remarkable personal appearance is more vital for Black women than for other women and men."[102]

One community college president stated that women of color, particularly Black women, have to be very careful about how they dress. "It is standard business attire," the executive said. "It can be the latest suit or the latest cut of pants, but it needs to look absolutely professional. You need to make a statement about who you are the minute you hit the door."[103]

Another Black woman community college president stated that her appearance was not only for herself, but for the women who come after her: "You're representing women of color that will come behind you and it's your shoulders and my shoulders on which they will climb, so we have to give them something to look up to."[104]

The African American community college presidents in the study identified interpersonal skills as "confidence, integrity, credibility, trustworthiness, ethics, and a sense of self" as critical for leaders.[105] Several respondents in the study asserted that the aforementioned interpersonal skills shaped their transformational communication styles. Moreover, the respondents agreed that all of the work completed to prepare for an executive-level position can be undone if the candidate fails to possess integrity, confidence, trustworthiness, credibility, a sense of self, and ethics.[106]

Yet another African American community college president in the study stated that Black women leaders gain respect by exhibiting confidence and not being intimidated. She stated that African American women executives must possess the ability to walk into a room of all White men and "handle your business."[107]

Still one other community college president interviewed for the study indicated that the interpersonal quality of trustworthiness is at the bedrock of professional relationships. The chief executive stated that African American women community college presidents must possess integrity, honesty, and openness.[108]

Constructing a well-developed professional image, with an emphasis on personal appearance and interpersonal skills, is at the core of the transformational leadership element of idealized influence, which provides a role model for high ethical behavior, instills pride, and gains respect and trust.[109] In a sense, the leader practices what she preaches, never says one thing and does something different, and lastly wouldn't ask followers to do something that she wouldn't do.[110]

African American women community college presidents said they were willing to take academic and professional risks on their road to the presidency.[111] Of all participants surveyed, five of eight cited risk-taking as a critical component of their upward mobility, including one president who offered this blunt assessment: "There's no such thing as a steady state, you're either moving an institution forward or it's going backward; there's no middle ground."[112]

The willingness to "take risks for learning and professional advancement" dovetails with the transformational leadership element of intellectual stimulation in which the leader challenges assumptions, takes risks, and solicits followers' ideas.[113] Transformational leaders are often misunderstood as "soft," but in reality, they are constantly challenging followers to higher levels of performance.[114]

All of the African American women community college presidents were forced to confront the twin demons of gender bias and racial discrimination in their ascent to the presidency at their institutions. All of the study's respondents acknowledged that they had experienced gender bias and racial discrimination either covertly or overtly. As a result of these incidences, they had to work above and beyond expectations to receive the level of respect they deserved.[115] One community college president reported that she has had to pay the "Black tax," a metaphor for working twice as hard as her White colleagues for the same reward.[116]

The external and internal pressures of dealing with both gender bias and racial discrimination are consistent with the transformational leadership element of idealized influence in which the leader provides a role model for high ethical behavior, instills pride, and gains respect and trust.[117] These women are overachievers in these areas, in an effort to assuage any doubt that they are not qualified for their positions, and to serve as a model of competence for their followers.[118]

FUTURE TRENDS: PATHWAYS TO DEVELOPING THE LEADER WITHIN

African American women seeking presidential appointments at community colleges should take advantage of opportunities to expand their professional, academic, and leadership potential by enrolling in educational programs that address those desires such as the Community College Leadership Doctoral Program at Morgan State University in Baltimore, Maryland.

Founded in 1998 by Dr. Christine Johnson McPhail, the doctoral program helps practitioners earn a doctorate in education so that they can advance to executive leadership roles at community colleges.[119] Since its inception two decades ago, the program has graduated 91 percent of its students, including 75 percent of whom are African American women.[120]

Under the leadership of Dr. Rosemary Gillett-Karam, former director and associate professor of higher education at Morgan State and former president of Louisburg College in Louisburg, North Carolina, the program expanded online in 2010 to widen the opportunity for more administrators of color seeking executive positions at two-year schools that serve a disproportionate number of African American and Latino students. An authority on community college leadership, Gillett-Karam has stated that the program debunks the myth that there are no qualified Blacks nor Latinos "coming through the pipeline" to assume executive leadership positions at community colleges.[121] The program, now directed by Dr. Myrtle E. B. Dorsey, is designed for working professionals and focuses on training professionals for the "unique situations encountered by senior administrators and faculty serving in community colleges."[122]

To ensure the continued upward trajectory of African American women community college presidents, it is necessary that an adequate support system be established and sustained to ensure their success. While there is no single panacea to close the gender and ethnicity leadership gap, there are several measures that can be employed to narrow the breach.

As individuals, African American women can become students of leadership through reading books and journals, watching educational videos and webinars, attending leadership training seminars, and taking advantage of volunteer opportunities that include leadership development to better position themselves to compete for leadership positions when they arise.[123]

African American women who aspire to the executive suites must speak up and negotiate for equal pay and fringe benefits with their White male and White female counterparts; establish clear leadership goals and work toward them with alacrity; keep a watchful eye for gender bias and stereotype threats and address them with all deliberate speed, and plan for potential career interruptions that may result in time away from the workforce.[124] Moreover, African American women who are seeking leadership roles must develop a transformational leadership style that embraces their cultural disposition toward caring, empathy, encouragement, motivation, positive reinforcement, ethics, integrity, trustworthiness, pride, and risk-taking.

NOTES

1. American Council on Education, "American College President Study 2017," last modified December 19, 2018, https://www.acenet.edu/news-room/Pages/American-College-President-Study.aspx.
2. American Council on Education, "American College President Study 2017."
3. Ibid.
4. Ibid.
5. Robbie Smith Latimore, "Rising to the Top: A National Study of Black Women Community College Presidents" (EdD diss., University of Georgia, 2009), 7.
6. Latimore, "Rising to the Top," 109.
7. American Association of Community College, "Executive Leadership Transitioning at Community Colleges," last modified December, 19, 2018, https://www.aacc.nche.edu/2018/04/30/executive-leadership-transitioning-at-community-colleges.
8. American Association of Community College, "Executive Leadership Transitioning at Community Colleges."
9. Ibid.

10. Ibid.

11. Catherine Hill and Kevin Miller, "Barriers and Bias: The Status of Women in Leadership," American Association of University Women, last modified December 18, 2018, https://www.aauw.org/research/barriers-and-bias.

12. Hill and Miller, "Barriers and Bias."

13. Ibid.

14. Ibid.

15. Langston University, "Transformational Leadership," last modified December 29, 2018, https://www.langston.edu/sites/default/files/basic-content-files/TransformationalLeadership.pdf.

16. Langston University, "Transformational Leadership."

17. Williams Political Science, "James MacGregor Burns Biography," last modified December 29, 2018, https://political-science.williams.edu/profile/jburns2.

18. Williams Political Science, "James MacGregor Burns Biography."

19. Langston University, "Transformational Leadership."

20. Ibid.

21. Ibid.

22. Ibid.

23. Ibid.

24. Bernard M. Bass, Bruce J. Avolio, Yair Berson, and Dong I. Jung, "Predicting Unit Performance by Assessing Transformational and Transactional Leadership," *Journal of Applied Psychology* 88, no. 2 (2003): 207–218. https://doi:10.1037/0021-9010.88.2.207.

25. Bass, Avolio, Berson, and Jung, "Predicting Unit Performance by Assessing Transformational and Transactional Leadership," 208.

26. Ibid., 208.

27. Ibid., 208.

28. Ibid., 208.

29. American Psychological Association, "Industrial and Organizational Psychology," last modified December 19, 2018, https://www.apa.org/ed/graduate/specialized/industrial.aspx.

30. American Psychological Association, "Industrial and Organizational Psychology."

31. Ibid.

32. Ibid.

33. Ibid.

34. Alice Walker, *In Search of Our Mother's Gardens: Womanist Prose* (New York, NY: Harcourt Brace Jovanovich, 1993), 94.

35. Dimpal Jain and Caroline Turner, "Purple is to Lavender: Womanism, Resistance, and the Politics of Naming," *The Negro Educational Review* 62/63, nos. 1–4 (Spring 2011/Winter 2012): 77.

36. Walker, *In Search of Our Mother's Gardens*, 94.

37. Linda Napikoski, "Womanist Feminism Definition," last modified February 28, 2018, https://www.thoughtco.com/womanist-feminism-definition-3528993.

38. Napikoski, "Womanist Feminism Definition."

39. Tamara Beauboeuf-Lafontant, "A Womanist Experience of Caring: Understanding the Pedagogy of Exemplary Black Women Teachers," *The Urban Review* 34, no. 1 (March 2002): 71–86. https://doi.org/10.1023/A:1014497228517.

40. Beauboeuf-Lafontant, "A Womanist Experience," 71–72.

41. Ibid., 72.

42. Ibid., 77.

43. Ibid., 78.

44. Ibid., 80.

45. Peter Northouse, *Leadership: Theory and Practice* (Los Angeles, CA: Sage Publications, 2015), 5.

46. Hill and Miller, "Barriers and Bias."

47. Ibid.

48. Ibid.

49. Ibid.

50. Janet S. Hyde, "Gender Similarities and Differences," *Annual Review of Psychology* 65 (2014): 373. https://doi.org/10.1146/annurev-psych-010213-115057.

51. Bass, Avolio, Berson, and Jung, "Predicting Unit Performance," 208.

52. Joan C. Williams and Rachel Dempsey, *What Works for Women at Work: Four Patterns Working Women Need to Know* (New York, NY: New York University Press, 2014), 221.

53. Lekan Oguntoyinbo, "Study: Female Leaders in Higher Ed Face Different Expectations than Males," *Diverse: Issues in Higher Education*, April 27, 2014, https://diverseeducation.com/article/63366.

54. Tiffani Lennon, "Benchmarking Women's Leadership in the United States," University of Denver, last modified December 19, 2018, https://womenscollege.du.edu/benchmarking-womens-leadership.

55. Hill and Miller, "Barriers and Bias."

56. Alice H. Eagly, Anne M. Koenig, Abigail A. Mitchell, and Tiina Ristikari, "Are Leader Stereotypes Masculine? A Meta-Analysis of Three Research Paradigms," *Psychological Bulletin* 137, no. 4 (May 2011): 616. http://dx.doi.org/10.1037/a0023557.

57. Hill and Miller, "Barriers and Bias."

58. Ibid.

59. Ibid.

60. Ibid.

61. Ibid.

62. Sylvia Ann Hewlett, "The Sponsor Effect: Breaking Through the Last Glass Ceiling," *Harvard Business Review*, last modified December 19, 2018, https://hbr.org/product/the-sponsor-effect-breaking-through-the-last-glass-ceiling/10428-PDF-ENG.

63. Hill and Miller, "Barriers and Bias."

64. Ibid.

65. Ibid.

66. Ibid.

67. Ibid.

68. Eagly, Koenig, Mitchell, and Ristikari, "Leader Stereotypes," 616. http://dx.doi.org/10.1037/a0023557.

69. Hill and Miller, "Barriers and Bias."
70. Ibid.
71. Ibid.
72. Ibid.
73. Ibid.
74. Project Implicit, "Frequently Asked Questions," last modified December 19, 2018, https://implicit.harvard.edu/implicit/faqs.html.
75. Hill and Miller, "Barriers and Bias."
76. Michelle M. Duguid, and Melissa C. Thomas-Hunt, "Condoning Stereotyping? How Awareness of Stereotyping Prevalence Impacts Expression of Stereotypes," *Journal of Applied Psychology* 100, no. 2 (2015): 343, https://doi:10.1037/a0037908.
77. Lennon, "Benchmarking Women's Leadership."
78. Shaki Asgari, Nilanjana Dasgupta, and Jane G. Stout, "When Do Counterstereotypic Ingroup Members Inspire Versus Deflate? The Effect of Successful Professional Women on Young Women's Leadership Self-Concept," *Personality and Social Psychology Bulletin* 38, no. 3 (December 2011): 370–371. https://doi.org/10.1177/0146167211431968.
79. "Executive Leadership."
80. Ibid.
81. Ibid.
82. Ibid.
83. Ibid.
84. Ibid.
85. Ibid.
86. Ibid.
87. "American College President Study."
88. Sandra Jackson, and Sandra Harris, "African-American Female College and University Presidents: Career Path to the Presidency," *Journal of Women in Educational Leadership* 165 (2005): 7, http://digitalcommons.unl.edu/jwel/165.
89. Jackson and Harris, "African-American Female College and University Presidents," 7.
90. Ruane Edwards-Wilson, "The Leadership Styles of African-American Female College Presidents at Four-Year Higher Education Institutions," (PhD diss., State University of New York at Buffalo, 1998), Dissertation Abstracts International, 28, 131.
91. Smith Latimore, "Rising to the Top," 109.
92. Ibid., 110.
93. Ibid., 110.
94. Ibid., 111.
95. "Transformational Leadership."
96. Smith Latimore, Rising to the Top," 126.
97. Ibid., 120.
98. "Transformational Leadership."
99. Ibid.
100. Ronald E. Riggio, "The Four Elements of Transformational Leaders," *Psychology Today,* last modified December 19, 2018, https://www.psychologytoday.com/us/blog/cutting-edge-leadership/201411/the-4-elements-transformational-leaders.

101. Smith Latimore, "Rising to the Top," 126.
102. Ibid., 126.
103. Ibid., 131.
104. Ibid., 127.
105. Ibid., 132.
106. Ibid.
107. Ibid.
108. Ibid., 133
109. "Transformational Leadership."
110. Riggio, "The Four Elements of Transformational Leaders."
111. Smith Latimore, "Rising to the Top," 135.
112. Ibid., 138.
113. "Transformational Leadership."
114. "Transformational Leadership."
115. Smith Latimore, "Rising to the Top," 139.
116. Ibid., 143.
117. "Transformational Leadership."
118. Riggio, "The Four Elements of Transformational Leaders."
119. Jamal Watson, "McPhail Rallies Around College Access," *Diverse: Issues in Higher Education*, April 16, 2018. https://diverseeducation.com/article/114428.
120. Ibid.
121. Malik Russell, "Morgan State Expands Community College Leadership Program Via Online," *Diverse: Issues in Higher Education*, November 18, 2010. https://diverseeducation.com/article/14409.
122. Morgan State University, "Community College Leadership Program," last modified December 19, 2018, https://www.morganstate.edu.
123. Hill and Miller, "Barriers and Bias."
124. Ibid.

BIBLIOGRAPHY

American Association of Community Colleges. "Executive Leadership Transitioning at Community Colleges." Last modified on December 19, 2018. https://www.aacc.nche.edu/2018/04/30/executive-leadership-transitioning-at-community-colleges.

American Council on Education. "American College President Study 2017." Last modified on December 19, 2018. https://www.acenet.edu/news-room/Pages/American-College-President-Study.aspx.

American Psychological Association. "Industrial and Organizational Psychology." Last modified on December 19, 2018. https://www.apa.org/ed/graduate/specialized/industrial.aspx.

Asgari, Shaki, Nilanjana Dasgupta, and Jane G. Stout. "When Do Counterstereotypic Ingroup Members Inspire Versus Deflate? The Effect of Successful Professional Women on Young Women's Leadership Self-Concept." *Personality and Social Psychology Bulletin* 38, no. 3 (December 2011): 370–383. https://doi.org/10.1177/0146167211431968.

Bass, Bernard M., Bruce J. Avolio, Yair Berson, and Dong I. Jung. "Predicting Unit Performance by Assessing Transformational and Transactional Leadership." *Journal of Applied Psychology* 88, no. 2 (2003): 207–218. https://doi:10.1037/0021-9010.88.2.207.

Beauboeuf-Lafontant, Tamara. "A Womanist Experience of Caring: Understanding the Pedagogy of Exemplary Black Women Teachers." *The Urban Review* 34, no. 1 (March 2002): 171–186. https://doi.org/10.1023/A:1014497228517.

Burns, James. *Leadership*. New York, NY: Harper & Row, 1978.

Duguid, Michelle M., and Melissa C. Thomas-Hunt. "Condoning Stereotyping? How Awareness of Stereotyping Prevalence Impacts Expression of Stereotypes." *Journal of Applied Psychology* 100, no. 2 (2015): 343–359. https://doi:10.1037/a0037908.

Eagly, Alice H., Anne M. Koenig, Abigail A. Mitchell, and Tiina Ristikari. "Are Leader Stereotypes Masculine? A Meta-Analysis of Three Research Paradigms." *Psychological Bulletin* 137, no. 4 (May 2011): 616–642. http://dx.doi.org/10.1037/a0023557.

Edwards-Wilson, R. "The Leadership Styles of African American Female College Presidents at Four-Year Higher Education Institutions." PhD diss., State University of New York at Buffalo, 1998. *Dissertation Abstracts International,* 28, 131.

Hewlett, Sylvia Ann, Kerry Peraino, Laura Sherbin, and Karen Sumberg. "The Sponsor Effect: Breaking Through the Last Glass Ceiling." *Harvard Business Review*. Last modified on December 19, 2018. https://hbr.org/product/the-sponsor-effect-breaking-through-the-last-glass-ceiling/10428-PDF-ENG.

Hill, Catherine, and Kevin Miller. "Barriers and Bias: The Status of Women in Leadership." American Association of University Women. Last modified on December 18, 2018. https://www.aauw.org/research/barriers-and-bias.

Hyde, Janet S. "Gender Similarities and Differences." *Annual Review of Psychology* 65 (2014): 373–398. https://doi.org/10.1146/annurev-psych-010213-115057.

Jackson, Sandra, and Sandra Harris. "African American Female College and University Presidents: Career Path to the Presidency." *Journal of Women in Educational Leadership* 165 (2005): 7–24. http://digitalcommons.unl.edu/jwel/165.

Jain, Dimpal, and Caroline Turner. "Purple is to Lavender: Womanism, Resistance, and the Politics of Naming." *The Negro Education Review* 62&63, nos.1–4 (2011&2012): 67–83.

Langston University. "Transformational Leadership." Last modified on December 29, 2018. https://www.langston.edu/sites/default/files/basic-content-files/TransformationalLeadership.pdf.

Lennon, Tiffani. "Benchmarking Women's Leadership in the United States." University of Denver. Last modified on December 19, 2018. https://womenscollege.du.edu/benchmarking-womens-leadership.

Morgan State University. "Community College Leadership Doctoral Program." Last modified on December 19, 2018. https://www.morganstate.edu.

Napikoski, Linda. "Womanist Feminism Definition." Last modified on February 28, 2018. ThoughtCo. https://www.thoughtco.com/womanist-feminism-definition-3528993.

Northouse, Peter G. *Leadership: Theory and Practice*. Los Angeles, CA: Sage Publications, 2015.

Oguntoyinbo, Lekan. "Study: Female Leaders in Higher Ed Face Different Expectations than Males." *Diverse: Issues in Higher Education*, April 27, 2014. https://diverseeducation.com/article/63366.

Project Implicit. "Frequently Asked Questions." Last modified on December 19, 2018. https://implicit.harvard.edu/implicit/faqs.html.

Riggio, Ronald E., "The Four Elements of Transformational Leaders." *Psychology Today*. Last modified on December 19, 2018. https://www.psychologytoday.com/us/blog/cutting-edge-leadership/201411/the-4-elements-transformational-leaders.

Russell, Malik. "Morgan State Expands Community College Leadership Program Via Online." *Diverse: Issues in Higher Education*, November 18, 2010. https://diverseeducation.com/article/14409.

Smith Latimore, Robbie. "Rising to the Top: A National Study of Black Women Community College Presidents." EdD diss., University of Georgia, 2009.

Walker, Alice. *In Search of Our Mother's Gardens: Womanist Prose*. New York, NY: Harcourt Brace Jovanovich, 1993.

Watson, Jamal. "McPhail Rallies Around College Access." *Diverse: Issues in Higher Education*, April 16, 2018. https://diverseeducation.com/article/114428.

Williams, Joan C., and Rachel Dempsey. *What Works for Women at Work: Four Patterns Working Women Need to Know*. New York, NY: New York University Press, 2014.

Williams Political Science. "James MacGregor Burns Biography." Last modified on December 29, 2018. https://political-science.williams.edu/profile/jburns2.

Chapter 4

The Impact of Maternity Leave Advice within the Academy on Work-Life Balance of Women Faculty and Administrators

Pavitra Kavya and Michael W. Kramer

Discussions about maternity leave policies became prominent in the United States with the implementation of the Family Medical and Leave Act (FMLA) in 1993. The FMLA provides instructions to both organizational leaders and employees on how to efficiently navigate family leave. The FMLA entitles employees to twelve weeks of leave and an opportunity to return to a job after the expiration of their leave.[1] Even though the FMLA has existed for more than two decades, organizational leaders still struggle to effectively manage family leave for employees.[2]

Family-leave policies were created to assist employees with maintaining work-life balance forming the triad of work-family policies alongside flexible work options and dependent-care benefits.[3] Clark defined work-life balance as "satisfaction and good functioning at work and at home, with a minimum of role conflict."[4] Based on empirical studies, work-life balance was linked positively to psychological well-being.[5]

In order to be perceived as fair and supportive of family-friendly practices, academic institutional leaders began adopting the *family* metaphor.[6] They hoped that using this metaphor would moderate the stress women and families experienced during the critical periods of pregnancy, childbirth, and postpartum. Since organizational leaders often lacked knowledge and understanding of individual work-life choices, the policies failed to alleviate these challenges.[7] Furthermore, the mere availability of a policy does not guarantee its utilization; organizational norms and peer pressure often influence practice far more than policy.[8] As a result, the actual impact of family-leave policy on work-life balance remains understudied.

Specific to the academy, the following illustration from *The Chronicle of Higher Education* highlights the struggles of faculty women:

> For instance, the year after my son was born, in the third year of my Ph.D. program, I found myself isolated, overwhelmed, and overlooked. I was replaced on projects I had previously worked on and wasn't invited to join others. I couldn't afford the money and time needed to travel to as many conferences. Even though I took no time off, enrolled my son in day care, and spent most days on campus working to meet deadlines, I was told that I wasn't serious about my research.[9]

Whitney Pirtle's experience shows that despite the adoption of FMLA, women continue to experience isolation and negative evaluations when they avail of leave benefits. The stigmas surrounding maternity leave create an environment where employers begin to talk in hushed tones behind the scenes. The second author, Dr. Michael Kramer, was department head at a university when four of the eleven faculty members experienced overlapping pregnancies. Vague policies and preexisting norms typecast the faculty as "pregnancy academics."[10] This label created uncertainty for the women as they navigated tenure and maternity. During this period, it was the pregnant faculty members who made the department head aware of the "phantom maternity policy."[11] The department chair labeled the policy this way as its essential tenets were never actively communicated by institutional leaders to department chairs or the university members at large. It was only through personal networks that some pregnant faculty became aware of the policy and communicated it to the department chair rather than the leadership communicating it to them. Lastly, the uncertainty of this period was enhanced by the members' struggle to balance their professional and personal identities.

Advice messages are a pervasive and universal form of social support across a wide range of relationships within organizations.[12] It is not surprising that faculty members seek advice from others, especially those in leadership positions or mentors filling leadership functions, to make sense of family-leave policies. Since the conception of FMLA, the need for maternity leave advice has become more necessary. Maternity leave advice from leaders and mentors, offered in good spirit and at the opportune moment, can play a mitigating role in helping women develop a sense of work-life balance. However, multiple factors relating to maternity, beginning with the time women plan to go on maternity leave, and including their return to work, dissatisfaction, work-family imbalance, requisite further examination.[13]

The focus of the present study is on communication surrounding family-leave policies, specifically maternity leave. The present study explores the advice given by leaders and mentors about maternity leave to women in the academy and its subsequent impact on their work–life balance. We focus on explicating the nature, properties, and characteristic features of maternity leave advice given by leaders and mentors through the retrospective accounts of ten female academic and administrative leaders.

REVIEW OF LITERATURE AND RESEARCH QUESTIONS

Maternity Leave Policies and Work-Life Balance

In 2016, according to the Bureau of Labor Statistics, only 19 percent of civil workers and 13 percent of private sector workers had access to paid parental leave.[14] Within the United States, only four states have paid maternity leave policies and laws: California, New Jersey, Massachusetts, and Rhode Island. Managing maternity leave continues to be among the toughest situations for organizational leaders as they are tasked with additional expenses, alongside loss of knowledgeable workers for a period of time. Miller, Jablin, Casey, Lamphear-Van Horn, and Ethington attributed the challenges to three main factors: (1) demographic changes within the United States resulting in an increase in women of childbearing age in the workforce; (2) biased attitudes held toward women actively utilizing their maternity leave; and (3) incompetent organizational leaders that are unable to create a smooth role-negotiation process for parents.[15]

New mothers are at risk for a variety of personal health and psychological challenges.[16] Often, society's "motherhood norm" sets the expectation on women to become the primary caretakers for the health of their newborn infant.[17] The situation is further aggravated by the problems women confront on their jobs, such as lack of a supportive organizational culture. Some coworkers have felt a sense of resentment as they were forced to "pick up the slack" for employees on leave.[18] Furthermore, most organizational leaders have not found an optimal solution to cope with the absence of female staffers on maternity leave. During the leave, women also experienced a sense of alienation from their organization which eventually made their transition back to work tougher.[19] Thus, women employees tend to associate maternity leave with downward incline in their careers.[20] Sometimes, the above perceptions influence women to dodge maternity leave.

Research indicates that women who do not receive some form of supportive culture from their organization post-maternity will leave their jobs, thereby losing a source of income for their families.[21] A 2014 *The New York Times* poll of non-employed adults (ages 25–54) in the United States showed that 67 percent of women polled as compared to 37 percent of men who were polled indicated family responsibilities as the number one factor preventing them from pursuing active employment.[22] The challenge of providing adequate support to women persists. Organizations struggle with constructing and implementing policies to create a culture that enables women to survive and thrive in the workplace post-maternity. In instances where equitable policies are constructed, leaders are unsure about how to communicate the benefits and limitations of the policy to employees. This results in a culture of ambiguity within the academy instead of a supportive one. By themselves, organizational policies cannot ameliorate the above problems. As a result, maternity leave has continued to cause significant career disruptions for women in both academia and business organizations.

Since 1966, there has been a steady growth in the number of women in academia.[23] Specifically, there has been a dramatic increase of female doctoral students from twelve to about forty-two percent. However, in spite of these trends, questions about gender equality in academia continue to be a concern. Mason and Goulden surveyed 8,500 active faculties in the University of California system and tracked approximately 30,000 PhDs in multiple disciplines across the National Science Foundation's (NSF) Survey of Doctorate Recipients (SDR).[24] They discovered that within the academy, the apathy of peers and administrators toward maternity leave alongside the presence of children negatively impacted the career trajectory of women. Thus, there is a high need to transform policy and attitudes of leaders and mentors to create a supportive culture for women experiencing maternity.

Maternity leave policies should tackle the numerous challenges of the maternity period alongside enhancing women's participation in the workforce. An ideal policy will address three main areas: (1) give women an opportunity to take care of their health alongside the needs of their child; (2) allow individuals to focus on the infant and family without any financial constraints; and (3) provide women a sense of job security and a pragmatic transition plan to resume work post their leave.

Models for such policies exist in countries outside the United States. For example, in India, the law allows women six months of paid maternity leave. Furthermore, in March 2014, SAP Lab India launched an application titled "Run Mummier" which allowed women on maternity leave to support each other.[25] Among first-time mothers, the initiative resulted in decreased attrition from thirty-one percent in 2010 to less than two percent in 2015.[26] Similarly, Epifanio and Troger analyzed 165 educational institutions in the United Kingdom and found a deep relationship between balanced family policies and faculty's productivity and research results.[27] The key element was that good policy implementation allowed faculty members to take rest during childbirth without worrying about the impact of the break on their career or tenure process. Consequently, the authors advocate for extended maternity leave as a means to enhance productivity in the workplace.

Advice, Leave Policy, and Work-Life Balance

When faced with interpersonal challenges, advice gained through face-to-face and online interactions becomes instrumental in providing care, encouragement, and guidance.[28] Advice reduces the beneficiaries' suffering alongside enhancing their coping mechanisms. For example, elderly women advise new mothers on infant care and organizational leaders advise subordinates on work-related challenges.[29] Advice is also central to mentoring and coaching relationships. Advice messages have the potential to create an apt space for brainstorming strategies to manage work problems[30] but it can threaten face/identity through generating defiance to the proposed ideas.[31]

Individuals often seek guidance and advice from organizational leaders and mentors while planning for both maternity and paternity leave. The potential positive effects of advice make it an essential feature for individuals grappling with the uncertainties of the family-leave process. Seeking maternity leave advice should be a simple process. Specifically, maternity leave advice offered in good spirit and at the opportune moment can play a mitigating role in understanding gender inequality and its pernicious effects. Appropriate advice seems essential for clarifying leave policies since individuals are typically hesitant to utilize existing policies, despite efforts by organizational leaders to make policies accessible.[32] In a 2008 special issue of the *Women Studies in Communication* journal, several faculty women wrote detailed experiences about the challenges of balancing personal care and career responsibilities.[33] These accounts highlight experiences, often negative, of individuals who did "academe differently" while circumnavigating the tenure process, pregnancy, childbirth, and maternity leave.

For example, McAlister's journey describes the biological reality of faculty women who struggle to realize the high expectations of the academy while simultaneously managing their "body clocks."[34] Dr. Melanie Mills was the first tenure track faculty in her department to experience pregnancy. Mills recounted, "I discovered very early that my institution did not have an explicit maternity leave. Instead I would use my 'sick' leave. So now having babies was not only frowned upon, it was 'sick'?"[35] Based on her experience Mills advises her students to examine the title (maternity, family, parental, disability, sick) of their future employer's leave policy as an indicator of their work culture. Sotirin's account describes the struggles of handling four pregnancies and a resultant low starting salary.[36] Her discussion about pay disparity makes salient the difficult choices faced by women, especially delaying childrearing. She recounts "maternity leaves at the university were (and still are) unpaid so I didn't consider taking time off for the birth. The department chair told me that covering classes was my responsibility, so I recruited people to cover for me for two weeks with materials that I put together for them."[37]

Waggoner's story touched on her journey as a new PhD seeking to work at an institution that would enable work-life balance.[38] She details the reality of work-life balance as a metaphor and concludes her story by asserting the need for new communication practices by organizational leaders to develop a work culture supportive of work-life balance.

Each of the narratives establish that work-life balance gets arbitrated, interpreted, and proclaimed through communication within the workplace.[39] The starting point for uncovering methods through which organizational policies and cultural practices may be made more conducive is the exploration of the intersection of women and the advice they are given versus their actual experiences when they take maternity leave. Examining the stories of women in academia seeking maternity leave advice provides an opportunity to view how *they* position themselves. These stories also enable us to examine how women employees perceive leaders, colleagues, administrators, and the policies they enact as positioning *them* as they request information regarding the benefits offered by family leave.

Furthermore, other factors related to maternity such as the decision by women to go on maternity leave, their return to work, and work-family balance strategies must also be addressed.[40] Effective maternity leave advice could be a strong moderator assisting women in managing work-life balance and pursuing leadership roles. While from an outsider's perspective the academy projects a culture of valuing work-life balance, this study sought to understand the specific advice members receive for navigating maternity leave and maintaining family and work balance from leaders and mentors in the academy.

Sensemaking and Positioning Theories

While navigating maternity leave and faced with uncertainty in organizational life, individuals engage in sensemaking, the process of retrospectively creating order and making meaning of events.[41] Combining sensemaking with positioning theory provides a theoretical overview for exploring academic women's accounts of giving and receiving maternity leave advice. Together, sensemaking and positioning theories explain how advice talk co-constructs academic women's agency in making important decisions which have implications for their life and career trajectories.

Sensemaking Theory

Sensemaking involves assigning meaning to situations or events that have already occurred.[42] As sensemaking helps individuals cope with disruptive occurrences within organizational life, it provides theoretical insight into women's experiences when faced with the ambiguity and anxiety of managing maternity leave and upholding a professional image/identity. Sensemaking becomes recognizable and apparent when there is uncertainty or ambiguity within the environment. For example, past research has examined sensemaking in contexts such as aircraft carriers and fire disasters among others.[43] Sensemaking is ongoing and reveals itself through communication among organizational members.[44] Individuals partake in this process by persistently asking themselves two interconnected questions: What is the story and what should we do next?[45] The two questions help individuals engage in backward-looking justifications for their past actions, along with articulating presumptions about future outcomes. Accordingly, the final story selected by individuals is one that is protective and/or reinforces the most significant and valued identity.[46]

Sensemaking is a social process. It tends to be about the questions, "How does something come to be an event for organizational members?"[47] Thus, it is a process that relies highly on extracted communicative cues. Sensemaking is also more focused on believability rather than precision.[48] The only expectation for sensemaking is that it should be relevant and appropriate to the organizational context, such that it is plausible rather than accurate. Maternity leave is one such organizational event in which sensemaking becomes salient due to the highly ambiguous and uncertain nature of the leave process and its outcomes. Faculty women who are attempting to navigate the labyrinth of polices and their department culture, against the backdrop of a male-dominated culture which provides ambiguous communication, start focusing on the cues extracted in their interactions with leading and mentors to understand their experience and make sense of organizational occurrences. Thus, sensemaking becomes a central theoretical framework in explaining how individuals attribute meaning to maternity leave experiences.[49] Sensemaking helps explain how advice plays a role in aiding faculty members understand expected standards of performance alongside managing work-life balance.

Discursive Positioning Theory

Since discursive approaches to organizations define how both our conversations and narratives help shape our social world, discursive positioning theory supplements sensemaking by focusing on the importance of specific communication messages, such as advice from leaders and mentors. Specific discourses can change the meaning of storylines and scenarios within the organizational life for members.[50] When organizational members seek advice from mentors and leaders, the specific narratives (or advice) enable sensemaking for individuals. Women may be infantilized as they are forced to go around using hushed voices lurking in the shadows of their institutions rather than having the voice and being welcomed to speak to authority about their circumstances. Overall, discourse (advice) can alter the possible outcomes for women who seek advice for maternity leave within the academy.

Positioning theory, as a form of discourse theory, enables researchers to examine how women faculty and administrators within the academy accept or challenge the assumptions and impact of maternity leave via interpersonal dialogues. These women often juggle multiple roles such as a mother and associate professor. Roles are often understood as fairly stable and static markers of identity. In contrast, positions are those identities which get invoked during specific discourses. Concerns around work-life balance start to emerge as individuals become overloaded with the responsibilities from a specific role.[51] Thereafter, every comment in the flow of conversation provides a context for summoning a position and thereby construct a new identity.[52] Similarly, advice about maternity leave gives individuals the opportunity for construction of various identities. For example, workers in a home healthcare and hospice organization resisted change via opposition to messages that created harsh and negative identities.[53] Similarly, maternity leave advice provides an opportunity to reinforce or reposition identities.

Positioning theory by Harre and Langenhove aids in examination of faculty accounts focused on construction of identity post-childbirth and -maternity leave within discourse episodes.[54] A positioning analysis explores the connections between positions, storylines, and speech acts.[55] For example, in an institution without a formal maternity leave policy, an organizational leader may provide advice and recommendations to enable new mothers to create work-life balance. This narrative creates a sense of equality and positions employees as both mothers and professionals. Alternatively, the leadership could promote advice messages that promote a culture that rewards extreme diligence at work and prioritizes the workplace. In either case, employees have the freedom to accept the position the advice creates or challenge the position and question the advice. Certain actions have the potential to be more resistant than others. Both options indicate that storylines are co-constructed by leaders and subordinates.

Research Questions

The literature review suggests examining the following two research questions. First, we focus on generating a list of the different kinds of advice that women received from administrators and mentors as they navigated childbirth and maternity leave. Specifically, we asked:

> RQ1: What kinds of maternity leave advice did women in the academy receive from university leaders and mentors?

Women in the academy must tackle a number of systemic challenges. According to the American Association of University Professors (AAUP), despite higher numbers of women procuring doctoral degrees, the number of women participating in the tenure process remains underrepresented.[56] Advice messages can have varying consequences ranging from an increase in distress levels to emotional support.[57] Consistent with sensemaking and positioning theory, we examined the positions that the storylines and narratives created for faculty women that led them to either tolerate or reject specific identities within the academy. Thus, we asked the second question:

RQ2: In what ways did the advice faculty women received from university leaders shape their understanding of their positions in the academy in relation to maternity leave policy and work-life balance?

METHOD

Participants

Participants were a subset of a larger study exploring how professional women navigated maternity leave across a range of organizations. To be included in this analysis, the participants met the following two criteria: (1) they held a tenure-track or an administrative position at a university; and (2) they experienced a maternity leave in some form during their career. Using her personal network, the first author recruited forty individuals for the larger study. Of those, ten were female faculty members or senior administrative leaders at multiple universities in the United States. Based on their personal experience of pursuing employment post-maternity leave, participants were well-poised to help address the relationship between advice and career trajectory post-maternity leave.

At the time of the interview, participants occupied positions such as dean, associate dean, associate professor, or assistant professor in the humanities, sciences, or social sciences at major research universities. They directly supervised between two to forty employees. In several instances, there were no official university policies pertaining to maternity leave. Thus, academic departments and units created their own policies and so there were no stated or established time period for maternity leave across participants. Most participants were relieved of their teaching requirements for one semester while receiving full pay, much like taking a sabbatical. A faculty member summarized the affordances offered by this policy as: "I think we're very fortunate in academia that there is a lot of flexibility in how we choose to do our jobs." Recalling when she was graduate student working on her PhD, another participant reported that she did not have access to maternity leave then. She mentioned: "So, I, you know, presented a paper at a conference ten days after my daughter was born and she went with me, and I was right back in the office working immediately." This statement suggests significant differences in policy for faculty and graduate students. These policies impacted the emotional response and overall well-being of women regarding their ability to focus fully on their families without worry for their financial and occupational futures.

Design

An interview schedule was developed to elicit participants' reflections from past, lived experiences.[58] Specifically, the questions focused on drawing out the advice participants received for navigating maternity leave and its impact on their lives. At the start of the interview, participants signed a consent form, as per Institutional Review Board (IRB) protocol. Interviews lasted from twenty-five to forty minutes. All interviews were digitally recorded. Transcriptions resulted in 190 double-spaced pages of transcript.

Interviews were conducted between September 2017 and May 2018. Participants had taken maternity leave six to forty years prior to the interviews. Each participant shared narratives from their first experience with maternity. Post-maternity leave some participants assumed leadership or administrative positions. Their role models during this time ranged from their grandmothers, mothers, and aunts to professional mentors, and included faculty men and women and office colleagues. Some role models served as examples of "what not to do." One participant reported this example of inappropriate work-life balance: "I distinctly remember hearing stories about one of them who was in his office working when his wife was in labor so not sure that was the best role model."

Analytic Strategy

To address the research question, a modified version of constant comparative analysis (CCA) was employed to conduct a thematic analysis in four main stages utilizing NVivo 12 software.[59] First, we engaged in data reduction, retaining only those data codes relevant to addressing the research questions.[60] For example, their descriptions of their duties were not analyzed, but a comment from a peer about maternity leave was because our primary focus was on identifying advice messages shared and received by the participants and the meaning participants assigned to that advice. Next, through a process of iterative open coding, the data were separated into categories and subcategories. Third, for focused coding, similarities and differences between the resultant categories from the open-coding process were examined resulting in condensed, overlapping categories.[61] Lastly, axial coding assigned meaningful labels to categories to demonstrate relationships between the final set of codes and the research questions and existing literature. There was back and forth between the four stages, signifying that the authors employed a nonlinear process to account for all the data.

Validation

Qualitative researchers are recommended to use at least two strategies for significantly increasing the quality of their research methods.[62] This study utilized the following three approaches. First, we used a theoretically constructed sample to inform emerging theory in the data.[63] Next, we provide thick, rich description by including direct quotes from the interviews to allow readers to evaluate our analysis. Lastly, the transcripts and findings were shared with three participants, at three checkpoints (post-transcription, preliminary coding and final analysis) for member check-in and reflection. Incorporating these tactics ensured and established the credibility of the results.[64]

RESULTS

According to Bisel and Barge advice messages provide opportune moments for women "to take up different positions."[65] A dean with a single maternity leave experience summarized that she made sense of pregnancy within the academy by focusing on tenure and waiting to have children. This was directly a result of the advice she received as a graduate student. As this anecdote indicates, advice to most of the participants included recommendations from mentors and leaders to delay maternity to the point when their careers were relatively stable, typically post-tenure which would cause them to be well into their thirties when childbearing is more challenging. This message also highlights the risk faculty women face in taking maternity leave by being typecast as choosing the "mommy track rather than the tenure track."[66]

RQ1: Types of Maternity Leave Advice

The thematic analysis revealed that faculty women received five major types of advice to assist them in making sense of and managing both their maternity and maternity leave. Those five included: (1) maternity leave as challenging; (2) attend to the child; (3) adapt to change; (4) conceal your pregnancy; and (5) no advice provided.

Advice from senior members of the academy frequently conveyed the message that maternity leave was a challenging process and hard to plan. One current associate dean noted, "the advice I got was it's very hard to plan when a child will come." This advice suggested women had limited control over maternity, which likely contributed to the anxiety felt by many faculty women. Another participant who had experienced two maternity leaves explained, "Literally on the day that I was in labor, my boss was calling to ask when I would be back at work." These advice messages highlighted the tough position academic women face. Furthermore, women made sense of these messages by concluding that a university work culture does not value work-life balance. It also made the presence of limited control salient and created a hostile work environment while they were trying to navigate care for their future child alongside their careers. Ultimately, both women resigned from their work positions within a few years of taking maternity leave. Their decision was driven by a desire to advance in their career as well as spend more time with their children. They later reentered the academy in different positions.

The second category of advice encouraged faculty women to focus on the child. Due to the limited time individuals could spend with their children, those in positions to give advice encouraged parents to spend time with their children in their formative years and enjoy each moment. An associate vice president recapped the advice she received as, "I think the biggest thing I got was take the time when you're off to be off and enjoy that time with your child. Work will be here when you get back; things will survive without you." Advice like this encouraged work-life balance by emphasizing the value of relationships with children over work. In spite of the hardship participants experienced having to sever ties with work for a temporary period, faculty women often trusted this advice and made sense of it by spending more time with their newborns and families. This demonstrated a relationship between the value of advice and the participants' desire to apply the recommended action.[67] In contrast to the first theme, focusing on the child meant that pregnancy, childbirth, and maternity were appreciated and treated as critical life events by universities.

Third, participants were encouraged to find ways to familiarize and adapt to their rapidly changing environment. Participants cherished their families and expressed passion toward their careers. They wanted to maintain work-life balance by managing their maternity leave in a manner that would not impact their careers. This advice suggested continual adaptation and involvement. A faculty woman currently serving in an administrative role recounts the following advice from a supervisor, "And he said this is a good lesson for you that from now on your time is not your own. Uh, you are not going to be the master of your own universe, but you have to learn to adapt." Advice messages like this supported faculty women in pursuing both the future career path they prized and their family roles but suggested that they needed to make sense of these dual careers as less predictable and controllable. This advice aided in establishing parenting norms through communicating the notion that it is acceptable for women to feel overwhelmed and conflicted on a basic human right. This category of advice focused on helping faculty members establish a bond with their universities by developing coping mechanism.[68] This senior administrator valued this advice and is still tenured at the same institution.

Next, faculty members were encouraged to conceal their ongoing maternity. A part-time adjunct instructor recalled the following advice from fellow colleagues to hide her pregnancy "as long as you can." This advice points to the stigma existing in academia toward maternity, portraying the new mother as lackadaisical about their career. This category of advice does not seem to aid in navigating maternity leave or developing a positive work-life balance. By encouraging concealment, it suggests maternity is contrary to the ideal worker norm that encourages complete commitment to work over other life activities.[69]

Lastly, a final theme that emerged from the analysis was that there was a lack of advice for some faculty women. Some participants stated that they did not receive formal advice from university leaders. One associate dean who experienced two maternity leaves concluded, "I should have gotten a lot more advice and I didn't." Participants suffered due to the lacunae of advice and felt any advice from the department or colleague would have been beneficial and advantageous. Another participant remembered, "So, I really didn't have any mentoring along the lines of maternity leave or how to navigate having a child in academia at all." An administrator who experienced two maternity leaves stated, "To be honest, I never got any advice." She attributed the stress she experienced to the lack of advice she received. These responses suggest that some faculty women must make sense of how to manage maternity on their own. This lack of advice from leaders communicates that women should figure out the balance between work and family by themselves.

Overall, faculty women had to make sense of maternity leave by reaching out to easily accessible experts. Examples included colleagues and administrators, as well as people outside their universities, such as friends and family members. Sometimes they had to make sense of their maternity leave without the benefit of advice and at other times, in the face of contradictory advice. Some advice encouraged a culture that supported work-life balance (e.g., focus on the child), some seemed to emphasize a culture that focused on work (e.g., maternity is challenging, conceal your pregnancy), while some was ambiguous (e.g., adapt to change). Although many faculty categorized much of the advice as helpful, many of them did not reach out proactively for advice.

RQ2: Influence on Understanding of Work-Life Balance

Women faculty members and leaders approached the process of maternity differently. This was prompted by diverse circumstances since participants had taken maternity leave across the past four decades, starting in the 1970s. Implementation and utilization of maternity leave policies has undergone significant transformation over that time. The analysis of each interview revealed that women in academia challenged or accepted the position they were offered through the structure of maternity leave in three distinct ways as they engaged with the policies while trying to accomplish work-life balance. The participants' maternity leave experiences further showcased that existence of policy did not necessarily result in work-life balance.[70]

Policy Users

Many individuals positioned themselves simply as policy users. In instances where there were clear guidelines and instructions given to them by organizational leaders about maternity leave policies, policy users focused on formulating a clear action plan to ensure a smooth childbirth and postpartum care within the restraints of the policy. A dean who had experienced one maternity leave advocated for new mothers to utilize every benefit afforded by the policy. She stressed the importance of maternity and the value of child care as a once in a lifetime moment that if underutilized would be filled with regrets. Participants like this acknowledged their privilege due to access to a great maternity leave plan. Communication of a clear and generous policy by university leaders helped prevent maternity from derailing their careers.

In situations where university leaders did not communicate clear policies, participants who were determined to be policy users created their own interpretation of policy. Subsequently, their stories demonstrated their hardiness as they overcame the ambiguity surrounding a vaguely communicated policy. For example, an administrator shared "it feels like I had to figure things out. And figure out what worked for our family, for our lifestyle." Faculty members like her demonstrated resilience by taking the initiative and used the lack of a clear policy to create their own position as a policy user. This enabled them to create the kind of work-life balance they preferred with the restrictions of an uncertain policy.

By utilizing the existing maternity leave policy, participants showcased their ability to assume a position as policy users, by making sense of either clearly communicated or ambiguous policies. They also expressed a clear desire to utilize the affordances available to them through the policies to manage work-life balance in the most advantageous way possible.

Policy Improvers

Instead of simply using policies communicated to them, some individuals positioned themselves as policy improvers. A dean with one maternity leave experience stated the importance of constantly improving policies as a way to provide the best care for people who were having children in their departments and offices. Individuals like this advocated for continued enhancement and development of maternity policies to better serve faculty women. By contrast, another department chair, who was a graduate student during her maternity, recalled with deep gratitude the help she received from a professor through a supportive relationship, during a tough pregnancy. The professor made accommodations for the participant in terms of attending classes and meeting with her privately at a more convenient moment, alongside giving her some very much appreciated extensions occasionally on assignments.

Individuals like the helpful faculty member did not work to formally change policies, but instead worked to improve the policy by focusing on serving the individuals experiencing maternity by being supportive and making accommodations. Their leadership and compassionate communicate style was instrumental in ensuring that the participant did not drop out of the academy, but rather progressed successfully and created a stellar career. Through formal methods of changing policies or informal methods of finding room to focus on serving individuals needing maternity leave, policy changers helped participants make sense of the obstacles around childbirth with the goal of minimizing the potential negative career outcomes of maternity.

Work-Life Balancers

Similarly, participants in the present study were eager to go beyond policy utilization to position themselves as capable of establishing work-life balance. Participants seemed to be inspired to manage work-life balance and attain stability and equilibrium through either their own mindset or via role models. For example, one current administrator with two maternity leaves each recalled, "I am career driven. I did want to have kids. My kids come first but my career is a really close second and so being able to manage that was going to be important to me." Similarly, an associate dean described her experience accordingly:

> I was able to take my time and I wasn't a work horse, or a robot and it was very fluid and organic. So, you know. I think if going forward if we do creative things we might have to choose either, or if we have a demanding job that needs sixty hours a week and 100% productivity, but I think that it can be done if, uh, it's gotta be culture.

Participants like these two position themselves as managing maternity leave in a way that supported both their career and family identities. To support both identities, work-life balancers relied on role models, particularly family and friends rather than organizational leaders. Another dean stated that she needed to "figure out what am I going to do having this child and being a professional. I just, that was modeled for me, my grandmother, you know, both of my grandmothers, my mom, were working people, and so I just never really questioned. I didn't really have many questions." Their narratives highlighted the significance of role models in helping them position themselves as achieving work-life balance during and after their maternity leave. Work-life balancers seemed motivated by their role models to accomplish work-life balance regardless of the organizational policy communicated to them.

Overall

Faculty women positioned themselves as managing their maternity leaves in ways that supported strong work and family identities either by using policies as communicated to them to their advantage, changing those policies formally or informally to meet their needs particularly when they were ambiguous, or by focusing on work-life balance apart from official policy. Despite making sense of their positions this way, the end result of their experiences seems to favor work over family identities. A senior administrator described the desperate urgency and what some would call down right abuse and the adverse impact of sudden emergencies during her maternity leave as: "Some of the things, in honesty, I had to do from my bed in the hospital while I had bedrest, you know, just to insure, you know, those things had to come in place." Another participant said, "you just have your babies, you suck it up, and you figure it out." Participants like these recounted experiences of personal sacrifices they had to undergo in order to remain on track for tenure or eligible for job elevations given their universities' culture. In the end, faculty women had to first make sense of maternity leave with limited—and even confusing—advice from university leaders and mentors and then assume subject positions in order to maintain a sense of agency over their maternity leave while managing their self-identities as both good organizational or professional citizens and parents. Balancing work-life in a manner that accomplishes the most good or causes the least harm to one's job and personal identities was challenging.

DISCUSSION

As universities focus their efforts on revamping parental-leave policies, it is important to capture the present struggles faced by faculty women. With its focus on communicative messages (advice), the present study first sought to uncover the types of advice faculty women received about their maternity leaves. Findings indicated that faculty women received five major categories of advice from multiple stakeholders such as university leaders and mentors to help them navigate the stress of the workplace during childbirth: (1) Individuals were told that maternity would be hard to plan; (2) They were also advised to spend time with their children; (3) They were often told to familiarize and adjust to their rapidly changing environment; (4) They were encouraged to conceal their pregnancy as long as possible; and (5) lastly, some participants declared they received no advice from university leaders. As expectant mothers, they were forced to make sense of the family-leave advice, constantly mindful of its impact on their work-life balance. Next, the study explored how in making sense of the advice, faculty women assumed one of three positions in relation to maternity leave policies communicated to them: policy users, policy improvers, and work-life balancers. The individual's interaction with maternity leave policy shaped their work-life identities and also performance of the job post-maternity leave.

Many but not all of these women received career advice from leaders, mentors, and family members when they approached an important career moment, maternity. Unfortunately, it is often after maternity leave that women's participation in leadership and organizational activities declines.[71] Thus, today we have a growing population of women in faculty positions, but not in senior faculty or administrative roles.[72] Advice received formally from leaders and informally from mentors serving in leadership roles was crucial to faculty women being able to pursue these career goals and overcome the constraints that maternity often creates for them. Advice can also create a downward spiral as it constrains an individual from progression or upward-movement if it disables further growth.[73]

The communication from organizational leaders and mentors creates an organizational culture surrounding maternity. Clearly stated policies can communicate support for maternity and work-life balance. By contrast, alternative messages can create a culture that rewards work over family. Ambiguous or contradictory messages or a lack of communication about maternity, a common experience for these women, creates a culture of uncertainty surrounding maternity and work-life balance leaving faculty women on their own to make sense of the culture. Many of these women demonstrated resilience by claiming positive work and family identities despite the mixed messages they received from organizational leaders and mentors. Furthermore, many of these women paved the way for future generations of scholars by working as organizational leaders to institute policies or practices surrounding maternity leave at their departments and institutions later in their careers.

Combining sensemaking and discursive positioning theories in the current study highlighted two important implications for future research into advice, maternity leave and work-life balance during academic careers. First, the narratives of these faculty women emphasize how the struggles they face as they battle the tenure clock are often created through the paradoxical advice they receive from organizational leaders that provides mixed messages on managing work-life balance.[74] The findings also highlight that a work culture can prioritize work-life balance rather than highlighting work. Some factors that would support a culture of work-life balance include greater family-leave policy development and supervisor training on understanding employee sensitivity at universities rather than administrators who expect faculty women to be productive during maternity.[75] A supportive work culture will likely ensure a higher retention rate and commitment from workers.

The categories of advice demonstrate the value of advice messages from organizational leaders in helping individuals manage challenges that may occur during additional perplexing interactions at the workplace. Past research showcased how advising strategies of peer tutors reflects on the philosophies of the workplace.[76] Similarly, the category of advice messages can be utilized as training material by universities. The categories easily reflect a list of do's (e.g., spend time with the child) and don'ts (e.g., conceal your pregnancy or no advice) in creating a culture that supports work-life balance. These findings can enable leaders and mentors to support workers by becoming more mindful of interpersonal interactions at the workplace, especially in the context of situations like maternity. Maternity is a nourishing period of life. In a study of Finish employees, those with beneficial work-life balance were found to have the highest psychological functioning and exhibited more professional belonging at work.[77] Future research could utilize empirical methods to investigate the impact of each type of advice message and its relationship with other important organizational outcomes.

Limitations and Future Research

Although the current sample size is a significant limitation, the rigorous interview schedule and an extensive interview process enabled the study to serve as an important, initial exploration into the research questions. In addition, the retrospective accounts, some collected years after the events occurred, means that the exact advice messages and subsequent conversation were not collected. However, the recollections likely represent participants' retrospective sensemaking of the advice they received from leaders and mentors. Lastly, since the majority of the participants were employed at large research universities, additional examinations across other university contexts are needed. Each interviewee chose to work at a research-intensive university rather than institutions with a stronger emphasis on teaching. The reasons for that choice were not explored in the interviews but may have influenced their maternity leave experiences. Future research may be conducted at various universities that offer concrete maternity leave polices and who pair expectant mothers with other faculty who have experienced similar circumstances. These policies and benefits are often communicated to new employees during the onboarding process at the universities who employ such practices.

CONCLUSION

This study generated research questions surrounding maternity leave advice and its impact for university faculty women based on previous research conducted on work-life balance and advice paradigms. Results indicated that participants struggled making sense from contradictory or incomplete advice messages from university leaders and mentors. Although they assumed various positions in relationship to the policies (or lack thereof), those positions did not inherently lead to accomplishing work-life balance. However, through their narratives, participants exhibited resilience and determination as they managed their career and family identities. Faculty women often challenged the policies and positions they were placed in with varying degrees of success and created alternate work and family identities that enabled them to continue in the academy as part of the next generation of scholars particularly when they assumed leadership roles. Even when these scholars did not hold a formal leadership position, they still advocated for fair practices surrounding maternity leave alongside treating all women with respect and dignity during this tough process.

NOTES

1. Kenza Bemis Nelson, "Employer Difficulty in FMLA Implementation: A Look at Eighth Circuit Interpretation of Serious Health Condition and Employee Notice Requirements," *Journal of Corporation Law* 30, no. 3 (Spring 2005): 609.

2. Kristin E. Smith and Amara Bachu, *Women's Labor Force Attachment Patterns and Maternity Leave: A Review of the Literature* (Population Division, U.S. Bureau of the Census, 1999).

3. Hal Morgan and Frances J. Milliken, "Keys to Action: Understanding Differences in Organizations' Responsiveness to Work-and-Family Issues," *Human Resource Management* 31, no. 3 (1992): 227.

4. Sue Campbell Clark, "Work/Family Border Theory: A New Theory of Work/Family Balance," *Human Relations* 53, no. 6 (2000): 751.

5. Maribeth C. Clarke, Laura C. Koch, and E. Jeffrey Hill, "The Work-Family Interface: Differentiating Balance and Fit," *Family and Consumer Sciences Research Journal* 33, no. 2 (2004): 136.

6. Catherine Egley Waggoner, "Academic Adultery: Surreptitious Performances of the Professor/Mother," *Women's Studies in Communication* 31, no. 2 (2008): 211.

7. Sharon Alisa Lobel, "Allocation of Investment in Work and Family Roles: Alternative Theories and Implications for Research," *Academy of Management Review* 16, no. 3 (1991): 509–510.

8. Erika Kirby, and Kathleen Krone, "The Policy Exists But You Can't Really Use It": Communication and the Structuration of Work-Family Policies," *Journal of Applied Communication Research* 30, no. 1 (2002): 68.

9. Whitney N. L. Pirtle, "Motherhood while Black," *The Chronicle of Higher Education*. April 5, 2018. Last modified December 20, 2018.

10. Jennifer Stevens Aubrey, Melissa A. Click, Debbie S. Dougherty, Mark A. Fine, Michael W. Kramer, Rebecca J. Meisenbach, Loreen N. Olson, and Mary-Jeanette Smythe, "We Do Babies! The Trials, Tribulations, and Triumphs of Pregnancy and Parenting in the Academy," *Women's Studies in Communication* 31, no. 2 (2008): 188.

11. Michael W. Kramer, "The Year of the Newborns: A Department Chair's Reflections," *Women's Studies in Communication* 31, no. 2 (2008): 197.

12. Erina L. MacGeorge, Bo Feng, and Lisa M. Guntzviller, "Advice: Expanding the Communication Paradigm," *Annals of the International Communication Association* 40, no. 1 (2016): 214.

13. Patrice M. Buzzanell and Meina Liu, "Struggling with Maternity Leave Policies and Practices: A Poststructuralist Feminist Analysis of Gendered Organizing," *Journal of Applied Communication Research* 33, no. 1 (2005): 19.

14. Drew Desilver, "Access to Paid Family Leave Varies Widely Across Employers, Industries," *Pew Research Center*, March 23, 2017.

15. Vernon D. Miller, Fredric M. Jablin, Mary K. Casey, Martha Lamphear-Van Horn, and Caroline Ethington, "The Maternity Leave as a Role Negotiation Process," *Journal of Managerial Issues* (1996): 286.

16. Mauricio Avendano, Lisa F. Berkman, Agar Brugiavini, and Giacomo Pasini, "The Long-run Effect of Maternity Leave Benefits on Mental Health: Evidence from European Countries," *Social Science & Medicine* 132 (2015): 45.

17. Robert William Drago, *Striking a Balance: Work, Family, Life* (Boston, MA: Dollars & Sense, 2007), 7.

18. Kirby and Krone, "The Policy Exists," 56.

19. Brinda Dasgupta and Saumya Bhattacharya, "Staff on Maternity Leave? Keep in Touch," *The Economic Times*, July 12, 2016.

20. Miller et al., "The Maternity Leave," 302.

21. Smith and Bachu, *Women's Labor Force*.

22. Claire C. Miller and Liz Alderman, "Why U.S. Women Are Leaving Jobs Behind," *The New York Times*, December 12, 2014.

23. Mary Ann Mason and Marc Goulden, "Marriage and Baby Blues: Redefining Gender Equity in the Academy," *The Annals of the American Academy of Political and Social Science* 596, no. 1 (2004): 86–87.

24. Mason and Goulden, "Marriage and Baby Blues," 88–89.

25. Dasgupta and Bhattacharya, "Staff on Maternity Leave?"

26. Ibid.

27. Mariaelisa Epifanio and Vera E. Troeger, *How Much Do Children Really Cost? Maternity Benefits and Career Opportunities of Women in academia*, CAGE Online Working Paper Series, 171. Competitive Advantage in the Global Economy (CAGE), 2013.

28. Erina L. MacGeorge, Bo Feng, Ginger L. Butler, and Sara K. Budarz, "Understanding Advice in Supportive Interactions: Beyond the Facework and Message Evaluation Paradigm," *Human Communication Research* 30, no. 1 (2004): 43.

29. MacGeorge et al., "Advice: Expanding the Communication Paradigm," 214.

30. Stacy Tye-Williams and Kathleen J. Krone, "Identifying and Re-imagining the Paradox of Workplace Bullying Advice," *Journal of Applied Communication Research* 45, no. 2 (2017): 218.

31. Daena J. Goldsmith and Kristine Fitch, "The Normative Context of Advice as Social Support," *Human Communication Research* 23, no. 4 (1997): 455.

32. Kirby and Krone, "The Policy Exists," 68.

33. Nikki C. Townsley and Kirsten J. Broadfoot, "Care, Career, and Academe: Heeding the Calls of a New Professoriate [Special Issue]," *Women's Studies in Communication* 31, no. 2 (2008): 133–134.

34. Joan Faber McAlister, "Lives of the Mind/Body: Alarming Notes on the Tenure and Biological Clocks," *Women's Studies in Communication* 31, no. 2 (2008): 218–219.

35. Melanie Bailey Mills, "Intersections between Work and Family: When a Playpen Can Be Office Furniture," *Women's Studies in Communication* 31, no. 2 (2008): 214.

36. Patty Sotirin, "Academic Momhood: In for the Long Haul," *Women's Studies in Communication* 31, no. 2 (2008): 264.

37. Sotirin, "Academic Momhood: In for the Long Haul."

38. Waggoner, "Academic Adultery: Surreptitious Performances," 209.

39. Claartje L. Ter Hoeven, Vernon D. Miller, Bram Peper, and Laura Den Dulk, "The Work Must Go On," *Management Communication Quarterly* 31, no. 2 (2017): 216.

40. Buzzanell and Liu, "Struggling with Maternity Leave Policies," 19.

41. Jennifer A. Scarduzio and Sarah J. Tracy, "Sensegiving and Sensebreaking via Emotion Cycles and Emotional Buffering: How Collective Communication Creates Order in the Courtroom," *Management Communication Quarterly* 29, no. 3 (2015): 332.

42. Karl E. Weick, *Sensemaking in Organizations* (Thousand Oaks, CA: Sage, 2005), 4.

43. Weick, *Sensemaking in Organizations*, 103.

44. Karl E. Weick, Kathleen M. Sutcliffe, and David Obstfeld, "Organizing and the Process of Sensemaking," *Organization Science* 16, no. 4 (2005): 409.

45. Weick, *Sensemaking in Organizations*, 103–104.

46. Weick et al., "Organizing and the Process," 416.

47. Ibid., 410.

48. Debbie Dougherty and Mary-Jeanette Smythe, "Sensemaking, Organizational Culture, and Sexual Harassment," *Journal of Applied Communication Research* 32, no. 4 (2004): 297.

49. Weick et al., "Organizing and the Process," 410.//
50. Robert J. Marshak and David Grant, "Transforming Talk: The Interplay of Discourse, Power, and Change," *Organization Development Journal* 26, no. 3 (2008).//
51. Rosalind C. Barnett and Grace K. Baruch, "Women's Involvement in Multiple Roles and Psychological Distress," *Journal of Personality and Social Psychology* 49, no. 1 (1985): 144.//
52. Ryan S. Bisel and J. Kevin Barge, "Discursive Positioning and Planned Change in Organizations," *Human Relations* 64, no. 2 (2011): 261.//
53. Bisel and Barge, "Discursive Positioning and Planned Change in Organizations," 276.//
54. Rom Harré, Fathali M. Moghaddam, Tracey Pilkerton Cairnie, Daniel Rothbart, and Steven R. Sabat, "Recent Advances in Positioning Theory," *Theory & Psychology* 19, no. 1 (2009): 20.//
55. Bisel and Barge, "Discursive Positioning and Planned Change," 259–260.//
56. Martha S. West and John W Curtis, *AAUP Faculty Gender Equity Indicators 2006* (Washington, DC: American Association of University Professors, 2006).//
57. MacGeorge et al., "Advice: Expanding the Communication Paradigm," 216–217.//
58. Sarah J. Tracy, *Qualitative Research Methods: Collecting Evidence, Crafting Analysis, Communicating Impact* (Hoboken, NJ: John Wiley & Sons, 2012), 139.//
59. Barney G. Glaser and Anselm L. Strauss, *The Discovery of Grounded Theory: Strategies for Qualitative Research* (Chicago, IL: Aldire, 1967), 105.//
60. Thomas R. Lindlof and Bryan C. Taylor, *Qualitative Communication Research Methods*, 3rd ed. (Thousand Oaks, CA: Sage), 2011.//
61. Kathy Charmaz and Liska Belgrave, "Qualitative Interviewing and Grounded Theory Analysis," *The Sage Handbook of Interview Research: The Complexity of the Craft* 2 (2012): 347–365.//
62. Tracy, *Qualitative Research Methods*, 228.//
63. Ibid., 136.//
64. Michael W. Kramer and David A. Crespy, "Communicating Collaborative Leadership," *The Leadership Quarterly* 22, no. 5 (2011): 1027.//
65. Bisel and Barge, "Discursive Positioning and Planned Change," 258.//
66. McAlister, "Lives of the Mind/Body," 221.//
67. MacGeorge et al., "Advice: Expanding the Communication Paradigm," 215.//
68. Erina L. MacGeorge, Lisa M. Guntzviller, Lisa K. Hanasono, and Bo Feng, "Testing Advice Response Theory in Interactions with Friends," *Communication Research* 43, no. 2 (2016): 212.//
69. Drago, *Striking a Balance*, 7–9.//
70. Kirby and Krone, "The Policy Exists," 74.//
71. Wen-Jui Han, Christopher J. Ruhm, Jane Waldfogel, and Elizabeth Washbrook, "The Timing of Mothers' Employment After Childbirth," *Monthly Labor Review/US Department of Labor, Bureau of Labor Statistics* 131, no. 6 (2008): 15.//
72. West and Curtis, *AAUP Faculty Gender Equity Indicators*.//
73. MacGeorge et al., "Advice: Expanding the Communication Paradigm," 215.//
74. McAlister, "Lives of the Mind/Body," 221.

75. Johanna Rantanen, Ulla Kinnunen, Saija Mauno, and Kati Tillemann, "Introducing Theoretical Approaches to Work-Life Balance and Testing a New Typology among Professionals," In *Creating Balance?*, 44.
76. Innhwa Park, "Seeking Advice: Epistemic Asymmetry and Learner Autonomy in Writing Conferences," *Journal of Pragmatics* 44, no. 14 (2012): 2010.
77. Johanna Rantanen, *Work-family Interface and Psychological Well-Being: A Personality and Longitudinal Perspective*. No. 346 (University of Jyväskylä, 2008).

BIBLIOGRAPHY

Alvesson, Mats, and Dan Karreman. "Varieties of Discourse: On the Study of Organizations through Discourse Analysis." *Human Relations* 53, no. 9 (2000): 1125–1149. doi: 10.1177/0018726700539002.

Aubrey, Jennifer Stevens, Melissa A. Click, Debbie S. Dougherty, Mark A. Fine, Michael W. Kramer, Rebecca J. Meisenbach, Loreen N. Olson, and Mary-Jeanette Smythe. "We Do Babies! The Trials, Tribulations, and Triumphs of Pregnancy and Parenting in the Academy." *Women's Studies in Communication* 31, no. 2 (2008): 186–195. doi: 10.1080/07491409.2008.10162531.

Avendano, Mauricio, Lisa F. Berkman, Agar Brugiavini, and Giacomo Pasini. "The Long-run Effect of Maternity Leave Benefits on Mental Health: Evidence from European Countries." *Social Science & Medicine* 132 (2015): 45–53. doi: 10.1016/j.socscimed.2015.02.037.

Barnett, Rosalind C., and Grace K. Baruch. "Women's Involvement in Multiple Roles and Psychological Distress." *Journal of Personality and Social Psychology* 49, no. 1 (1985): 135–145. http://dx.doi.org/10.1037/0022-3514.49.1.135.

Bisel, Ryan S., and J. Kevin Barge. "Discursive Positioning and Planned Change in Organizations." *Human Relations* 64, no. 2 (2011): 257–283. doi: 10.1177/0018726710375996.

Bulger, Carrie A., Russell A. Matthews, Mark E. Hoffman, and Louis E. Tetrick. "Work and Personal Life Boundary Management: Boundary Strength, Work/Personal Life Balance, and the Segmentation–Integration Continuum." *Journal of Occupational Health Psychology* 12, no. 4 (2007): 365–375. doi: 10.1037/1076-8998.12.4.365.

Buzzanell, Patrice M., and Meina Liu. "Struggling with Maternity Leave Policies and Practices: A Poststructuralist Feminist Analysis of Gendered Organizing." *Journal of Applied Communication Research* 33, no. 1 (2005): 1–25. doi: 10.1080/00909880420003 18495.

Buzzanell, Patrice M., Rebecca Meisenbach, Robyn Remke, Meina Liu, Venessa Bowers, and Cindy Conn. "The Good Working Mother: Managerial Women's Sensemaking and Feelings about Work–Family Issues." *Communication Studies* 56, no. 3 (2005): 261–285. doi: 10.1080/10510970500181389.

Buzzanell, Patrice M., Robyn V. Remke, Rebecca Meisenbach, Meina Liu, Venessa Bowers, and Cindy Conn. "Standpoints of Maternity Leave: Discourses of Temporality and Ability." *Women's Studies in Communication* 40, no. 1 (2017): 67–90. doi: 10.1080/07491409.2015.1113451.

Charmaz, Kathy, and Liska Belgrave. "Qualitative Interviewing and Grounded Theory Analysis." *The SAGE Handbook of Interview Research: The Complexity of the Craft* 2, 347–365. Thousand Oaks, CA: Sage, 2012.

Clark, Sue Campbell. "Work/Family Border Theory: A New Theory of Work/Family Balance." *Human Relations* 53, no. 6 (2000): 747–770. doi: 10.1177/0018726700536001.

Clarke, Maribeth C., Laura C. Koch, and E. Jeffrey Hill. "The Work-family Interface: Differentiating Balance and Fit." *Family and Consumer Sciences Research Journal* 33, no. 2 (2004): 121–140. doi: 10.1177/1077727X04269610.

Dasgupta, Brinda, and Saumya Bhattacharya. "Staff on Maternity Leave? Keep in Touch." *The Economic Times*, July 12, 2016. Last modified December 20, 2018. https://economictimes.indiatimes.com/jobs/staff-on-maternity-leave-keep-in-touch/articleshow/53164364.cms.

Desilver, Drew. "Access to Paid Family Leave Varies Widely Across Employers, Industries." *Pew Research Center*, March 23, 2017. Last modified December 18, 2018. http://www.pewresearch.org/fact-tank/2017/03/23/access-to-paid-family-leave-varies-widely-across-employers-industries/.

Dougherty, Debbie, and Mary-Jeanette Smythe. "Sensemaking, Organizational Culture, and Sexual Harassment." *Journal of Applied Communication Research* 32, no. 4 (2004): 293–317. doi: 10.1080/0090988042000275998.

Drago, Robert William. *Striking a Balance: Work, Family, Life*. Boston, MA: Dollars & Sense, 2007.

Epifanio, Mariaelisa, and Vera E. Troeger. *How Much do Children Really Cost? Maternity Benefits and Career Opportunities of Women in Academia*. CAGE Online Working Paper Series 171. Competitive Advantage in the Global Economy (CAGE), 2013.

Glaser, Barney G., and Anselm L. Strauss. *The Discovery of Grounded Theory: Strategies for Qualitative Research*. Chicago, IL: Aldire, 1967.

Goldsmith, Daena J. *Communicating Social Support*. Cambridge, United Kingdom: Cambridge University Press, 2004.

Goldsmith, Daena J., and Kristine Fitch. "The Normative Context of Advice as Social Support." *Human Communication Research* 23, no. 4 (1997): 454–476. doi: 10.1111/j.1468-2958.1997.tb00406.x.Han, Wen-Jui, Christopher J. Ruhm, Jane Waldfogel, and Elizabeth Washbrook. "The Timing of Mothers' Employment after Childbirth." *Monthly Labor Review/US Department of Labor, Bureau of Labor Statistics* 131, no. 6 (2008): 15.

Harré, Rom. "Positioning Theory: Moral Dimensions of Social-Cultural Psychology." In *The Oxford Handbook of Culture and Psychology*. New York, NY: Oxford University Press, 2012.

Harré, Rom, and Luk V. Langenhove. *Positioning Theory: Moral Context of Intentional Action*. Malden, MA: Blackwell, 1999.

Harré, Rom, Fathali M. Moghaddam, Tracey Pilkerton Cairnie, Daniel Rothbart, and Steven R. Sabat. "Recent Advances in Positioning Theory." *Theory & Psychology* 19, no. 1 (2009): 5–31. doi: 10.1177/0959354308101417.

Jackson, Lorraine D. "Reflections on Obstacles and Opportunities: Suggestions for Improving the Retention of Female Faculty." *Women's Studies in Communication* 31, no. 2 (2008): 226–232. doi: 10.1080/07491409.2008.10162537.

Kirby, Erika, and Kathleen Krone. "The Policy Exists But You Can't Really Use It: Communication and the Structuration of Work-Family Policies." *Journal of Applied Communication Research* 30, no. 1 (2002): 50–77. doi: 10.1080/00909880216577.

Kramer, Michael W. "The Year of the Newborns: A Department Chair's Reflections." *Women's Studies in Communication* 31, no. 2 (2008): 196–202. doi:10.1080/07491409.2008.10162532.

Kramer, Michael W., and David A. Crespy. "Communicating Collaborative Leadership." *The Leadership Quarterly* 22, no. 5 (2011): 1024–1037. doi: 10.1016/j.leaqua.2011.07.021.

Lindlof, Thomas R., and Bryan C. Taylor. *Qualitative Communication Research Methods*, 3rd ed. Thousand Oaks, CA: SAGE, 2011.

Lobel, Sharon Alisa. "Allocation of Investment in Work and Family Roles: Alternative Theories and Implications for Research." *Academy of Management Review* 16, no. 3 (1991): 507–521. doi: 10.5465/amr.1991.4279467.

Lucas, Kristen, and Patrice M. Buzzanell. "Employees 'Without' Families: Discourses of Family as an External Constraint to Work-Life Balance." In Lynn H. Turner and Richard West (Eds.), *The Family Communication Sourcebook* (335–352). Thousand Oaks, CA: Sage, 2006.

Lucas, Kristen, Suzy D'enbeau, and Erica P. Heiden. "Generational Growing Pains as Resistance to Feminine Gendering of Organization? An Archival Analysis of Human Resource Management Discourses." *Journal of Management Inquiry* 25, no. 3 (2016): 322–37. doi: 10.1177/1056492615616692.

MacGeorge, Erina L., Bo Feng, Ginger L. Butler, and Sara K. Budarz. "Understanding Advice in Supportive Interactions: Beyond the Facework and Message Evaluation Paradigm." *Human Communication Research* 30, no. 1 (2004): 42–70. 10.1111/j.1468-2958.2004.tb00724.x.

MacGeorge, Erina L., Bo Feng, and Lisa M. Guntzviller. "Advice: Expanding the Communication Paradigm." *Annals of the International Communication Association* 40, no. 1 (2016): 213–243. doi: 10.1080/23808985.2015.11735261.

MacGeorge, Erina L., Lisa M. Guntzviller, Lisa K. Hanasono, and Bo Feng. "Testing Advice Response Theory in Interactions with Friends." *Communication Research* 43, no. 2 (2016): 211–231. doi: 10.1177/0093650213510938.

Marshak, Robert J., and David Grant. "Transforming Talk: The Interplay of Discourse, Power, and Change." *Organization Development Journal* 26, no. 3 (2008): 33–40. doi: https://search.proquest.com/docview/197996895?accountid=12964.

Mason, Mary Ann, and Marc Goulden. "Do Babies Matter?" *Academe* 88, no. 6 (2002): 21.

Mason, Mary Ann, and Marc Goulden. "Marriage and Baby Blues: Redefining Gender Equity in the Academy." *The Annals of the American Academy of Political and Social Science* 596, no. 1 (2004): 86–103. doi:10.1177/0002716204268744.

McAlister, Joan Faber. "Lives of the Mind/Body: Alarming Notes on the Tenure and Biological Clocks." *Women's Studies in Communication* 31, no. 2 (2008): 218–225. doi: 10.1080/07491409.2008.10162536.

Meisenbach, Rebecca J., Robyn V. Remke, Patrice Buzzanell, and Meina Liu. "'They Allowed': Pentadic Mapping of Women's Maternity Leave Discourse as Organizational Rhetoric." *Communication Monographs* 75, no. 1 (2008): 1–24. doi: 10.1080/03637750801952727.

Miller, Claire C., and Liz Alderman. "Why U.S. Women are Leaving Jobs Behind." *The New York Times*, December 12, 2014. Last modified December 20, 2018. https://www.nytimes.com/2014/12/14/upshot/us-employment-women-not-working.html.

Miller, Vernon D., Fredric M. Jablin, Mary K. Casey, Martha Lamphear-Van Horn, and Caroline Ethington. "The Maternity Leave as a Role Negotiation Process." *Journal of Managerial Issues* (1996): 286–309. doi: http://www.jstor.org/stable/40604108.

Mills, Melanie Bailey. "Intersections between Work and Family: When a Playpen Can Be Office Furniture." *Women's Studies in Communication* 31, no. 2 (2008): 213–217. doi: 10.1080/07491409.2008.10162535.

Morgan, Hal, and Frances J. Milliken. "Keys to Action: Understanding Differences in Organizations' Responsiveness to Work-and-family Issues." *Human Resource Management* 31, no. 3 (1992): 227–248. doi: 10.1002/hrm.3930310308.

Nelson, Kenza Bemis. "Employer Difficulty in FMLA Implementation: A Look at Eighth Circuit Interpretation of Serious Health Condition and Employee Notice Requirements." *Journal of Corporation Law* 30, no. 3 (Spring 2005): 609–626.

Park, Innhwa. "Seeking Advice: Epistemic Asymmetry and Learner Autonomy in Writing Conferences." *Journal of Pragmatics* 44, no. 14 (2012): 2004–2021. doi: 10.1016/j.pragma.2012.09.012.

Pirtle, Whitney N. L. "Motherhood while Black." *The Chronicle of Higher Education*. April 5, 2018. Last modified December 20, 2018. https://www.chronicle.com/interactives/the-awakening.

Rantanen, Johanna. *Work-Family Interface and Psychological Well-Being: A Personality and Longitudinal Perspective*. No. 346. University of Jyväskylä, 2008.

Rantanen, Johanna, Ulla Kinnunen, Saija Mauno, and Kati Tillemann. "Introducing Theoretical Approaches to Work-Life Balance and Testing a New Typology Among Professionals." In S. Kaiser, M. Ringlstetter, D. Eikof, M. Pina e Cunha (Eds.), *Creating Balance?* pp. 27–46. Berlin, Germany: Springer, 2011.

Scarduzio, Jennifer A., and Sarah J. Tracy. "Sensegiving and Sensebreaking via Emotion Cycles and Emotional Buffering: How Collective Communication Creates Order in the Courtroom." *Management Communication Quarterly* 29, no. 3 (2015): 331–357. doi: 10.1177/0893318915581647.

Smith, Kristin E., and Amara Bachu. *Women's Labor Force Attachment Patterns and Maternity Leave: A Review of the Literature*. Population Division, US Bureau of the Census, 1999.

Smithson, Janet, and Elizabeth H. Stokoe. "Discourses of Work–Life Balance: Negotiating 'Genderblind' Terms in Organizations." *Gender, Work & Organization* 12, no. 2 (2005): 147–168. doi: 10.1111/j.1468-0432.2005.00267.x.

Sotirin, Patty. "Academic Momhood: In for the Long Haul." *Women's Studies in Communication* 31, no. 2 (2008): 258–267. doi:10.1080/07491409.2008.10162541.

Ter Hoeven, Claartje L., Vernon D. Miller, Bram Peper, and Laura Den Dulk. "The Work Must Go On." *Management Communication Quarterly* 31, no. 2 (2017): 194–229. doi: 10.1177/0893318916684980.

Townsley, Nikki C., and Kirsten J. Broadfoot. "Care, Career, and Academe: Heeding the Calls of a New Professoriate [Special Issue]." *Women's Studies in Communication* 31, no. 2 (2008): 133–286. doi: 10.1080/07491409.2008.10162525.

Tracy, Sarah J. *Qualitative Research Methods: Collecting Evidence, Crafting Analysis, Communicating Impact.* Hoboken, NJ: John Wiley & Sons, 2012.

Tracy, Sarah J., and Clifton Scott. "Sexuality, Masculinity, and Taint Management among Firefighters and Correctional Officers: Getting Down and Dirty with 'America's heroes' and the 'scum of law enforcement.'" *Management Communication Quarterly* 20, no. 1 (2006): 6–38. doi: 10.1177/0893318906287898.

Tye-Williams, Stacy, and Kathleen J. Krone. "Identifying and Re-imagining the Paradox of Workplace Bullying Advice." *Journal of Applied Communication Research* 45, no. 2 (2017): 218–235. doi: 10.1080/00909882.2017.1288291.

Waggoner, Catherine Egley. "Academic Adultery: Surreptitious Performances of the Professor/Mother." *Women's Studies in Communication* 31, no. 2 (2008): 209–212. doi: 10.1080/07491409.2008.10162534.

Weick, K. E. *Sensemaking in Organizations.* Thousand Oaks, CA: Sage, 2005.

Weick, Karl E., Kathleen M. Sutcliffe, and David Obstfeld. "Organizing and the Process of Sensemaking." *Organization Science* 16, no. 4 (2005): 409–421. doi: 10.1287/orsc.1050.0133.

West, Martha S., and John W Curtis. *AAUP Faculty Gender Equity Indicators 2006.* Washington, DC: American Association of University Professors, 2006.

Chapter 5

When External Networks Bolster Internal Prestige

Establishing and Sustaining Support Systems for Black Women in the Academy

Sheryl Kennedy Haydel and Shearon D. Roberts

INTRODUCTION

The following Twitter post on January 24, 2019, set off hundreds of engagements:

> Academic freedom is truly dead @WakeForest. Two days after a public MLK address where I called into question the university's labor practices Provost
>
> @rtkersh sends an email "inviting" me to eliminate @AJCCenter as a university entity & offering "goodwill" payoff. #notforsale.[1]

Of the hundreds of responses to the above tweet, Dr. Sara Goldrick-Rab replied on January 25:

> Provost, let's be clear: You should be grateful she's willing to spend time on your campus. The debt is yours, not hers. Wake up—its 2019. Respect MHP or quit. #RealCollege.[2]
>
> She, or rather, MHP is Melissa Harris-Perry.

Melissa Harris-Perry is a recent example of a Black woman in academia who developed her brand (prestige), outside of the academy, that allowed her to bolster her public standing and advance within the academy. Harris-Perry's tool for public support and advancement was the mainstream media first, and then second through social media. These media platforms provided her the reach to communicate to and to coalesce existing online and offline networks (established and loose affiliations) of academics, professionals, and activists around her work. Like Black women before her, she modeled Black feminism, which aimed to combine intellectual critiques with real-world approaches to fighting systemic and institutionalized oppressions for marginalized people. She used her prestige as a national media personality to communicate these approaches and to amplify the lived experiences of people of color, particularly of African American women. Those networks of academics, professionals, and activists that Harris-Perry uplifted through her media work then in turn sustained her efforts within the academy. They also did so in difficult moments when she faced opposition and silencing for her projects that pursued Black feminism both in the academy and in the public eye. She therefore demonstrates the importance of cultivating allies as networks (through the sharing of Narrative)[3] to sustain Black women in the academy as they aim to advance their intellectual and professional endeavors in a space that has often marginalized and silenced them.

Melissa Harris-Perry had rarely shied away from using a platform that was in front of her. Harris-Perry's career is notable because as an academic she pioneered in a space where few academics in general go: national television. As a daughter of academics (her father being the first University of Virginia Dean of African American Affairs),[4] she moved across elite universities since earning her Ph.D. from Duke University in 1999 with both tenured and administrative positions at: The University of Chicago, Princeton University, and Tulane University where she launched the Anna Julia Cooper project that studies the intersection of race and gender in politics.[5] Finally she returned to her alma mater Wake Forest University in 2014 as a full professor holding the presidential chair for politics and international affairs.[6]

Her ability to navigate across elite academic institutions and to launch intellectual work that embodied Black feminist ideals was aided by the external networks of allies Harris-Perry supported either in the public eye as a media personality and directly through her collaborations with social groups, many of them founded and led by Black women. In her book *Sister Citizen*, she recognized her "sister professors" Elizabeth Alexander and Kimberlé Crenshaw and her network of other African American colleagues in academia who have equipped her with support and the tools for advancement.[7] She underscored the importance of these networks, arguing that the work of Black women is political. She noted that "the internal, psychological, emotional, and personal experiences of black women are inherently political... because black women in America have always had to wrestle with derogatory assumptions about their character and identity."[8] As a result, Black women, Harris-Perry wrote, needed to and must continue to find ways to "accommodate and resist" to "preserve their authentic selves" and to earn "recognition as citizens."[9] This is what Black women's networks provide in allowing Black women to progress both professionally and personally, as this chapter will explore.

Harris-Perry navigated her shifts across elite academia while hosting *The Melissa Harris-Perry* show from 2012 to 2016. She provided a contemporary model of how Black women in academia use communicative tools to display their intellect, advance their work, and gain prestige. During her time as host, she demonstrated how women of color can distinguish themselves in the academy by using external, visible platforms to advance their work. Her public visibility resulted in her gaining leadership positions at the institutions she was affiliated with, particularly as the founding director of the Anna Cooper Julia Center on Gender, Race & Politics at Wake Forest University. As a media personality, Harris-Perry was able to emerge as a leading voice on issues of race and gender, and also support other women of color, many of whom she invited as guests to her show. This strong base of women allies, particularly among women of color, would continue to be a form of support for Harris-Perry in the highs and lows of her professional endeavors.

Her departure from her eponymous show made national headlines when MSNBC cancelled Harris-Perry's program in February 2016. Harris-Perry had initially expressed her disapproval of the network's preempting of her show, a few weeks prior, for what she described as the network privileging election "horserace" coverage, over the types of issues featured in her show. She also noted recent "disappearances" of hosts of color or programming that looked at issues of social justice, in favor of "horserace" coverage. In a *National Public Radio* interview Harris-Perry told NPR's David Folkenflik in a segment for "All Things Considered" that she felt MSNBC became

> less concerned with questions of racial and social justice and less interested in highlighting a variety of concerns that shows like mine and others had been focused on over the past couple of years.[10]

After refusing to appear on her program, Harris-Perry sent an email that was later published in *The New York Times*,[11] where she stated to the show's staff: "I will not be used as a tool for their purposes. I am not a token, a mammy, or little brown bubble head. I am not owned by Lack Griffin or MSNBC. I love our show. I want it back."[12]

Further in her email she described how her expertise had been ignored by the network.

> I have stayed in the same hotels where MSNBC has been broadcasting in Iowa, in New Hampshire, and in South Carolina, yet I have been shut out from coverage. I have a PhD in political science and have taught American voting and elections at some of the nation's top universities for nearly two decades, yet I have been deemed less worthy to weigh in than relative novices and certified liars.[13]

When MSNBC sought to settle the terms of Harris-Perry's contract, she described the negotiations as a "gag order." She stated in a CNN-Money interview:

> They wanted me to sign a non-disparagement clause, and we had a deep disagreement over what constituted the non-disparagement clause. They wanted me to not speak about MSNBC. I said no. . . . I will never get another penny from MSNBC.[14]

And in taking to her digital platforms with more than 600,000-plus followers, she posted a meme of Angela Bassett's character Bernadine "Bernie" Harris in the film "Waiting to Exhale," as she walks away from a car ablaze after setting it on fire when her unfaithful husband leaves her for a White woman. In contextualizing the meme to her own battles, Harris-Perry tweeted at her detractors:

> So #MSNBC y'all keep making cable great again. I'll be staying challenging & unpredictable. #NerdlandForever.[15]

Three years after her very public ousting from MSNBC, Harris-Perry sustained her national audience as a contributor for *The Nation* and *Elle.com* where she continued to address controversial intellectual and social conversations around race and gender. Through her work with the Anna Julia Cooper Center, she was able to channel her academic work to national audiences after her MSNBC departure. What has maintained Harris-Perry's position in the academy, despite her experiences described above, is arguably two factors: first, her uncompromising willingness to speak on women of color's lived experiences and second, her support among women of color networks and primarily, African American women networks in the academy.

She cultivated her #Nerdland, described as a "mix of academic theory, social issues, and deep substantive cultural topics."[16] Supporters of her show noted that she opened her platform up for other marginalized groups from academia to activism to be heard within political and social discourse where other shows often shied away from difficult conversations:

> Harris-Perry walked the walk, consistently booking an incredible array of smart, often highly scholarly guests, from academia and activism—the most diverse slate of guests on any news channel, by a long shot. As a woman of color, Harris-Perry spoke from experience as well as deep knowledge on matters of racial oppression, holding frank discussions about how bias, privilege and endemic systems affected black and brown bodies.[17]

Journalist and author Sheila Simmons wrote that Harris-Perry's Nerdland—the brand she built, was a strong following who dedicated Saturday and Sunday afternoons for "smart political, cultural and social discussion."[18]

I miss Melissa Harris-Perry. I miss her eloquent commentary, her "Black Girl Magic" references, her wide, girlish smile and the panel of African American intellectuals she gathered.[19]

Harris-Perry's networks became a support base not just for her show, but also for the work she has pioneered in academia. Journalist Joy Reid, who eventually replaced Harris-Perry had worked with her before through the Anna Julia Cooper Center, filled in as a guest host for Harris-Perry and continued to participate in Harris-Perry's projects after she had replaced her. The Nerdland network she developed, which was a mix of academics, professionals, and activists continued to support her and her endeavors through social media and through offline projects in part because Harris-Perry used her platform to elevate them during her time as a national media personality.[20] This group rallied to her support in 2016, and did so again in 2019. This chapter revisits how networks support and sustain African American women in academia in recent times and how these networks reinforce the credentials of Black women, offering them prestige that bolsters their standings in academic and other spaces.

In this chapter, we examine the writings of Black feminist scholars on navigating the academy. We acknowledge recent uses of digital media as a tool for (a) the sharing of narratives and (b) the external support for the work within oppressed spaces for Black women in academia. We also summarize through auto-ethnography how networks support the advancement of Black women in academia. We argue that the combined digital spaces, and offline personal networks provide a form of legitimizing of bonafides to support the work women of color must do in the academy. When hundreds of women scholars supported Harris-Perry's public critique of her provost's attempt to close the Anna Julia Cooper Center, they publicly affirmed Harris-Perry's credentials. These external communications from networks support another woman's lived experiences of "silencing." The collective voices that new digital networks provide women in academia were reinforcements for Harris-Perry that allowed her to sustain herself in the academy and in her own words to remain "challenging & unpredictable."

BLACK WOMEN NARRATIVES

In defining Black feminist thought, social theorist Patricia Hill Collins[21] outlined that Black women embody a distinct lived experience. Their lives are constant navigations of how to overcome compounded oppressions. Collins noted that while feminism emerged as a tool for all women to achieve "emancipation" and "empowerment," Black feminism more specifically reflected Black women's efforts to come to terms with lived experiences within "intersecting oppositions of race, class, gender, sexuality, ethnicity, nation and religion."[22] Collins added that Black feminist thought goes beyond simply identifying this intersectionality. Collins wrote that this "social theory lies in its commitment to justice."[23]

Black women communicate "visionary pragmatism"[24] through their lived experiences. They move beyond simply a critique of the system by setting their imaginations of what's possible for them, much further than their existing realities suggest.[25] Black women's aspirations are grounded in "stressing the pragmatic, it reveals how current actions are part of some larger, more meaningful struggle."[26]

Therefore, studies of Black women's lived experiences identify both the forms of injustice, as well as it outlines how Black women, as a collective, combat these injustices. This is at the core of Black feminist studies. A primary tool for doing so is "narrative." Jewel Amoah noted that narrative "is the method of Black Feminist Theory."[27] Narrative allows oppressed groups to "reclaim their voices."[28] In "the telling of one's own story"[29] Amoah wrote that "oppressed peoples are able to create their own sphere of theorized existence."[30] This *story telling* provides pathways to navigating their own oppression, and pioneering into new spaces that society had not originally afforded them. More important, the more stories are shared, the more theories are developed around lived experiences that challenge "white male patriarchal" theories.[31]

Amoah notes in a theorizing of the use of narratives as method:

> The lessons of life are learned faster and told better by those who experienced them. The strength of the network stems from an understanding that human experiences is the basis for Narrative, and that Narrative is, in turn, a credible basis for theory.[32]

In her work on intellectual activism, Collins notes two ways in which this is done. First, Collins wrote that in "speaking truth to power" it often means using the legitimacy that the academy provides those lower in the social hierarchy to advance ideas that often conflict the space in which they are operating. She noted that this strategy involved "learning to speak multiple languages of power convincingly."[33] Second, she wrote that "intellectual activism aims to speak the truth directly to people."[34] In the digital landscape, it is even more possible to do so, but often those who do so often "pay a high price."[35] Intellectual activism is often "speaking in multiple registers."[36] This involved engaging both academic and nonacademic audiences, and the pursuit of intellectual work that is a form of "dual truth telling" for not just Black women in one space of society but also in multiple spaces.[37]

Therefore, it is not surprising that Collins had moved much of her intellectual work into public spaces. Likewise, Black women in the academy have used public spaces as a way to bolster and sustain their work and advancement within the academy. In the practice of Black feminism, Black women in academia see their work not bound only by the academy but see the effecting of social justice as boundary less. Therefore, it is natural for external spaces to support academic spaces, as the intellectual work of Black women seeks to address inequalities.

Therefore this chapter used narratives to expand on how networks, built from the sharing of lived experiences, provide legitimacy and advancement for Black women in academia.

Networks as Safe Spaces for Narratives

It is through "narrative" that Black women develop "networks." Several scholars have outlined the ways in which networks play a pivotal role in allowing Black women to navigate systemic oppression in society and in professions.[38] Black women networks can be intergenerational,[39] employ non-White patriarchal strategies,[40] are structured around how a group socializes,[41] and provide access for members within the group to find opportunity.[42]

Yet, the most fundamental role that networks can play is it is the first place where stories are told, and it is these stories that piece together the importance of the network for Black women.[43] Networks allow Black women to learn the "pragmatism" part, while supporting each other in the pursuit of the "visionary" in "visionary pragmatism." The network serves as a space for mentoring, referral, support, and advocacy.[44] Scholars also study how the network is a space for the teaching and practice of communication tools, particularly the learning and defining of organizational communication.[45] It is through the sharing of stories and testimonials within networks that both best and coping practices are learned and formed. It provides a way to communicate not just the injustice, but also on "how to" combat the injustice.

This chapter draws on the tradition of scholarship in Black feminist theory in looking at narrative as a communicative tool[46] for advancing Black women in the academy. In examining narrative, the authors look at how sharing within Black women digital networks is a form of communication strategy training that translates into actionable outcomes. The authors also consider how narrative allows Black women to then recast themselves within the academy to those outside "the network," and to those who reinforce these structures of oppression in academia.

As a communicative space, networks support the establishment and development of credentials and legitimacy. Black women learn how to use credentials to communicate competence, suitability, and acceptability for leadership. This is the narrative of communicating leadership acceptability for Black women in academia.

The network therefore equips, arms, and prepares Black women in academia to position their credentials for advancement. Black women then use these bonafides to earn and advance in positions, and then to overcome the undermining and delegitimizing of their position by the individuals they were hired to lead.

In this chapter, we examine how in the current context digital networks serve as a tool for a pathway to advancement through its inherent structure as a social, communicative resource. We also examine how offline networks sustain Black women in academia and allow them to progress with "visionary pragmatism" in a space that is still producing firsts today.

While the practice of "working twice as hard" results in burnout and retention issues that explains the low numbers of Black women who do ascend to positions of leadership, it underscores the realities of Black women in patriarchal spaces, and works to theorize the inequality.[47] Although we affirm that it should be enough for Black women to perform at levels comparable to men or even White women, the injustice is that the structures in place still work against Black women's advancement.[48] However, Black feminism outlines the continued and persistent fight by Black women to overcome a combination of "othering" that draws on stereotypes of both their race, and their gender, as a form of oppression. Therefore Black feminist thought is both a construct and a tool, suggesting the work at hand is still underway. Academia is an institutional sphere where both intellect and leadership are qualifying measurements (bonafides) for advancement. The nurturing of external networks for Black women allow them to communicate to institutions that they have no shortage of either.

NARRATIVES OF BLACK WOMEN IN THE ACADEMY

Women of color in general outline in narratives their "lived contradictions" or their "ambiguous empowerment."[49] Such experiences are often ignored in the academy and results in "multiple marginalizations."[50] Both as faculty and administrators, Black women describe isolation, both from White colleagues and from the few other Black women colleagues who they need support from to avoid pitfalls in the so-called rights of passage. What is consistent across the experiences of Black women in academia is the role of "external support in building allies."[51]

Black women's experiences in the academy are also intersectional. Yolanda Moses[52] examined how oppressions can occur at both predominantly White institutions and historically Black ones, and not just for Black women faculty and administrators, but also for Black female students and Black female staff.

At predominantly White institutions, Black women are isolated from access to networks from White colleagues for publishing, receiving grants or receiving support for advancement.[53] They are often burdened with "tokenism" having to speak on behalf of, or represent all Black voices, instead of being recognized for their individual perspectives.[54] Interestingly, these experiences result in alliances that go across hierarchies, with Black women recognizing that support within the institution comes from Black women who are not in their positions, such as Black women staff members and students.[55]

At HBCUs (Historically Black Colleges and Universities), Moses noted that historically, Black women have had stronger numbers as professors of varying rank and as instructors. Where the numbers have been fewer are at the highest administrative levels.[56] Men are able to rise to become chief administrators in their forties, and most women mostly achieved these positions at HBCUs at older ages and far later on in their careers than men. So at HBCUs, while race may not be a primary factor, gender and age often work against Black women who seek to advance within this Black space. Finally, when Black women do become leaders at HBCUs, their work expectations and administrative tasks differ from those from men, and their salaries are lower than men.[57]

More importantly to hindering Black women's advancements is the unspoken tax of "balancing competing obligations."[58] Moses wrote that since Black women teach, counsel, do more committee work, and serve their communities more so than White men and women in the academy, they do less research, and are considered less prestigious in the academy because of this. This places obstacles for their legitimacy when seeking advancement.

The burnout from balancing overcommitments in the academy, while also managing families and personal lives, with the desire for "civic-consciousness"[59] is ignored when evaluating the experiences of Black women in the academy by their peers. Black women also wrestle with the demands to "publish or perish" not because they are unable to do so, but because it comes at the expense, in many cases, of substantive teaching and service to the community and to students. This is particularly true in historically black universities, where the mission is to "teach with social responsibility and vision" and to pursue "socially pertinent research."[60]

Altogether, these "lived contradictions" and the tax exacted from them figure into why Black women remain underrepresented at White institutions, and only advance later on at Black institutions. However, Black feminism seeks to wrestle with the struggles and the pursuit of a social justice that is often "visionary" while using "pragmatism" to attain what is often considered unattainable for those who fall at the intersection of the lowest social hierarchies. Many Black women in the academy recorded their lived experiences in ethnographic studies of the late nineties and early 2000s.[61] Their truth-telling provided insights that have allowed for a generation of Black women to advance to not only elite positions today as intellects, but also to professional positions and to leadership positions in the academy.

As Hill Collins noted herself as she pursues her current public intellectual work, new media has provided new opportunities for us to communicate. Hill Collins wrote: "New technologies have opened up formerly unimaginable ways for us to talk to one another."[62] How we use these new digital spaces to support intellectual activism is what Hill Collins considered as new expressions of the work of Black feminism. Therefore, this chapter considered what networks have offered Black women in academia in terms of legitimacy and advancement. Black women benefit from their professional networks because these connections allow them to remain encouraged in the face of discrimination, serve as a respite from the peering eyes of their White counterparts and serve as a valued pipeline to employment, communal resources and emotional support. Second, this chapter summarizes recent examples of narratives of Black women in academia, and how networks also support and sustain Black women who actively use them to continue to communicate strategies and support for mutual advancement.

THE ROLE OF NETWORKS

They Come by It Honestly

Black women have used interconnected networks for advancements in three spheres: Black intelligentsia, Black social organizations, and Black professional associations. In these three spaces that will be addressed next, Black women have found ways to execute "visionary pragmatism" through Black feminism.

Black Intelligentsia

African American women have longed for spaces to not only intellectually tussle with issues, but also to fellowship free from the gaze of their White counterparts. Throughout history, their yearning to be free from the social construct of race, gender, and socioeconomic binaries is undeniable. As if chased by nagging stereotypes as well as unrealistic expectations to overcome often-suffocating oppression, Black women have always looked for private yet collective moments to protect themselves from scathing judgments and to better serve their communities. More importantly, Black women have found ways to historically connect their work in academic spaces with the larger work for social justice. Therefore, the work of Black women's intellectual networks has always gone beyond institutional hallways and into the public domain.

In the early twentieth century, African Americans found refuge as well as empowerment within informal and formal women's enclaves and organizations. These women were diverse in background. Some were educated, married, affluent or working class, but galvanized around the promise of authentic community cemented by friendship, service and social advancement. These movements were connected in intellectual exercises rooted in Black feminism, stemming from Black women's intelligentsia. Because of its close connections to events in the public sphere, Black women's intelligentsia could never have been classified as an academic exercise. It was a public-facing work that brought scholarship and activism together.

Dovetailing into a national movement that formalized itself in the early 1900s, gender liberation was launched by African American women journalists such as Pauline Hopkins and Josephine St. Ruffin, and continued throughout the first half of the twentieth century with the pen of Ida B. Wells and Charlotta Bass. Like Wells and Bass, other civil rights and journalism luminaries including Irene McCoy Gaines, A'lelia Walker, Mary McDowell, Mary Church Terrell, and Mary McLeod Bethune supported the efforts of working class men's organizations (like the Brotherhood of Sleeping Car Porters) and their auxiliary working women's clubs through their memberships on the Citizens' Committee, however, very few such "club women" regularly joined the local city chapters. In fact, "Even among the wives of the BSCP national organizers, only Walter (Mrs. C.L.) Dellums actively participated in Oakland's local's activities. Other organizers like Lucille Randolph [Mrs. A. Phillip], Elizabeth Webster, and Hazel Smith had their own circles of social service and club friends and did not [initially] belong to their local Women's Economic Councils. Historian Deborah Gray White argued that such divisions were 'the cost of club work, the price of black feminism.'"[63] Some twenty years later (1946), Lucille Randolph joined the local New York Ladies' Auxiliary "when her husband paid for her dues."[64]

Reminiscent of Black women clubs that Hill Collins wrote about in *Black Feminist Thought*, African American women recognized that they needed their own networks and spaces within both civil rights and gender movements. Black women created a subculture for themselves because mainstream society had exploited them in ways that it had not done to Black men. Collins referred to Black women as "outsiders within," where "black women have a distinct view of the contradictions between the dominant group's actions and ideologies."[65] For example, "If women are allegedly passive and fragile, then why are black women treated as mules and assigned heavy cleaning chores?"[66]

Betty Collier-Thomas and Vincent P. Franklin[67] wrote about a well-established and intricate network of Black women's organizations and the intellectual framework that grounded it. These groups were designed to combat rampant injustice including racial and gender inequality. Collier and Franklin noted that these women's groups represented "teachers and business women and the wives of lawyers, physicians, and the other professionals"; however, "there were also many representatives who were domestic servants, day laborers, and other service workers."[68] These networks emerged to become a federation of organizations that used their vision to draw attention to the needs of the Black community when Whites did their best to ignore the systemic damage caused by segregation.[69]

For example, the National Association of Colored Women (NACW) held its twenty-first biennial convention in the summer of 1939 in Boston where Black women's intellectual critiques shaped public actions they would then pursue.[70] And while the term "civil rights" did not become widely used until the 1940s, African American women, in particular, were actively protesting "racial discrimination in education, voting, public accommodations, armed services, and housing."[71] Women's organizations were the nucleus for developing national strategies to eradicate social injustice in their communities. Other women's groups such as the Alpha Kappa Alpha Sorority's Non-Partisan Council on Human Rights, the New Jersey Federation of Colored Women's Clubs, the National Council for Negro Women, and the National Association of Colored Women were all working from similar agendas to liberate their communities from oppression.[72] They all were shaped by a unique intellectual discourse of Black women's intelligentsia, forged out of their lived experiences.

This history explains why the work of Black women today in the academy is still connected to the real-world fights to address marginalization of Black women in all spheres.

Black Social Organizations

Scholars who have conducted research or written on the importance of Black organizations like Walter M. Kimbrough, Andre McKenzie, Susan Marcus-Mendoza, and Dary T. Erwin[73] have noted that students engaged in "campus organizations are more action-oriented."[74] This same assertion can be extended to African American women who developed their work first as part of a pool of student advocates while attending college, and who then brought this same level of energy and commitment to their academic careers as professors and administrators. The aforementioned group of scholars agreed "that such participation relates directly to higher levels of both cognitive and leadership development,"[75] and supports the notion that a sense of belonging for Black women is historically rooted. For example, national Black Greek-letter organizations influenced undeniable professionalism on college campuses as well as created an expectation that there should be a place for their public voice that was undergirded by calls for justice, equality, and protection.[76]

Since the genesis of belonging flourished on college campuses, it is not unusual that college-educated African American women would bring these same aspirations with them as they ascended to leadership roles in the very places that nurtured their longing for respectability. As student activists, these Black women saw what was missing in leadership, and now as academics, they aspire to execute the changes they agitated during their quest to become PhDs, the first required credential for the academy, and then their quest to make meaningful change in the academy. While rife with "organizational and problem-solving skills," many members of these esteemed organizations "believed that forming and joining" sororities and fraternities "could be beneficial to them both socially and developmentally."[77] So even though many women are not affiliated with a Black Greek-letter organization, their training was influenced by the drum beat of these organizations which espoused excellence, created and maintained safe spaces to share vulnerabilities, and challenged the status quo along with finding strength in intelligence.

On the national front, members of Black Greek-letter organizations undeniably escalated the "Counterfraternal" and "Black Counterpublic" movements that rapidly unfolded across the country in the first half of the twentieth century and continued into the present day.[78] Many leaders who advanced in multiple spaces were bolstered by their membership in Greek-letter organizations. These stakeholders were also the framers of Black women's intelligentsia and they labored to gain unfettered access to "the public sphere for political action" and societal respect.[79] Counterhegemonic by design, Black social organizations usurped the power of the "dominant culture"[80] and refused to let White standards define them as academically, emotionally, and physically inferior citizens.[81] To Black college women and men, these groups proved a gateway to "reinsert themselves into the channels of public discourse."[82]

This sentiment continues to be pronounced even today. For instance, the Black Greek-letter organizations' communal benevolence, civic-engagement, and commitment to fellowship validated the members' voice in the "cultural and counterpublic sphere."[83] Marginalized African Americans understood the political imperative to create "parallel discursive arenas where those excluded from dominant discourses, invent and circulate counterdiscourses" that form "oppositional interpretations of their identities, interests, and needs."[84]

Black Professional Networks

From the might of the Black Greek-letter organizations to the need to be heard, the common thread was gaining access as well as building and maintaining the appropriate professional network. Within each discipline, Black professional groups have emerged from the sciences to the humanities. Others have spanned diverse professional areas and have specifically become professional spaces for Black women such as The Links, Incorporated, and 100 Black Women. In both cases, the desire to connect based on race, gender, culture, and community advocacy is not a new phenomenon but one that has been reinvigorated in today's contentious political climate.

Black women in higher education have become protective of their sacred spaces. They have equally become more aware of how professional networks fill in the gaps created in porous places in the academy. Oftentimes, professional organizations provide career development, and serve as a respite. For example, when looking at the National Association of Black Journalists (NABJ), the organization's annual national convention draws Black journalists from across the country because it is a refuge from the isolation many attendees feel in newsrooms. The swapping of stories of failed promotion bids to their ideas being co-opted by White counterparts serves as a cathartic release. While these experiences are demeaning, the ability to connect with scattered Black professionals at a conference far away from the peering eyes of White counterparts becomes liberating. This notion is supported by the sentiments of attendees like journalism educator and freelance digital journalist Nakia Hill who wrote before attending the 2012 NABJ Convention in New Orleans:

> NABJ's convention is like the Oscars for Black journalists. There are endless possibilities for a budding reporter like myself who is hungry for knowledge, crawfish, and opportunities. I look forward to rubbing elbows with seasoned professionals like, Mr. Controversy himself—no not Kanye West, but Roland S. Martin, MSNBC host, Melissa Harris Perry, and political leaders Joe Biden and Reverend Al. Sharpton (I probably won't get close to Biden, but it's nice to dream). It's rumored that President Barack Obama will be attending this year's event, so I'm beyond elated to be in attendance.[85]

Within this mix, in just one organization alone, Black celebrities, activists, civil rights leaders, and members of Black intelligentsia all converge in a space designated as a Black professional organization that is closest to the First Amendment. This demonstrates that although these three network spaces: Black Intelligentsia, Black social organizations, and Black professional networks, are distinct, these are not mutually exclusive spaces, but extensions of each other all serving as connected doors for Black advancement and Black empowerment.

Black professional organizations work to be that place for intellectual and professional freedom and unconditional support. When Jemele Hill was suspended from ESPN in 2017 because of comments she made about President Donald J. Trump, NABJ's professionals and academics came to her aide. Months later they named her Journalist of the Year in her hometown of Detroit during their national convention. In giving this award, NABJ president Sarah Glover noted Hill's perseverance.

> Jemele Hill is a gem. She exhibits strength, grace, and doggedness. NABJ appreciates the courage and steadfastness Jemele has demonstrated as a journalist and commentator speaking truth to power.[86]

LIVED NARRATIVES AND THE USE OF NETWORKS

Within these three spaces, we summarize next how networks allow Black women in academia to advance. We draw on lived experiences, auto-ethnographies,[87] of moving through such networks to explain why their existence is crucial for combatting structures that impede and restrict Black women in academia. As they have been historically, networks today, aided by new platforms, serve as communicative roles internally and externally for developing credentials, and for sustaining Black women in positions of power.

Black Intelligentsia

Networks that bolster Black women's thoughts and scholarship from related marginalized field. In recent times, Black women's intellectual networks have coalesced to challenge the appropriation of Black women's theorizing from going uncredited or "othered" by scholars in critical studies. Part of gaining prestige for academic advancement is the prominence of one's scholarship, manifested by the frequency of citations of a scholar's work. This has often been a tool for White male advancement in the academy, because they are able to gain legitimacy in the academy by how well-cited their work has become in their respective disciplines. Black women's intellectual frameworks have existed from the beginning of their civic work, as outlined earlier, yet the history of academia is that Black women's intellectual frameworks have been ignored in the academy or appropriated in scholarship without providing credit to Black women as the originators of such theoretical concepts and methodologies.

Digital platforms today have provided spaces to communicate this form of academic marginalization and have resulted in bringing many past and new Black women scholars much overdue public and academic recognition. Even Hill Collins recognized more recently the work digital networks have played in re-crediting her work, and that of other Black feminist scholars as being central to gender and critical race scholarship. One example of how digital networks focus on Black women's intelligentsia is by bringing visibility to Black Women's work through the hashtags #CiteBlackWomen and #CiteBlackWomenSunday. Cite Black Women are public-facing calls by both formal and informal networks to restore appropriated or coopted theories from Black women back to their proper context and to halt the erasure and marginalizing of Black women in recent critical studies. Black feminist scholar Christen A. Smith began the Cite Black Women Collective in 2017 through using social media networks to credit Black women in scholarship as a form of "radical praxis."[88] The collective notes that

> Cite Black Women engages with social media, aesthetic representation (our t-shirts) and public dialogue to push people to critically rethink the politics of race, gender and knowledge production.[89]

Another such movement is the work of critical scholars to ensure that the work of "intersectionality" and the scholar behind it, Kimberlé Crenshaw, is first recognized as a Black woman's critical work, and applied within its appropriate contexts.[90] Intersectionality, as a concept, has now moved beyond its original applications and has become a language that is now the mainstream in social justice movements and even for political platforms. Black intellectual networks, many of whom are Black women academics among Black Twitter, continue to work with other Black digital networks to combat the erasure of Crenshaw in the widening use of the term "intersectionality" and the principles first articulated in its theorizing by Crenshaw.

Black women now use intellectual networks to carve out spaces within larger academic associations or disciplinary areas. Within mainstream academic organizations, Black women networks have allowed for Black women scholars to garner support to earn elected positions. These academic networks also increasingly provide spaces for Black women to present on scholarship specific to their unique research, to cite each other, to collaborate on critical studies, and to support Black women who seek to be published in traditional peer-reviewed journals. It has led to the creation of more niche disciplinary meetings, symposia and colloquia that harken back to the early work of the NACW and that specifically seek to advance Black women's scholarship. In fact, Harris-Perry's Anna Julia Cooper Center was among such spaces that supported designated intellectual meetings around Black feminist scholarship and practice and how it connected to the larger work of Black upliftment.

In addition to supporting their scholarly output and participation, Black women intellectual networks provide spaces for mentorship, the passing of the baton, the lobbying for long-overdue recognitions in White dominated associations, and the sharing of strategies for advancement. These strategies are connected to Hill Collins's praxis that Black women learn to navigate by speaking "multiple languages of power convincingly," and "speaking in multiple registers" in addition to doing the work of "dual truth telling."[91]

Black Social Organizations

One of the reasons Black women often do not advance is the burnout and checking out that comes with working twice as hard. Here, Black social organizations provide networks that provide safe spaces for the overall development and sustaining of "the work." Black social organizations comprise Black Greek-letter organizations, the Black church, and a wide array of Black community organizations. While their makeup are women working in a variety of professions, not just academia, they serve as a broader collective of reliable camaraderie.

The camaraderie is a safe space for Black women to unpack their intersectionality free from the judgment of the norms of the professions they belong to. Black women become visible and seen in Black social networks as not just beings who must shoulder their communities or their households, or who must represent for their people. They are seen as human beings, and Black social networks are a second circle of security and advocacy for the well-being of the whole woman.[92]

Social networks support healthy living, some form fitness groups and healthcare support. They promote work-life balance. They ensure Black women feel safe to let down their defenses and indulge all of their sensibilities. Black women's networks in religious spaces like the Black church fortify the desire to be a nurturer in a space that celebrates this and praises this, but does not look at such traits as vulnerabilities. Nonreligious social networks then free Black women from the confines of some doctrine, allowing them to be accepted to pursue their professional growth without the condescension of religious patrimony.

Social networks also bring Black women from different professional backgrounds together. This provides a financial resource for funding community-based projects and other endeavors requiring some form of capital. These projects allow Black women to work on initiatives external to their institutions that gives them leverage with their communities, meaningful collaborations with corporations or other entities, and even public recognitions and awards that allow them to gain prestige and to build a reputation in their cities and states, nationally and globally. Where they may be passed over at an institution, their public standing can be elevated through these social networks. These external social networks allow them to return to their institutions with prestige that provides credibility for their pursuit of advancement.

Professional Networks

Finally, since Black women see their work in the academy as an extension of their professional work, they remain connected to networks outside of academic associations. For instance, it would be common for a Black nursing professor to still work directly with or be a member of a Black nursing professional organization. A Black political science professor may still work with the NAACP. A Black chemistry, or engineering woman professor may be a part of a national association for Black chemists or engineers. Likewise, a Black communications professor would also be a member of the NABJ and so forth. The work they do of training future professionals is shaped by their real-time participation in professional networks. This impacts their teaching, research and broader service to their discipline as they serve in a professional capacity, and are able to advance pedagogy in their disciplines by being current on developments in their respective positions.

The credibility they gain from the positions they still maintain as professionals working in academia sets them apart. They are not merely members of an academic ivory tower. They are relevant educators in touch with evolving pedagogy and practices for the professions and academic programs they train their students in. Professional networks serve as references for the relevancy of Black women academics. They carry certifications, job pipelines for students, and real-world references to bolster the credentials of their members. More importantly, they give Black women a competitive edge in seeking career advancement because they are able to articulate a vision for their leadership that allows institutions to develop and grow to meet the future educational needs of students.

STRENGTH IN NUMBERS

Black women networks are multifaceted and with diverse fixtures of Black women's support structures for retention and advancement. They can be public-facing (like digital networks), and at other times, they aim to be more discreet (like social networks). Both serve their functions for bolstering those who form their ranks as the work of edifying Black women requires both public advocacy and private respite as safe spaces. Black women's networks exist within their own institutions and beyond their own institutions. These networks are multidisciplinary spaces bringing Black women together from the sciences to the humanities who are tasked to execute Black feminism in spheres of medicine all the way to the arts. Black women are bound by their marginalization, regardless of their fields, and their execution of Black feminism is a practice that is discipline-neutral.

Black women's networks are lastly interconnected. They connect the work of Black women in the academy with the professional domain. They connect intellectual work to real-time movements. They extend beyond class or economic structures in social networks. And they are largely extensions of the same domain. While Black associations in general have been spaces for the work of Black empowerment, Black women's networks in particular have been distinct spaces for Black women to also wrestle with the unique marginalization that comes with being both a woman and being Black.

As outlined earlier, even at Black academic spaces, like HBCUs, Black women have had to wait longer and take on more menial job portfolios as part of advancement, compared to Black men in academia. Therefore the work of Black women's networks are also distinct among Black empowerment associations in general, because they support the work of advancement in both White and Black institutional spaces.

This diversity of Black women's networks therefore makes them spaces for articulating Hill Collins's "visionary pragmatism." They allow Black women to creatively imagine paths for Black upliftment, which is the "visionary" component of Black feminism. However, they are knowledge spaces, through narrative sharing of lived experiences for teaching "pragmatism." Networks are therefore not only the supportive resources to articulate advancement, but they also serve as spaces to chart this advancement. This can come from the collective bolstering by networks that recognize Black women's achievements, or the more quiet work that sustains and retains Black women from the oppressions they face. They provide communication within their spaces and outside their spaces that constitute a sisterhood that allow their members to move up their ranks and to stay in positions of power. They are spaces of mentorship, camaraderie, and respite that have historically and to the present day sustained the work of Black feminism and that address the unique lived experiences of being a Black woman.

NOTES

1. Melissa Harris-Perry, "Academic freedom is truly dead @WakeForest. Two days after a public MLK address where I called into question the university's labor practices Provost @rtkersh sends an email 'inviting' me to eliminate @AJCCenter as a university entity & offering a "goodwill" payoff. #notforsale", January 24, 2019, 7:30 a.m., https://twitter.com/MHarrisPerry/status/1088459120494108672.

2. Sara Goldrick-Rab, "Provost, let's be clear: You should be grateful she's willing to spend time on your campus. The debt is yours, not hers. Wake up—it's 2019. Respect MHP or quit. #RealCollege" January 25, 2019, 1:50 p.m., https://twitter.com/saragoldrickrab/status/1088917058069372928.

3. Jewel Amoah, "Narrative: The Road to Black Feminist Theory," *Berkeley Women's LJ* 12 (1997): 85, https://doi.org/10.15779/Z38FP3B.

4. *The History Makers*, "Melissa Harris-Perry," Last Modified September 12, 2014, https://www.thehistorymakers.org/biography/melissa-harris-perry.

5. *The History Makers*, "Melissa Harris-Perry."

6. Ibid.

7. Melissa V. Harris-Perry, *Sister Citizen: Shame, Stereotypes, and Black Women in America* (New Haven, CT: Yale University Press, 2011), xi.

8. Harris-Perry, *Sister Citizen*, 5.

9. Ibid.

10. David Folkenflik, "MSNBC Fires Host Melissa Harris-Perry over Controversial Memo," *NPR*, Last modified, March 9, 2016, https://www.npr.org/2016/03/09/469837015/msnbc-fires-host-melissa-harris-perry-over-controversial-memo.

11. John Koblin, "Melissa Harris-Perry Walks Off her MSNBC Show after Pre-emptions," *The New York Times*, Last modified, February 26, 2016, https://www.nytimes.com/2016/02/27/business/media/melissa-harris-perry-walks-off-her-msnbc-show-after-pre-emptions.html.

12. Paul Farhi, "MSNBC Will Cut Ties with Show Host who Wrote Critical Email to Colleagues," *The Washington Post*, Last modified, February 28, 2016, https://www.washingtonpost.com/lifestyle/style/msnbc-will-cut-ties-with-show-host-who-wrote-critical-email-to-colleagues/2016/02/27/bce30c8e-dd82-11e5-891a-4ed04f4213e8_story.html?utm_term=.20af06698214.

13. Jamil Smith, "Melissa Harris Perry's email to her Nerdland Staff," *Medium*, Last modified, February 26, 2016, https://medium.com/@JamilSmith/melissa-harris-perry-s-email-to-her-nerdland-staff-11292bdc27cb.

14. Dylan Byers, "Melissa Harris-Perry Rejects MSNBC Deal in a Scathing Farewell," *CNN.com*, Last modified, January 3, 2016, https://money.cnn.com/2016/03/01/media/melissa-harris-perry-msnbc-farewell/index.html.

15. Byers, "Melissa Harris-Perry Rejects MSNBC Deal in a Scathing Farewell."

16. Rachel Skylar, "Why We Need Melissa Harris-Perry. The End of #Nerdland Marks Sad Times for Diversity on Cable News," *Elle.com*, Last modified, March 4, 2016. https://www.elle.com/culture/career-politics/news/a34595/melissa-harris-perry-end-of-show-nerdland/.

17. Skylar, "Why We Need Melissa Harris-Perry."

18. Sheila Simmons, "Farewell Melissa Harris-Perry, 'Nerdland,'" *The Philadelphia Tribune*, Last modified, March 11, 2016, https://www.phillytrib.com/commentary/farewell-melissa-harris-perry-nerdland/article_b3dedbda-26cb-5ffc-9781-5fd245527541.html.

19. Simmons, "Farewell Melissa Harris-Perry, 'Nerdland.'"

20. Skylar, "Why We Need Melissa Harris-Perry."

21. Patricia Hill Collins, *Black Feminist Thought: Knowledge, Consciousness, and the Politics of Empowerment* (Abingdon, U.K.: Routledge, 2002), 9.

22. Hill Collins, *Black Feminist Thought*, 9.

23. Ibid., 9.; see also Gwendolyn M. Combs, "The Duality of Race and Gender for Managerial African American Women: Implications of Informal Social Networks on Career Advancement," *Human Resource Development Review* 2, no. 4 (2003):

385–405, https://doi.org/10.1177/1534484303257949; Janis V. Sanchez-Hucles and Donald D. Davis, "Women and Women of Color in Leadership: Complexity, Identity, and Intersectionality," *American Psychologist* 65, no. 3 (2010): 171, doi:10.1037/a0017459; Naz Rassool, "Black Women as 'Other' in the Academy," *Feminist Academics: Creative Agents for Change* (1995): 22, doi:10.2304/pfie.2006.4.2.101; Caroline Sotello Viernes Turner, "Women of Color in Academe: Living with Multiple Marginality," *The Journal of Higher Education* 73, no. 1 (2002): 74–93, doi:10.1353/jhe.2002.0013.

24. Patricia Hill Collins, *Black Woman and the Search for Justice* (Minneapolis, MN: University of Minnesota, 1998), 189.
25. Hill Collins, *Black Woman and the Search for Justice*, 190.
26. Ibid.
27. Amoah, "Narrative: The Road to Black Feminist Theory," 85.
28. Amoah, "Narrative: The Road to Black Feminist Theory," 85.
29. Ibid.
30. Ibid.
31. Ibid.
32. Ibid.
33. Patricia Hill Collins, "Truth-telling and Intellectual Activism," *Contexts* 12, no. 1 (2013): 38, doi:10.1177/1536504213476244.
34. Hill Collins, "Truth-telling and Intellectual Activism," 38.
35. Ibid.
36. Ibid., 39.
37. Ibid.
38. Sharon Fries-Britt and Bridget Turner Kelly, "Retaining Each Other: Narratives of Two African American Women in the Academy," *The Urban Review* 37, no. 3 (2005): 221–242, doi:10.1007/s11256-005-0006-2; Cosette M. Grant and Juanita Cleaver Simmons, "Narratives on Experiences of African-American Women in the Academy: Conceptualizing Effective Mentoring Relationships of Doctoral Student and Faculty," *International Journal of Qualitative Studies in Education* 21, no. 5 (2008): 501–517, https://doi.org/10.1080/09518390802297789; Monica C. Higgins and Kathy E. Kram, "Reconceptualizing Mentoring at Work: A Developmental Network Perspective," *Academy of Management Review* 26, no. 2 (2001): 264–288, https://doi.org/10.5465/amr.2001.4378023; Steve McDonald, Nan Lin, and Dan Ao, "Networks of Opportunity: Gender, Race, and Job Leads," *Social Problems* 56, no. 3 (2009): 385–402, doi:10.1525/sp.2009.56.3.385.
39. Fries-Britt and Turner Kelly, "Retaining Each Other: Narratives of Two African American Women in the Academy."
40. Grant and Simmons, "Narratives on Experiences of African-American Women in the Academy: Conceptualizing Effective Mentoring Relationships of Doctoral Student and Faculty."
41. Higgins and Kram, "Reconceptualizing Mentoring at Work: A Developmental Network Perspective."
42. McDonald, Lin, and Ao, "Networks of Opportunity: Gender, Race, and Job Leads."
43. Amoah, "Narrative: The Road to Black Feminist Theory," 85.

44. Jeannine E. Dingus, "'I'm Learning the Trade' Mentoring Networks of Black Women Teachers," *Urban Education* 43, no. 3 (2008): 361–377, https://doi.org/10.1177/0042085907311794; Joanne Kilgour Dowdy, "Fire and Ice: The Wisdom of Black Women in the Academy," *New Horizons in Adult Education and Human Resource Development* 22, no. 1 (2008): 24–43, doi:10.1002/nha3.10297; Gina L. Evans, and Kevin O. Cokley, "African American Women and the Academy: Using Career Mentoring to Increase Research Productivity," *Training and Education in Professional Psychology* 2, no. 1 (2008): 50, doi:10.1037/1931-3918.2.1.50; Cheryl Evans Green and Valarie Greene King, "Sisters Mentoring Sisters: Africentric Leadership Development for Black Women in the Academy," *The Journal of Negro Education* 70, no. 3 (2001): 156, doi:10.2307/3211207; Tammy L. Henderson, Andrea G. Hunter, and Gladys J. Hildreth, "Outsiders Within the Academy: Strategies for Resistance and Mentoring African American Women," *Michigan Family Review* 14, no. 1 (2010), http://dx.doi.org/10.3998/mfr.4919087.0014.105.

45. Margaret M. Hopkins, Deborah O'Neil, Angela Passarelli, and Diana Bilimoria. "Women's Leadership Development Strategic Practices for Women and Organizations." *Consulting Psychology Journal: Practice and Research* 60, no. 4 (2008): 348, http://dx.doi.org/10.1037/a0014093.

46. Florence Bonner and Veronica G. Thomas, "New and Continuing Challenges and Opportunities for Black Women in the Academy," *The Journal of Negro Education* 70, no. 3 (2001): 121–123, doi:10.2307/3211204; Winnifred R. Brown-Glaude, "But Some of Us are Brave: Black Women Faculty Transforming the Academy," *Signs: Journal of Women in Culture and Society* 35, no. 4 (2010): 801–809, doi:10.1086/651035; Joanne Kilgour Dowdy, "Fire and Ice: The Wisdom of Black Women in the Academy," 24–43, doi:10.1002/nha3.10297; Sheila T. Gregory, "Black Faculty Women in the Academy: History, Status and Future," *The Journal of Negro Education* 70, no. 3 (2001): 124, doi:10.2307/3211205; Julia S. Jordan-Zachery, "Reflections on Mentoring: Black Women and the Academy," *Political Science & Politics* 37, no. 4 (2004): 875–877, https://doi.org/10.1017/S1049096504045317; Reitumetse Obakeng Mabokela and Anna Lucille Green, *Sisters of the Academy: Emergent Black Women Scholars in Higher Education* (Herndon, Stylus Publishing, LLC., 2001); Heidi Safia Mirza, "Transcendence Over Diversity: Black Women in the Academy," *Policy Futures in Education* 4, no. 2 (2006): 101–113, doi:10.2304/pfie.2006.4.2.101.

47. Robert J. Menges and William H. Exum, "Barriers to the Progress of Women and Minority Faculty," *The Journal of Higher Education* 54, no. 2 (1983): 123–144, https://doi.org/10.1080/00221546.1983.11778167; Carol Logan Patitu and Kandace G. Hinton, "The Experiences of African American Women Faculty and Administrators in Higher Education: Has Anything Changed?" *New Directions for Student Services* 2003, no. 104 (2003): 79–93, https://doi.org/10.1002/ss.109.

48. Patitu and Hinton, "The Experiences of African American Women Faculty and Administrators in Higher Education: Has Anything Changed?"

49. Turner, "Women of Color in Academe: Living with Multiple Marginality," 75.

50. Ibid., p. 76.

51. Green and King, "Sisters Mentoring Sisters: Africentric Leadership Development for Black Women in the Academy," 158, doi:10.1080/00064246.1998.11430912.

52. Yolanda T. Moses, *Black Women in Academe. Issues and Strategies* (Washington, DC: Project on the Status of Women, Association of American Colleges, 1989), 23.
53. Moses, *Black Women in Academe. Issues and Strategies*, 27.
54. Ibid., 36.
55. Ibid., 27.
56. Ibid.
57. Ibid., 28.
58. Ibid., 29.
59. Ibid., 30.
60. Ibid.
61. Lois Benjamin, *Black Women in the Academy. Promises and Perils* (Gainesville, FL: University Press of Florida, 1997); Gregory, "Black Faculty Women in the Academy: History, Status, and Future," 124–138; Sheila T. Gregory, *Black Women in the Academy: The Secrets to Success and Achievement.* (Lanham, MD: University Press of America, 1999); Green and King, "Sisters Mentoring Sisters: Africentric Leadership Development for Black Women in the Academy."
62. Hill Collins, "Truth-telling and Intellectual Activism," 37.
63. Melinda Chateauvert, *Marching Together: Women of the Sleeping Car Porters* (Chicago, IL: University of Illinois Press, 1998), 45–46.
64. Ibid., 14.
65. Hill Collins, *Black Feminist Thought*, 10.
66. Ibid.
67. Bettye Collier-Thomas and Vincent P. Franklin, *Sisters in the Struggle: African American Women in the Civil Rights – Black Power Movement* (New York, NY: New York University Press, 2001), 21.
68. Ibid., 11.
69. Ibid., 12.
70. Ibid., 21.
71. Ibid., 22.
72. Ibid., 23.
73. André McKenzie, "Community Service and Social Action: Using the Past to Guide the Future of Black Greek-letter Fraternities," *NASPA Journal* 28, no. 1 (1990): 30–36, doi:10.1080/00220973.1990.11072184; Dary T. Erwin and Susan T. Marcus-Mendoza, "Motivation and Students' Participation in Leadership and Group Activities," *Journal of College Student Development* 29, no. 4 (1988): 356–361, https://eric.ed.gov/?id=EJ383512.
74. Kimbrough, "Self-assessment, Participation, and Value of Leadership Skills, Activities, and Experiences for Black Students Relative to their Membership in Historically Black Fraternities and Sororities," 63.
75. Ibid.
76. Ibid.
77. Ibid., 63–65.
78. Deborah Elizabeth Whaley, *Disciplining Women: Alpha Kappa Alpha, Black Counterpublics, and the Cultural Politics of Black Sororities* (Albany, NY: State University of New York Press, 2010), 6.

79. Ibid.
80. Ibid., 6–7.
81. Ibid.
82. Michael C. Dawson, "A Black Counterpublic? Economic Earthquakes, Racial Agenda(s), and Black Politics," in *The Black Public Sphere*, ed. Black Public Sphere Collective (Chicago, IL: University of Chicago Press, 1995), 204.
83. Whaley, *Disciplining Women: Alpha Kappa Alpha, Black Counterpublics, and the Cultural Politics of Black Sororities*, 118.
84. Nancy Fraser, "Rethinking the Public Sphere," in *The Phantom Public Sphere*, ed. Bruce Robbins (Minneapolis, MN: University of Minnesota, 1993), 14.
85. Nakia Hill, "On My Way to NABJ," *The Huffington Post*, Last modified, August 8, 2012, https://www.huffpost.com/entry/nabj-2012_b_1606997.
86. James Durrah, "Jemele Hill Named 2018 NABJ Journalist of the Year," *NABJ.org*, Last modified, May 18, 2018, https://www.nabj.org/news/401602/Jemele-Hill-named-2018-NABJ-Journalist-of-the-Year-.htm.
87. Benjamin, *Black Women in the Academy. Promises and Perils*.
88. Cite Black Women Collective, "Our Story," https://www.citeblackwomencollective.org, 2017.
89. Ibid.
90. Devon W. Carbado, Kimberlé Williams Crenshaw, Vickie M. Mays, and Barbara Tomlinson, "Intersectionality: Mapping the Movements of a Theory," *Du Bois Review: Social Science Research on Race* 10, no. 2 (2013): 303–312, doi:10/1017/S1742058X13000349.
91. Hill Collins, "Truth-telling and Intellectual Activism," 38.
92. Harris-Perry, *Sister Citizen*, 5.

BIBLIOGRAPHY

Amoah, Jewel. "Narrative: The Road to Black Feminist Theory." *Berkeley Women's Law Journal* 12 (1997): 84. https://doi.org/10.15779/Z38FP3B.

Benjamin, Lois. *Black Women in the Academy. Promises and Perils*. Gainesville, FL: University Press of Florida, 1997.

Bonner, Florence B., and Veronica G. Thomas. "New and Continuing Challenges and Opportunities for Black Women in the Academy." *The Journal of Negro Education* 70, no. 3 (2001): 121–123. doi:10.2307/3211204.

Brown-Glaude, Winnifred R. "But Some of Us Are Brave: Black Women Faculty Transforming the Academy." *Signs: Journal of Women in Culture and Society* 35, no. 4 (2010): 801–809. doi:10.1086/651035.

Byers, Dylan. "Melissa Harris-Perry Rejects MSNBC Deal in a Scathing Farewell." *CNN.com*, Last Modified January 3, 2016. https://money.cnn.com/2016/03/01/media/melissa-harris-perry-msnbc-farewell/index.html.

Carbado, Devon W., Kimberlé Williams Crenshaw, Vickie M. Mays, and Barbara Tomlinson. "Intersectionality: Mapping the Movements of a Theory." *Du Bois*

Review: Social Science Research on Race 10, no. 2 (2013): 303–312. doi:10/1017/S1742058X13000349.

Chateauvert, Melinda. *Marching Together: Women of the Sleeping Car Porters.* Chicago, IL: University of Illinois Press, 1998.

Cite Black Women Collective, "Our Story." Last Modified, 2017 https://www.citeblackwomencollective.org.

Collier-Thomas, Bettye, and Vincent P. Franklin. *Sisters in the Struggle: African American Women in the Civil Rights—Black Power Movement.* New York, NY: New York University Press, 2001.

Combs, Gwendolyn M. "The Duality of Race and Gender for Managerial African American Women: Implications of Informal Social Networks on Career Advancement." *Human Resource Development Review* 2, no. 4 (2003): 385–405. https://doi.org/10.1177/1534484303257949.

Davis, Dannielle Joy, Rema Reynolds, and Tamara Bertrand Jones. "Promoting the Inclusion of Tenure Earning Black Women in Academe: Lessons for Leaders in Education." *Florida Journal of Educational Administration & Policy* 5, no. 1 (2011): 28–41. https://eric.ed.gov/?id=EJ961224.

Dawson, Michael C. "A Black Counterpublic? Economic Earthquakes, Racial Agenda(s), and Black Politics," in *The Black Public Sphere*, ed. Black Public Sphere Collective. Chicago, IL: University of Chicago Press, 1995.

Dingus, Jeannine E. "'I'm Learning the Trade.' Mentoring Networks of Black Women Teachers." *Urban Education* 43, no. 3 (2008): 361–377. https://doi.org/10.1177/0042085907311794.

Dowdy, Joanne Kilgour. "Fire and Ice: The Wisdom of Black Women in the Academy." *New Horizons in Adult Education and Human Resource Development* 22, no. 1 (2008): 24–43. doi:10.1002/nha3.10297.

Durrah, James. "Jemele Hill Named 2018 NABJ Journalist of the Year." *NABJ.org*, Last Modified, May 18, 2018. https://www.nabj.org/news/401602/Jemele-Hill-named-2018-NABJ-Journalist-of-the-Year-.htm.

Erwin, T. Dary, and Susan T. Marcus-Mendoza. "Motivation and Students' Participation in Leadership and Group Activities." *Journal of College Student Development* 29, no. 4 (1988): 356–361. https://eric.ed.gov/?id=EJ383512.

Evans, Gina L., and Kevin O. Cokley. "African American Women and the Academy: Using Career Mentoring to Increase Research Productivity." *Training and Education in Professional Psychology* 2, no. 1 (2008): 50. doi:10.1037/1931-3918.2.1.50.

Farhi, Paul. "MSNBC Will Cut Ties with Show Host Who Wrote Critical Email to Colleagues." *The Washington Post*, Last Modified, February 28, 2016. https://www.washingtonpost.com/lifestyle/style/msnbc-will-cut-ties-with-show-host-who-wrote-critical-email-to-colleagues/2016/02/27/bce30c8e-dd82-11e5-891a-4ed04f4213e8_story.html?utm_term=.20af06698214.

Folkenflik, David. "MSNBC Fires Host Melissa Harris Perry Over Controversial Memo." *NPR*, Last Modified, March 9, 2016. https://www.npr.org/2016/03/09/469837015/msnbc-fires-host-melissa-harris-perry-over-controversial-memo.

Fraser, Nancy. "Rethinking the Public Sphere," in *The Phantom Public Sphere*, Ed. Bruce Robbins. Minneapolis, MN: University of Minnesota, 1993.

Fries-Britt, Sharon, and Bridget Turner Kelly. "Retaining Each Other: Narratives of Two African American Women in the Academy." *The Urban Review* 37, no. 3 (2005): 221–242. doi:10.1007/s11256-005-0006-2.

Grant, Cosette M., and Juanita Cleaver Simmons. "Narratives on Experiences of African-American Women in the Academy: Conceptualizing Effective Mentoring Relationships of Doctoral Student and Faculty." *International Journal of Qualitative Studies in Education* 21, no. 5 (2008): 501–517. https://doi.org/10.1080/09518390802297789.

Gregory, Sheila T. "Black Faculty Women in the Academy: History, Status and Future." *The Journal of Negro Education* 70, no. 3 (2001): 124. doi:10.2307/3211205.

Green, Cheryl Evans, and Valarie Greene King. "Sisters Mentoring Sisters: Africentric Leadership Development for Black Women in the Academy." *The Journal of Negro Education* 70, no. 3 (2001): 156. doi:10.2307/3211207.

Harris-Perry, Melissa V. *Sister citizen: Shame, Stereotypes, and Black Women in America*. New Haven, CT: Yale University Press, 2011.

Henderson, Tammy L., Andrea G. Hunter, and Gladys J. Hildreth. "Outsiders Within the Academy: Strategies for Resistance and Mentoring African American Women." *Michigan Family Review* 14, no. 1 (2010). http://dx.doi.org/10.3998/mfr.4919087.0014.105.

Higgins, Monica C., and Kathy E. Kram. "Reconceptualizing Mentoring at Work: A Developmental Network Perspective." *Academy of Management Review* 26, no. 2 (2001): 264–288. https://doi.org/10.5465/amr.2001.4378023.

Hill Collins, Patricia. *Black Feminist Thought: Knowledge, Consciousness, and the Politics of Empowerment*. Abingdon, U.K.: Routledge, 2002.

Hill Collins, Patricia. *Fighting Words. Black Woman and the Search for Justice*. Minneapolis, MN: University of Minnesota, 1998.

Hill Collins, Patricia. "Truth-telling and Intellectual Activism." *Contexts* 12, no. 1 (2013): 36–41. doi:10.1177/1536504213476244.

Hill, Nakia. "On My Way to NABJ." *The Huffington Post,* Last Modified, August 8, 2012. https://www.huffpost.com/entry/nabj-2012_b_1606997.

Hopkins, Margaret M., Deborah O'Neil, Angela Passarelli, and Diana Bilimoria. "Women's Leadership Development Strategic Practices for Women and Organizations." *Consulting Psychology Journal: Practice and Research* 60, no. 4 (2008): 348. http://dx.doi.org/10.1037/a0014093.

Jordan-Zachery, Julia S. "Reflections on Mentoring: Black Women and the Academy." *Political Science & Politics* 37, no. 4 (2004): 875–877. https://doi.org/10.1017/S1049096504045317.

Kennedy Haydel, Sheryl. "Our Voice, Our Choice: Race, Politics and Community Building on the Page of Five Historically Black College and University Newspapers from 1930 to 1959." PhD diss., University of Southern Mississippi, 2016. https://aquila.usm.edu/dissertations/341/.

Kimbrough, Walter M. "Self-assessment, Participation, and Value of Leadership Skills, Activities, and Experiences for Black Students Relative to their Membership in Historically Black Fraternities and Sororities." *Journal of Negro Education* (1995): 63–74. doi:10.2307/2967285.

Koblin, John. "Melissa Harris-Perry Walks off her MSNBC Show after Pre-emptions." *The New York Times*, Last Modified, February 26, 2016. https://www.nytimes.com/2016/02/27/business/media/melissa-harris-perry-walks-off-her-msnbc-show-after-pre-emptions.html.
Mabokela, Reitumetse Obakeng, and Anna Lucille Green. *Sisters of the Academy: Emergent Black Women Scholars in Higher Education*. Herndon, VA: Stylus Publishing, LLC., 2001.
Menges, Robert J., and William H. Exum. "Barriers to the Progress of Women and Minority Faculty." *The Journal of Higher Education* 54, no. 2 (1983): 123–144. https://doi.org/10.1080/00221546.1983.11778167.
McDonald, Steve, Nan Lin, and Dan Ao. "Networks of Opportunity: Gender, Race, and Job Leads." *Social Problems* 56, no. 3 (2009): 385–402. doi:10.1525/sp.2009.56.3.385.
McKenzie, André. "Community Service and Social Action: Using the Past to Guide the Future of Black Greek-letter Fraternities." *NASPA Journal* 28, no. 1 (1990): 30–36. doi:10.1080/00220973.1990.11072184.
Mirza, Heidi Safia. "Transcendence over Diversity: Black Women in the Academy." *Policy Futures in Education* 4, no. 2 (2006): 101–113. doi:10.2304/pfie.2006.4.2.101.
Moses, Yolanda T. *Black Women in Academe. Issues and Strategies*, Washington, DC: Project on the Status of Women, Association of American Colleges, 1989.
Payne, Charles, M. *I've Got the Light of Freedom: The Organizing Tradition and the Mississippi Freedom Struggle*. Berkeley, CA: University of California Press, 1996.
Patitu, Carol Logan, and Kandace G. Hinton. "The Experiences of African American Women Faculty and Administrators in Higher Education: Has Anything Changed?" *New Directions for Student Services* 2003, no. 104 (2003): 79–93. https://doi.org/10.1002/ss.109.
Sanchez-Hucles, Janis V., and Donald D. Davis. "Women and Women of Color in Leadership: Complexity, Identity, and Intersectionality." *American Psychologist* 65, no. 3 (2010): 171. doi:10.1037/a0017459.
Simmons, Sheila. "Farewell Melissa Harris-Perry, 'Nerdland'." *The Philadelphia Tribune*. Last Modified, March 11, 2016, https://www.phillytrib.com/commentary/farewell-melissa-harris-perry-nerdland/article_b3dedbda-26cb-5ffc-9781-5fd245527541.html.
Skylar, Rachel. Why We Need Melissa Harris-Perry. "The End of #Nerdland Marks Sad Times for Diversity on Cable News." *Elle.com*, Last Modified, March 4, 2016, https://www.elle.com/culture/career-politics/news/a34595/melissa-harris-perry-end-of-show-nerdland/.
Smith, Jamil. "Melissa Harris Perry's Email to her Nerdland Staff." *Medium*, Last Modified, February 26, 2016. https://medium.com/@JamilSmith/melissa-harris-perry-s-email-to-her-nerdland-staff-11292bdc27cb.
Rassool, Naz. "Black Women as 'Other' in the Academy." *Feminist Academics: Creative Agents for Change* (1995): 22. doi:10.2304/pfie.2006.4.2.101.
Taylor, Ula Y. "Making Waves: the Theory and Practice of Black Feminism." *The Black Scholar* 28, no. 2, Black Social Issues (Summer 1998). Reprint: *The Black Scholar* 44, no. 3 (2014): 32–47. doi:10.1080/00064246.1998.11430912.

The History Makers. "Melissa Harris-Perry." Last Modified, September 12, 2014. https://www.thehistorymakers.org/biography/melissa-harris-perry.

Turner, Caroline Sotello Viernes. "Women of Color in Academe: Living with Multiple Marginality." *The Journal of Higher Education* 73, no. 1 (2002): 74–93. doi:10.1353/jhe.2002.0013.

Whaley, Deborah Elizabeth. *Disciplining Women: Alpha Kappa Alpha, Black Counterpublics, and the Cultural Politics of Black Sororities*. Albany, NY: SUNY Press, 2010.

Chapter 6

Cultivating Feminist Reflexivity and Resilience in Leadership Communication

Stephanie Norander

Leadership challenges, paradoxes, and tensions manifest themselves in a multitude of ways for women in academia. Burgeoning discourse and research on the advancement of women in higher education substantiates the salience of these challenges. Such analyses often emphasize interventions designed to increase the numbers of females in leadership positions and pipelines. Moreover, there is no shortage of advice directed at women leaders and potential leaders. In practice, though, it is not quite so straightforward to navigate the daily intersections of identity, career, organizational culture, and relationships. Despite such efforts, "women are still underrepresented, underpaid, and commanding a fraction of the leadership space."[1] Instead, broader and deeper shifts in organizational cultures are needed in order to empower women and men "to think, speak, and act to create the bold moves" (see note 1).

Gender is embedded throughout all organizing practices and many scholars have proposed feminist approaches to examining, deconstructing, resisting, and changing patriarchal, gendered norms of organizational communication.[2] As such, communication scholars have much to contribute to initiating and sustaining transformations in higher education organizations that support women as leaders and emerge from women's experiences. I argue that feminist organizational communication theories provide a robust departure point for developing leadership communication strategies for women in academia because they are grounded in everyday, personal, gendered experiences.[3] When women's experiences, in particular, are taken seriously and considered generative of organizational knowledge, organizational scholarship and practice stand to transform gender inequities that persist in the abovementioned leadership space of academia.

In this chapter, I demonstrate how emergent organizational feminist praxis generates leadership communication strategies for women in academia. By grounding the development of leadership strategies in both theory and practice, I align this work with contemporary feminist scholarship that moves beyond a singular focus on outcomes to highlight, instead, organizational processes.[4] This chapter revolves around key themes of my inquiry and life experiences over the past fifteen years. Questions such as "What allows women to thrive in organizations? How do women negotiate tensions surrounding self-organization, self-other, and personal-professional? What communication strategies and resources facilitate success for women leaders?" characterize this line of inquiry. In past work, I developed a feminist theory of organizational reflexivity which explored symbolic and material privileges and vulnerabilities that flow from inhabiting a White, female, academic subject position and analyzed gendered media portrayals of high-profile female leaders.[5] The focus in this chapter on cultivating leadership communication strategies for women in academia reflects the unfolding of my own career trajectory and resonates with contemporary feminist perspectives on leadership communication.

Ultimately, my goal is two-fold: (1) to articulate a process for developing an emergent feminist leadership praxis and (2) to offer communication strategies useful for enacting feminist leadership across contexts. I begin by describing theoretical developments in leadership communication that highlight meaning-centered approaches. Then, I discuss how the communicative processes of reflexivity and resilience are essential to a meaning-centered feminist leadership praxis. These processes emphasize and help us make sense of disruptions both common and extraordinary to organizational life. I then narrate my own organizational experiences with disruption and share communication strategies that emerge from ongoing attention to reflexivity and resilience in enacting leadership.

LEADERSHIP COMMUNICATION

A current wave of communication scholarship theorizes leadership through a communicative, meaning-centered lens. In contrast to long-held and popular psychological and managerial perspectives on leadership, meaning-centered approaches shift focus to the discursive, relational, and constructionist dimensions of organizational leadership.[6] As such, leadership sensemaking processes and products are the focus of inquiry, rather than, for example, individualistic cognitive leadership traits or surefire "rules" and "tips" that guarantee leadership success. Emergent leadership communication perspectives do not offer a comprehensive, unified theory. Instead, a consistent theme across communication leadership research is that it "shows communication to be central, defining and constitutive of leadership."[7]

Feminist organizational communication scholarship has contributed much to alternative and meaning-centered perspectives on leadership.[8] Not only is gender of specific concern, but also the intersectionality of gender, race, and class are considered crucial to the ways we experience organizational life and our sensemaking of those processes.[9] As such, feminist ways of knowing, such as personal narratives, are considered viable and rich sites for meaning making and engaging difference.[10] Alternative logics feature centrally in this scholarship. Drawing on aesthetic, relational, and egalitarian ways of organizing creates possibilities for knowing and doing organizational life differently than in traditional, patriarchal, and hierarchical forms.[11] Finally, although there are many different feminist philosophical foundations drawn upon across this research, a common theme shows that paradoxes, tensions, contradictions, and complexities are *normal*.[12] This move encourages scholars to both embrace and explore the messiness of organizing.

Examples of this messiness can be found in the contradictions that abound in higher education where progressive ideals are often espoused but not necessarily intrinsic to the institutional culture. Wilson summarizes well the conflicted nature of academic organizational culture as "rigid, inhibiting, and progressive."[13] For women, enacting leadership within a historically patriarchal and contradictory culture poses distinct challenges, especially when women's experiences reveal narratives counter to progressive ideals. A recent collection of narratives, for instance, highlights the experiences of women of color in the academy and reveals harrowing accounts of specific ways that race, gender, and class remain sources of discrimination and marginalization.[14] The #MeToo movement has also shone a light on how academic organizations are far from immune to gendered hierarchies, inequities, and harassment.[15] A significant challenge in enacting feminist leadership, then, is doing so in ways that are politically aware and simultaneously open to ongoing learning, adaptation, and transformation.

Taken together, leadership communication and feminist organizational research provide a basis from which to develop communication strategies for academic women that are situated, nuanced, and both grounded in and generative of praxis. If we want to understand how women can thrive, it makes sense to explore disruption, failure, and tension as both expected challenges and significant sites of learning about leadership communication and contradictory organizational cultures. I propose that the cultivation of reflexivity and resilience are essential communication strategies to build stronger, supportive discursive and material organizational resources for female leaders to thrive amid such disruptions. I turn now to a brief conceptual overview of reflexivity and resilience.

REFLEXIVITY AND RESILIENCE: A BRIEF CONCEPTUAL OVERVIEW

Reflexivity. Reflexivity is also an emerging concept in organizational theorizing. Scholars, for the most part, distinguish and elevate reflexivity over reflection as a meta-process that encompasses and is reliant on active reflection.[16] Like reflection, reflexivity involves an active interest in how we construct ourselves socially and is a process of accounting for and sensemaking of organizational experience.[17] Reflexivity, conversely, implicates and connects those reflections to engage contradictions, assess reflective processes (i.e., what orientations and assumptions belie my reflections?), and generate knowledge and action.[18] In this way, reflexivity is both an analytical concept and a way of being.[19] Alvesson and Skoldberg emphasize that reflexivity is about a commitment to unpacking theory-praxis relationships and ways of doing knowledge.[20] For leaders, frequently examining one's own experiences and communicative actions, considering how theoretical and philosophical commitments influence those actions and their interpretations, and intentionally integrating reflections on past experience into future actions are some ways to accomplish this.

Enacting relational, meaning-centered leadership thus requires a commitment to reflexivity and active reflection on our observations, language use, actions, and contexts. Barge makes this connection clear in his depiction of leaders and leadership as constituted through multiple relationships rather than through traits or prescriptions.[21] Everyday reflexive practice is constructed in daily conversation with others, and involves steadfast attention to the relationships between meaning, assumptions, and context. Reflexive leadership, then, means being accountable to all those involved in the relationship and in remaining open to possibilities for alternative courses of action. Norander and Harter take these ideas a step further in articulating a feminist approach to cultivating organizational reflexivity that involves "not only problematizing dominant knowledge structures but also reclaiming subjugated knowledges."[22]

Resilience. Several academic disciplines currently research and theorize resilience as a human construct. Most relevant to this chapter is recent work on developing a communicative approach to resilience. Resilience is the "process of reintegrating from disruptions in life."[23] Recent communication theorizing shifts focus away from resilient individuals to resilience as a communicative resource that can be explored and cultivated at and across individual, relational, and organizational levels.[24] In organizations, for example, "resilience encompasses the processes by which individuals and organizations reintegrate and foster productive change during and after career setbacks, material and personnel losses, disasters, and other obstacles."[25]

Key to situating resilience processes to the development of leadership communication strategies are the communicative dimensions of feminist leadership considered thus far: disruption, action, and reflexivity. First, resilience processes are responsive to disruptions, disruptions that can be embedded in a wide range of organizational episodes that vary in scope and scale, from everyday interactions to acute crises.[26] Of particular interest to communication scholars are the contextually embedded messages, discourses, narratives, and material resources part of reintegration processes.[27]

Second, Buzzanell[28] outlined five processes that characterize resilience in action:

1. Crafting a new normalcy
2. Affirming important identities
3. Using/maintaining networks
4. Putting alternative logics to work
5. Foregrounding productive action, backgrounding unproductive behaviors

As mentioned above, these processes are contextual and will unfold differently across various temporal, spatial, and cultural dimensions of organizational life. For example, creating a new normal after a large-scale institutional crisis like racial violence on campus will be different, likely, from doing so after an individual crisis. Likewise, organizational cultures and individual roles and career stages will influence resiliency processes.

Finally, and of particular importance to this inquiry, is the notion that these resilience processes embody reflexivity.[29] The capacity for organizations, groups, and individuals to develop and mobilize communicative and material resources for integrating disruption into their narrative relies on their ability to practice reflexivity.

To develop strategies for cultivating reflexivity and resilience in leadership communication, I next discuss the methodological commitments and analytic process involved in doing so. Then, I share three stories of organizational disruption and situate those experiences, and my sensemaking of those processes, through a leadership communication lens. Finally, I suggest further questions for research and praxis.

KNOWLEDGE/EXPERIENCE: PERFORMING REFLEXIVITY AND RESILIENCE

In this chapter, I draw upon my own life experiences and communication theories to generate crystallized insights on leadership communication for academic women.[30] I argue that in order to cultivate feminist leadership strategies we must be willing to embrace the messiness and contradictions of organizational life. One way to do so is to conceptualize leadership as a learning process punctuated, and nourished by, setbacks and disruptions. Thus, I organize my personal sensemaking around three significant disruptions in my career that continue to influence my leadership philosophy. Such autoethnographic productions of knowledge have a strong tradition in feminist scholarship.[31] I join this tradition in mining meaning from my organizational experiences with negotiating maternity leave, intractable conflict, and career transitions.

Bodies and Bureaucracies

It was late August, just the before the start of my second year as a tenure-track assistant professor. I had just discovered, with a bit of surprise, that I was pregnant with my second child, who would hopefully arrive in April. My first year had been emotionally and physically exhausting. Moving twelve hours away from family, friends, and the support of all that was familiar with my husband and a then nine-month-old was a more dramatic life change than I ever could have predicted. A new city, state, institution, career, colleagues, neighbors, daycare, and house was a lot to encounter and navigate in ways both positive and challenging. I felt that I had barely survived.

And now. Joy. Wonder. Fear. I was barely managing life and career with one child. How would I possibly do this with two? I landed in an institutional and department culture where women tenure-track professors taking leave, for childbirth, was an anomaly. From my perspective, this was not a product of a hard-charging research and publication culture. The publication requirements for tenure were modest, however, the teaching (three courses per semester) and service requirements were significant. Instead, the organizational culture, or lack thereof, around parental leave seemed to be a product of a slow-to-change, heavily entrenched patriarchal expectations of how (and who is expected) to do an academic career.

For example, at the start of my first year, I was placed in a cubicle in a shared office space with three others. I asked, albeit meekly, about where I could pump as I was still breastfeeding. The response belied a bit of bafflement. When I shared that my graduate school institution had just opened a women's center and breastfeeding room to much fanfare in my last semester, I was told that because space was at such a premium here there was little chance of that ever happening. Not wanting to draw unwelcome attention to my breastfeeding self in the first days of my new career, I opted not to pursue a private space to pump at work, running home (thankfully I lived quite close to campus) when necessary and decreasing the amount of breastfeeding I was doing.

Now, I would again have to draw attention to myself, and my female body. First, I spoke with my faculty mentor, who was kind, supportive, and also pragmatic in sharing that this was not "normal" for a pre-tenure professor and she helped me strategize ways to present the news to the chair and department. I then met with my chair, also female, who asked that I work with human resources (HR) on putting together a proposed leave plan that followed the appropriate policies and present it to her. I encountered a lack of knowledge about, and experience with, my situation more than I did a lack of support. I was one of the only female tenure-track professors to have children, and the first in the department, I believe, to ever request leave for childbirth.

Reaching out to human resources was a bit surprising as I learned they also had rarely encountered such a request for leave for a nine-month tenure-track employee giving birth during the academic year. The person I spoke with suggested I look through the employee handbook and that she would too before we met in person. Upon scouring the handbook, I found the one-to-two sentences referencing leave for nine-month employees and childbirth under "Disability Leave." I highlighted this and brought it to the meeting. The HR official printed out the disability paperwork. Then, I typed up a two-page overview for my chair, and department (namely, the tenured professors on the annual evaluation committee), of three different scenarios and their accompanying policy explanations: one where I would take disability leave only for the final six weeks of the spring semester and return full time the following fall, one where I would apply for Family Medical and Leave Act (FMLA) to use in the fall semester, and a third where I would apply for additional FMLA time.

A tenured male full professor offered, kindly, to cover my classes for the last six weeks of the spring semester. Another full professor offered to meet with the provost's office to discuss how leave would impact my annual evaluation and progress toward tenure, and how the department should handle it. Her efforts were appreciated, but the results of that meeting were ambiguous and seemed to be largely a subjective opinion of the then male associate provost. I received handwritten notes indicating that I could request an additional year on my tenure clock along with a warning that if I did so, my case should be very solid by the time I applied for tenure. Also, I was warned that if I requested additional time, but then decided I didn't need it, I should be certain that my case would be successful because I would not be given an additional chance. Ad hoc advice, opinions, and policy-making were integrated and annotated into my "proposal."

Fast forward one year later. I returned to work three months after my healthy, beautiful daughter was born with no complications. As time unfolded, numerous women on campus in the same situation were asked by their department chairs to get in touch with me because they heard I could help them put together a "proposal" for taking maternity leave. I willingly shared my experiences and advice, and developed some strong friendship bonds over initial interactions about how to navigate the system successfully.

Pregnant bodies disrupt bureaucratic orders, accenting gendered identities and organizational structures and policies, and making public personal life dimensions.[32] Female academics who experience pregnancy are subject to particular assumptions and questions about career commitments.[33] Despite progressive ideals, such as egalitarianism and equality, that abound in higher education, institutions can still be slow to change practices and update policies that would create more flexibility equity around parenting. In the narrative above, as well as in my broader experiences seeking advice from others, I have learned that many of us in these situations just find a way to make it work—one handles the disruption of pregnancy and parenthood by finding ways, and people, to navigate organizations that at best have some institutional support for such situations and at worst little to none.

Bullies and Bad Behaviors

Anyone who has spent time in organizations has encountered or will encounter an array of bad behaviors that range from annoying to unethical to even illegal. Over the past twenty years, much attention has been given to "bad" organizational behaviors, often defined as deviance, aggression, antisocial behavior, and violence.[34] Higher education is by no means immune to the proliferation of such behaviors. There is mounting evidence, for example, that organizational bullying behaviors such as threatening one's professional status and obstructing one's ability to achieve professional goals occur frequently relative to nonacademic organizations.[35]

Some "bad" organizational behaviors in higher education that I have experienced and witnessed together with colleagues include:

- Abusing power to manipulate job searches
- Sowing discord among faculty by talking badly about individuals to their colleagues
- Using perks, such as research assistant assignments, as rewards and punishments
- Retaliating against individuals in annual evaluation processes
- Elevating one's own career ambitions over the good of the unit or department
- Silencing those who ask questions or ask for better transparency
- Kissing up to higher administrators and kicking down faculty

The rigid hierarchical structure that characterizes most institutions of higher learning in the United States means that the behaviors of those in formal leadership positions can have significant impacts on, for good and bad, the daily working lives of employees and especially those whom they supervise. The literature on how to negotiate power in supervisory relationships in academic organizations is fairly sparse and the literature on navigating and protecting oneself from unethical behaviors even more so.[36] This is perhaps because there is a facade of egalitarianism surrounding academic work culture, and a common bristling by many to terms such as "supervisor." I argue, though, that such a facade conceals the material and symbolic realities of a hierarchical institutional structures and limits our abilities to develop strategies to deal with them. To pretend that the abuse of power in academic organizations is an anomaly, or that any of the above behaviors (as well as many more egregious than listed) should come as a surprise or unexpected is to ignore years of narratives and experiences from academic women.[37] I make the case here that bullying and other communicative behaviors cause organizational disruption, in varying degrees of severity.

I have experienced one particularly acute abuse of power early in my academic career. A White male administrator engaged in manipulative, deceptive, and bullying behaviors targeted at a small group of female faculty (including me) and one male faculty member. The instigation of these targeted behaviors seemed to be questioning, by faculty members, of the lack of transparency in decision-making, allocation of department resources, and repeated falsehoods. Although the personal motives for such behaviors remain unknown, the outcomes on the targets included silencing, physical and emotional distress, fear of retaliation through performance evaluation processes, and discord within a department that heretofore had been relatively peaceful and supportive. To paint this episode in broad strokes, the magnitude of disruption was both personal in that it affected individual careers and collective in that it shifted a department's cultural norms.

As I reflect now on this experience, I wonder about the choices women especially have when faced with such disruptive situations. As a feminist, I felt principled not to remain silent, and to speak up at witnessing the attempts at silencing directed at me and others. And yet, I also wanted to commit to taking care of myself. Meetings after meetings, with the dean's and provost's office, the office of legal affairs, and the office of institutional equity, dragged on for months. The experience was emotionally and physically draining, as well as all-consuming. I questioned, often, "Was I fighting the power? Or, was I giving disproportionate intellectual, social, and emotional energy toward one White male administrator?" The answer to both, I believe, was yes.

One of the major lessons I learned in this was how willing organizations are to look the other way, to make false equivalencies when presented with evidence of wrongdoing (well, there are two sides to every story), and to put it bluntly, to let White males who seem to be shining stars off the hook. This should come as no surprise, as one does not have to look hard to find organizational narratives that buttress this claim.[38] The challenge then becomes how to handle such commonplace disruptions, and contribute to "new normal" that ideally, albeit slowly, change this dynamic.

In looking at what it meant to construct resilience in the above context, it is important to understand that context is cultural, spatial, and temporal. Each of us involved took different actions to try to create a more workable relationship with our self, our career, our organization. We were able to draw on each other for strength, support, and to engage in meaning making. For example, I engaged in a job search that was ultimately successful, another took a position in the provost's office, another focused on what remained before she wanted to retire and finally another invested her energy elsewhere. We all had to find our new normal, and how to foreground productive action.

The experience of going through deep conflict has had a significant impact on my approach to organizational life. Having witnessed the "dark side" of organizational behaviors, I am much more careful in my approach to relationships to supervisors, choosing to keep interactions formal and professional rather than informal and personal. This helps me better preserve my autonomy and independence to speak up when and if I have questions and concerns about organizational policies or the decision-making process.

Second, it has impressed upon me the importance of taking care of myself. To be a successful academic leader, female, and human, I have to make decisions, daily, about how and where and in whom to invest my time and energy. Deciding how much power and space I give to other people, and to organizational issues, has become a daily concern for me as I endeavor to have meaningful relationships and engage in meaningful activities across all life spheres.

Finally, it has given me a sense of bureaucratic savvy and perspective. First, I have learned that as an organizational member, one can follow processes and adhere to the integrity of organizational policies. But, one cannot control the outcomes of doing so. I learned through this process, that organizations, and yes, even lofty academic ones, excuse, allow, enable, normalize, and even promote all kinds of bad behaviors. This experience gave me, also, a healthy sense of perspective of the scope and scale of organizational conflict and unhealthy behaviors. And, I can gauge my reaction, as well as my emotional investment accordingly. I have a better appreciation, from an organizational perspective, of what constitutes serious and potentially harmful transgressions, such as bullying, and what constitutes everyday organizational tensions, such as frustrations with another's administrative philosophy.

Promotions and Pivots

A year after earning tenure and promotion, I applied for and was offered a position as the executive director of a communication across the curriculum program. The position allowed me to maintain tenure and associate professor status, live within closer driving distance of family, and engage in work that reenergized me post-tenure. And, the new role was a leap in both status and salary. All of a sudden, my competence was valued, I was meeting with administrators, offering insights and ideas on curriculum, and dwelling in a large, beautiful office with natural light. I arrived in a new role and new institutional context, eager to thrive in this environment.

I threw myself into the role and the new campus culture. As an organizational communication scholar, I felt I had a reasonable grasp of socialization processes and that because of this my experience of trying to enter a new culture would be mitigated. Instead, I realized the enormity of disruption, much of it positive, of moving one's family twelve hours across the country, transitioning from an associate professor to a program administrator/associate professor. All the while, I felt incredible internal pressure to project outwardly that it was not disruptive, and that, I was "fine." Amid navigating a new city, home, neighborhood, social life, public school system, jobs for myself and my spouse, healthcare system—I was both incredibly excited and grateful for this new career phase and when I think back now on that experience, I sense that the struggle was borne of deep-seated notions that professional success means not acknowledging disruption (especially on a personal level). For me to acknowledge, in this case, that such a transition was both difficult and exciting, felt as though it would also be for me to risk being perceived as unprepared, and even worse, an imposter.

Imposter syndrome is well documented in the literature on women and leadership, and especially in academic contexts.[39] The disruption I explore in this section has foregrounded for me the ways in which aspects of my social identity intersect in ways that bring about acute dimensions of imposter syndrome. A promotion and pivot to administration at a new, larger institution with a different academic culture brought to light for me the way that gender and class intersect in particular ways. This career disruption allowed the frictions of integrating working class origins into an elitist, academic world to surface anew.

I found myself adrift, and awash in imposter syndrome, among administrative elite and colleagues who could begin a faculty presentation, nonchalantly, with "like many of us, I grew up in an academic family," or lament how difficult it was to "make it" on a professor's salary. Interactions like these rendered my expression frozen in a smile and faraway stare. At the same time, my mind worked hard to hold competing and contradictory thoughts and feelings like relief at passing as someone who belongs, indignation that someone with my background should feel so alien, and curious about what others would think if they knew of my humble backgrounds. My experience of the invisibility of and the need to suppress class identity in the academy resonates with that of other women who have written about coming from working class backgrounds to academia. As Anthony candidly states, "You can take the woman out of the working class, but you cannot take the working class out of the woman,"[40] suggesting that class identity influences women's experiences of leadership and academia in significant ways.

For example, I remember preparing for a high stakes meeting with an administrator to request additional resources early on in this new phase of my career. The night before, I revisited my well-worn copy of "Women Don't Ask" and proofread my six-page proposal. Driving my morning commute, I cranked up the volume to my feminist anthem, or fight song at that time, and belted out the chorus with Lily Allen.[41] Butterflies danced in my stomach as I walk from the parking lot to my office. I experience the familiar sensation of playing a role that was maybe given to me by mistake. Will today be the day that others realize I am only pretending to be a successful female leader, administrator, academic? Viewing this and other critical moments of my leadership career through a feminist, class-conscious lens allows me to see how gender, class identity, and imposter syndrome can play out in daily interactions and helps me make sense of lessons learned.

For example, the deepest lessons for me out of this disruptive career transition were about context and the importance of finding ways to recognize, and subsequently anchor myself, in parts of my identity that perhaps I had not before attuned myself so clearly. As mentioned previously, the ability to act into and from context involves temporal, spatial, and cultural dimensions.[42] I was learning a new institutional culture and all of its identity-based norms and expectations. At the same time, I was learning how to act like an administrator by showing that I was capable, confident, and that I "belonged" in the academic world in a way more enveloping than I had previously experienced as a faculty member. Temporally, I was in the midst of what I refer to as the "muddy middle" of academic careers, the post-tenure, "how do I define myself now?" phase. In order to more fully affirm my identity, I had to decide which parts to let go of, and which parts to grow. As a result of encountering my class identity poignantly in this transition, for example, I have made moves to embrace it more intentionally in enacting and reflecting upon my leadership as an administrator, mentor, and scholar (i.e., including it in this chapter).

LEARNING ABOUT LEADERSHIP THROUGH DISRUPTIONS

As I journey through different phases in my career, I become interested, increasingly, in developing and living a meaning-centered leadership philosophy that embodies feminist ideals. I propose such a philosophy and its accordant communication practices are best grounded in a deep sense of and appreciation for disruption. The mining of my own disruptive experiences in this chapter is not meant to suggest a representative narrative for all female academic leaders. Rather, I suggest that the process of exploring our disruptions, failures, and career fissures gives a blueprint for future actions as leaders. And, I suggest that reflexivity—seeking alternative organizational communication paths through questioning dominant structures—and resilience—using reflexivity to integrate disruptive experiences into future actions—are indispensable leadership communication processes.

I began this chapter by sharing the central concern, "How can female academic leaders thrive?" Then, I connected leadership communication to reflexivity and resilience before sharing my own organizational experiences of thriving and not thriving. Mining my own disruptions for meaning, through a leadership communication lens, has led me to suggest five communicative dimensions of organizational life necessary for female leaders to thrive:

1. *Support Networks:* Female leaders need strong informal and formal support networks of other females and males in which they can give and receive support and process their experiences.
2. *Care of Self:* Physical, mental, and spiritual well-being are not luxuries one can put off until later in one's leadership journey and career. Rather, care of self is an integral part of cultivating reflexivity and resilience in leadership practice.[43]
3. *Identity Integration:* Women's experiences vary widely, both across and within our individual lives. Attention to the intersectionality of our different aspects of identity and awareness of the organizational constraints and affordances for integrating our identities are necessary in order to leverage, affirm, and anchor our identities in times of disruption.
4. *Intentional Reflection:* Reflection on experience and learning is a necessary part of adopting reflexive approaches to leadership that enable adaptive-transformative, resilience processes.
5. *Forward Momentum:* Just as reflection on past experience is necessary, so is a consistent focus on forward vision and motion.

Developing feminist leadership communication strategies for academic women draws attention to irresolvable tensions between self and organization, personal and professional, and discourse and embodied needs. I suggest that the communicative dimensions put forward above are necessary in order to engage those tensions and cultivate reflexivity and resilience as foundational leadership practices encompassing the five dimensions above.

First, seeking supportive networks continues to be an avenue of leadership growth and development. I have experienced growth when I approach support as a reciprocal process, and seek ways both to support other female leaders and be supported. Especially as I gain more seniority in my career, I invest time in relationships where my support can be most useful to cultivating resiliency in others. Second, I take seriously the idea that self-care is essential, not optional, to one's whole life, including career. As a leader, I believe it is my responsibility to model this for others and I try to push back, actively, against the notion that we need to deny ourselves in order to be successful. This does not always go over well in a culture wherein it is common to talk about how overworked one is and to privilege work above other life realms. But, self-care is a practice that helps me on a daily basis cultivate the mental space to be reflexive and the motivation to build and sustain resiliency. Third, I continue to pay attention to how different aspects of my identity influence my organizational experiences. This includes attention to privileges attached to different aspects of my identity as well as hindering stereotypes. By also including reflection, mostly through journaling, as part of my leadership practice, I'm able to assess frequently when I need to affirm different parts of my identity. Finally, it is difficult for me to understate the power of forward momentum in enacting reflexive and resilient leadership. Grounded in sensemaking of the past through reflection and feminist commitments that alternative ways of doing organizational life are possible, forward oriented leadership is both realistic and hopeful. For me, this is a particularly necessary stance during and after disruption and change.

Ultimately, enacting feminist leadership by centering reflexivity and resiliency in everyday practices offer women a way to engage the inevitable disruptions of academic life. The practices I have suggested do not replace the need for systemic change to institutional structures. Rather, they provide a day-to-day praxis approach to female leadership that can contribute to shifting traditional, gendered ideas about what constitutes success as an academic leader.

NOTES

1. Lynn M. Gangone, "Reflections on Advancing Women in Higher Education," last modified January 11, 2016, https://www.acenet.edu/the-presidency/columns-and-features/Pages/Reflections-on-Advancing-Women-in-Higher-Education.aspx

2. Karen L. Ashcraft, and Dennis K. Mumby, *Reworking Gender: A Feminist Communicology of Organization* (Thousand Oaks, CA: Sage, 2004); Patrice

M. Buzzanell, *Rethinking Organizational and Managerial Communication from Feminist Perspectives* (Thousand Oaks, CA: Sage, 2000); Patrice M. Buzzanell et al., "Positioning Gender as Fundamental in Applied Communication Research," in *Routledge Handbook of Applied Communication Research*, ed. Lawrence R. Frey and Kenneth N. Cissna (New York: Taylor & Francis, 2009), 181–202. Sarah E. Dempsey, Patricia S. Parker, and Kathleen J. Krone, "Navigating Socio-spatial Difference, Constructing Counter-space: Insights from Transnational Feminist Praxis," *Journal of International and Intercultural Communication* 4 (2011): 201–220.

3. Buzzanell et al., "Positioning Gender as Fundamental," 181.

4. Buzzanell et al., "Positioning Gender as Fundamental," 181–183.

5. Stephanie Norander, and Lynn M. Harter, "Reflexivity in Practice: Challenges and Potentials of Transnational Organizing," *Management Communication Quarterly* 26, no. 1 (2012): 74–105.; Stephanie Norander, "Complicating Empowerment and Privilege," *Women & Language* 34 (2011): 121–124.; Stephanie Norander, "Embodied Moments: Revisiting the Field of Writing Vulnerably," *Journal of Applied Communication Research* 45, no. 3 (2017a): 346–351.; Stephanie Norander, "Surveillance/Discipline/Resistance: Carly Fiorina Under the Gaze of *The Wall Street Journal*," *Communication Studies* 59 (2008): 99–113.; Stephanie Norander, "Kamala Harris and the Interruptions Heard Around the Internet," *Feminist Media Studies* 17 (2017b): 1104–1107.

6. J. Kevin Barge, "Pivotal Leadership and the Art of Conversation," *Leadership* 10, no. 1 (2014): 60; Gail T. Fairhurst, and Stacey L. Connaughton, "Leadership: A Communicative Perspective," *Leadership* 10, no. 1 (2014): 9–15.

7. Fairhurst and Connaughton, "Leadership," 8.

8. Buzzanell, *Rethinking Organizational and Managerial Communication*, 334–358.; Gail T. Fairhurst et al., "Leadership Discourses of Difference: Executive Coaching and the Alpha Male Syndrome," in *Reframing Difference in Organizational Communication Studies: Research, Pedagogy, Practice*, ed. Dennis K. Mumby (Thousand Oaks, CA: Sage, 2011), 77–100.; Marlene G. Fine, and Patrice M. Buzzanell, "Walking the High Wire: Leadership Theorizing, Daily Acts, and Tensions," in *Rethinking Organizational and Managerial Communication from Feminist Perspectives*, ed. Patrice M. Buzzanell (Thousand Oaks, CA: Sage, 2000), 128–156.

9. Karen L. Ashcraft, and Brenda J. Allen, "The Racial Foundation of Organizational Communication," *Communication Theory* 13 no. 1 (2003): 28–33.; Patricia S. Parker, *Race, Gender, and Leadership: Re-envisioning Organizational Leadership from the Perspectives of African American Women Executives* (Mahwah, NJ: Lawrence Erlbaum Associates, Inc., 2005).

10. Fine and Buzzanell, "Walking the High Wire," 133–138.

11. Karen L. Ashcraft, "Organized Dissonance: Feminist Bureaucracy as Hybrid Form," *Academy of Management Journal* 44, 1301–1322; Karen L. Ashcraft, "Feminist-Bureaucratic Control and Other Adversarial Allies: Extending Organized Dissonance to the Practice of 'New' Forms," *Communication Monographs* 73, 55–86.

12. Lynn M. Harter et al., "The Intermingling of Aesthetic Sensibilities and Instrumental Rationalities in a Collaborative Arts Studio," *Management Communication Quarterly* 21, no. 4 (2008): 423–453.

13. Tanisca M. Wilson, "Complexities of Female Leadership for the Novice Leader in Higher Education Settings," in *Women as Leaders in Higher Education:*

Succeeding Despite Inequity, Discrimination, and Other Challenges Volume One, ed. Jennifer L. Martin (Santa Barbara, CA: Praeger, 2011), 263.

14. Gabriella Gutiérrez y Muhs et al., *Presumed Incompetent: The Intersections of Race and Class for Women in Academia* (Boulder, CO: University Press of Colorado, 2012).

15. Lindsay Ellis, and Sarah Brown, "How a Department Took on the Next Frontier in the #MeToo Movement," *The Chronicle of Higher Education*, November 9, 2018, https://www.chronicle.com/article/How-a-Department-Took-On-the/245050.; Athene Donald, "Are Universities Finally Moving Toward Their #MeToo Movement?," *The Guardian*, July 27, 2018, https://www.theguardian.com/higher-education-network/2018/jul/27/are-universities-finally-moving-towards-their-metoo-moment.

16. Ian Sutherland, "Arts-Based Methods in Leadership Development: Affording Aesthetic Workspaces, Reflexivity and Memories with Momentum," *Management Learning* 44, no. 1 (2012): 27.

17. Ann L. Cunliffe, "Reflexive Dialogical Practice in Management Learning," *Management Learning* 33, no. 1 (2002): 35–61.

18. J. Kevin Barge, "Reflexivity and Managerial Practice," *Communication Monographs* 71 (2004): 72–73.

19. Norander and Harter, "Reflexivity in Practice," 80–82.

20. Mats Alvesson and Kaj Sköldberg, *Reflexive Methodology: New Vistas for Qualitative Research* (London: Sage, 2000).

21. Barge, "Reflexivity," 75.

22. Norander and Harter, "Reflexivity in Practice," 80.

23. Glenn E. Richardson, "The Metatheory of Resilience and Resiliency," *Journal of Clinical Psychology* 58 (2002): 309; Patrice M. Buzzanell, "Resilience: Talking, Resisting, and Imagining New Normalcies into Being," *Journal of Communication* 60, no. 1 (2010): 2.

24. Patrice M. Buzzanell and J. Brian Houston, "Communication and Resilience: Multilevel Applications and Insights," *Journal of Applied Communication Research* 46, no. 1 (2018): 1–4.

25. Patrice M. Buzzanell, "Organizing Resilience as Adaptive-Transformational Tensions," *Journal of Applied Communication Research* 46, no. 1 (2018): 14.

26. Patrice M. Buzzanell and J. Brian Houston, "Communication and Resilience," 1–4.

27. Buzzanell, "Resilience: Talking, Resistance, and Imagining," 2.

28. Buzzanell, "Resilience: Talking, Resistance, and Imagining," 3.

29. Buzzanell, "Organizing Resilience," 15.

30. Laura L. Ellingson, *Engaging Crystallization in Qualitative Research: An Introduction* (Thousand Oaks, CA: Sage, 2009): 10–14.

31. Suzy D'Enbeau and Patrice M. Buzzanell, "Caregiving and Female Embodiment: Scrutinizing (Professional) Female Bodies in Media, Academe, and the Neighborhood Bar," *Women & Language* 33, no 1 (2010): 32–33; Gutiérrez et al., "Introduction," 1; Norander, "Complicating Empowerment," 121–122.

32. Norander, "Embodied Moments," 346–347; Jennifer A. Reich, "Pregnant With Possibility: Reflections on Embodiment, Access, and Inclusion in Field Research," *Qualitative Sociology* 26, no. 3 (2003): 357–359.

33. Paige K. Turner and Kristen Norwood, "Unbound Motherhood: Embodying A Good Working Mother Identity," *Management Communication Quarterly* 27, no. 3 (2013): 396–424.

34. Ricky P. Griffin and Yvette P. Lopez, "'Bad Behavior' in Organizations: A Review and Typology for Future Research," *Journal of Management* 31, no. 6 (2005): 990–992.

35. Loraleigh Keashly and Joel H. Neuman, "Faculty Experiences with Bullying in Higher Education," *Administrative Theory & Praxis* 32, no. 1 (2010): 53.

36. Keashly and Neuman, "Bullying in Higher Education," 61–63; Penelope M. Early, Jane H. Applegate, and Jill M. Tarule, "Relationship Building and Higher Education Women: Stories and Observations," in *Women as Leaders in Higher Education: Succeeding Despite Inequity, Discrimination, and Other Challenges Volume One*, ed. Jennifer L. Martin (Santa Barbara, CA: Praeger, 2011), 251–261.

37. Heipua Kaopua, and Joanne Cooper, "Toxic to the Heart: Barriers to Tenure and Leadership for Women of Faculty of Color," in *Women as Leaders in Higher Education: Succeeding Despite Inequity, Discrimination, and Other Challenges Volume One*, ed. Jennifer L. Martin (Santa Barbara, CA: Praeger, 2011), 110–114.

38. Gutiérrez y Muhs et. al., *Presumed Incompetent*.

39. Holly M. Hutchins, and Hilary Rainbolt, "What Triggers Imposter Phenomenon Among Academic Faculty? A Critical Incident Study Exploring Antecedents, Coping, and Development Opportunities," *Human Resource Development International* 20, no. 3 (2017): 194–214.; Anna Parkman, "The Imposter Phenomenon in Higher Education: Incidence and Impact," *Journal of Higher Education Theory and Practice* 16, no. 1 (2016): 51–60.

40. Constance G. Anthony, "The Port Hueneme of My Mind: The Geography of Working-Class Consciousness in One Academic Career," in *Presumed Incompetent*, ed. Gabriella Gutiérrez y Muhs et al. (Boulder, CO: University Press of Colorado, 2012): 301.

41. Lily Allen, "Hard Out Here," recorded 2013, track 12 on *Sheezus*, Parlophone, compact disc.

42. Barge, "Pivotal Leadership," 62.

43. Adrien K. Wing, "Lessons from A Portrait: Keep Calm and Carry On," in *Presumed Incompetent: The Intersections of Race and Class for Women in Academia*, ed. Gabriella Gutiérrez y Muhs et al. (Boulder, CO: University Press of Colorado, 2012): 369.

BIBLIOGRAPHY

Allen, Lily. "Hard out here." On *Sheezus* (2013). Parlophone.

Alvesson, Mats, and Kaj Sköldberg. *Reflexive Methodology: New Vistas for Qualitative Research*. London, UK: Sage, 2000.

Anthony, Constance G. "The Port Hueneme of My Mind: The Geography of Working-class Consciousness in One Academic Career." In *Presumed Incompetent: The Intersections of Race and Class for Women in Academia*, edited by Gabriella

Gutiérrez y Muhs, Yolanda Flores Niemann, Carmen G. González, and Angela P. Harris, 300–312. Boulder, CO: University Press of Colorado.

Ashcraft, Karen L. "Organized Dissonance: Feminist Bureaucracy as Hybrid Form." *Academy of Management Journal* 44, no. 6 (2001): 1301–1322. https://doi.org/10.5465/3069402.

Ashcraft, Karen L. "Feminist-Bureaucratic Control and Other Adversarial Allies: Extending Organized Dissonance to the Practice of 'New' Forms." *Communication Monographs* 73, no. 1 (2006): 55–86. https://doi.org/10.1080/03637750600557081.

Ashcraft, Karen L., and Brenda J. Allen. "The Racial Foundation of Organizational Communication." *Communication Theory* 13, no. 1 (2003): 5–38. https://doi.org/10.1111/j.1468-2885.2003.tb00280.x.

Ashcraft, Karen L. and Dennis K. Mumby. *Reworking Gender: A Feminist Communicology of Organization*. Thousand Oaks, CA: Sage, 2004.

Barge, J. Kevin. "Reflexivity and Managerial Practice." *Communication Monographs* 71, no. 1 (2004): 70–96. https://doi.org/10.1080/03634520410001691465.

Barge, J. Kevin. "Pivotal Leadership and the Art of Conversation." *Leadership* 10, no. 1 (2014): 56–78. https://doi.org/10.1177/1742715013511739 .

Buzzanell, Patrice M. "Gaining a Voice." *Management Communication Quarterly* 7, no. 4 (1994): 339–383. https://doi.org/10.1177/0893318994007004001 .

Buzzanell, Patrice M. "Reframing the Glass Ceiling as a Socially Constructed Process: Implications for Understanding and Change." *Communication Monographs* 62, no. 4 (1995): 327–354. https://doi.org/10.1080/03637759509376366.

Buzzanell, Patrice M. *Rethinking Organizational and Managerial Communication from Feminist Perspectives*. Thousand Oaks, CA: Sage, 2000.

Buzzanell, Patrice M. "Resilience: Talking, Resisting, and Imagining New Normalcies Into Being." *Journal of Communication* 60, no. 1 (2010): 1–14, https://doi.org/10.1111/j.1460-2466.2009.01469.x.

Buzzanell, Patrice M. "Organizing Resilience as Adaptive-Transformational Tensions." *Journal of Applied Communication Research* 46, no. 1 (2018): 14–18. https://doi.org/10.1080/00909882.2018.1426711 .

Buzzanell, Patrice M., and Brian J. Houston. "Communication and Resilience: Multilevel Applications and Insights – A Journal of Applied Communication Research Forum." *Journal of Applied Communication Research* 46, no. 1 (2018): 1–4. https://doi.org/10.1080/00909882.2017.1412086

Buzzanell, Patrice M., Rebecca J. Meisenbach, Robyn Remke, Helen Sterk, and Lynn H. Turner, Lynn "Positioning Gender as Fundamental in Applied Communication Research." In *Routledge Handbook of Applied Communication*, edited by Lawrence R. Frey and Kenneth N. Cissna, 181–202. New York, NY: Routledge, 2009.

Cunliffe, Ann L. "Reflexive Dialogical Practice in Management Learning." *Management Learning* 33, no. 1 (2002): 35–61. https://doi.org/10.1177/1350507602331002.

Dempsey, Sarah E., Patricia S. Parker, and Kathleen J. Krone. "Navigating Socio-Spatial Difference, Constructing Counter-Space: Insights from Transnational Feminist Praxis." *Journal of International and Intercultural Communication* 4, no. 3 (2011): 201–220. https://doi.org/10.1080/17513057.2011.569973.

D'Enbeau, Suzy, and Patrice M. Buzzanell. "Caregiving and Female Embodiment: Scrutinizing (Professional) Female Bodies in Media, Academe, and the Neighborhood Bar." *Women and Language* 33, no. 1 (April 1, 2010): 29–52.
Donald, Athene. "Are Universities Finally Moving Toward Their #MeToo Movement?" *The Guardian*, last modified on July 27, 2018, https://www.theguardian.com/higher-education-network/2018/jul/27/are-universities-finally-moving-towards-their-metoo-moment.
Ellingson, Laura L. *Engaging Crystallization in Qualitative Research: An Introduction.* Thousand Oaks, CA: Sage, 2009.
Ellis, Lindsay, and Sarah Brown. "How a Department Took on the Next Frontier in the #MeToo Movement." *The Chronicle of Higher Education*, last modified on November 9, 2018, https://www.chronicle.com/article/How-a-Department-Took-On-the/245050.
Fairhurst, Gail T., Marthe L. Church, Danielle E. Hagan, and Joseph T. Levi. "Leadership Discourses of Difference: Executive Coaching and the Alpha Male Syndrome." In *Reframing Difference in Organizational Communication Studies: Research, Pedagogy, Practice,* edited by Dennis K. Mumby, 77–100. Thousand Oaks, CA: Sage, 2011.
Fairhurst, Gail T., and Stacey L. Connaughton. "Leadership: A Communicative Perspective." *Leadership* 10, no. 1 (February 2014): 7–35. https://doi.org/10.1177/1742715013509396.
Fine, Marlene G., and Patrice M. Buzzanell. "Walking the High Wire: Leadership Theorizing, Daily Acts, and Tensions." In *Rethinking Organizational and Managerial Communication from Feminist Perspectives,* edited by Patrice M. Buzzanell, 128–156. Thousand Oaks, CA: Sage, 2000.
Gangone, Lynn M. "Reflections on Advancing Women in Higher Education." Last modified January 11, 2016. https://www.acenet.edu/the-presidency/columns-and-features/Pages/Reflections-on-Advancing-Women-in-Higher-Education.aspx
Griffin, Ricky W., and Yvette P. Lopez. "'Bad Behavior' in Organizations: A Review and Typology for Future Research." *Journal of Management,* 31, no. 6 (December 2005): 988–1005. https://doi.org/10.1177/0149206305279942 .
Gutiérrez y Muhs, Gabriella, Yolanda Flores Niemann, Carmen G. González, and Angela P. Harris, *Presumed Incompetent: The Intersections of Race and Class for Women in Academia.* Boulder, CO: University Press of Colorado, 2012.
Harter, Lynn M., Mark Leeman, Stephanie Norander, Stephanie L. Young, and William K. Rawlins, "The Intermingling of Aesthetic Sensibilities and Instrumental Rationalities in a Collaborative Arts Studio." *Management Communication Quarterly* 21, no. 4 (May 2008): 423–453. https://doi.org/10.1177/0893318907313711.
Hutchins, Holly M., and Hilary Rainbolt. "What Triggers Imposter Phenomenon Among Academic Faculty? A Critical Incident Study Exploring Antecedents, Coping, and Development Opportunities." *Human Resource Development International* 20, no. 3 (2017): 194–214. https://doi.org/10.1080/13678868.2016.1248205 .
Kaopua, Heipua, and Joanne Cooper. "Toxic to the Heart: Barriers to Tenure and Leadership for Women of Faculty of Color." In *Women as Leaders in Higher Education: Succeeding Despite Inequity, Discrimination, and Other Challenges, Vol. 1*, edited by Jennifer L. Martin, 107–130. Santa Barbara, CA: Praeger, 2011.

Keashly, Loraleigh, and Joel Neuman. "Faculty Experiences with Bullying in Higher Education: Causes, Consequences, and Management." *Administrative Theory & Praxis* 32, no. 1 (2010): 48–70. https://doi.org/10.2753/atp1084-1806320103.

Norander, Stephanie. "Surveillance/Discipline/Resistance: Carly Fiorina Under the Gaze of The *Wall Street Journal*." *Communication Studies* 59, no. 2 (2008): 99–113. https://doi.org/10.1080/10510970802062394.

Norander, Stephanie. "Complicating Empowerment and Privilege/Commentary." *Women and Language* 34, no. 2 (2011): 121–124.

Norander, Stephanie. "Embodied Moments: Revisiting the Field and Writing Vulnerably." *Journal of Applied Communication Research* 45, no. 3 (May 27, 2017a): 346–351. https://doi.org/10.1080/00909882.2017.1320572.

Norander, Stephanie. "Kamala Harris and the Interruptions Heard Around the Internet." *Feminist Media Studies* 17, no. 6 (2017b): 1104–1107. https://doi.org/10.1080/14680777.2017.1380427.

Norander, Stephanie, and Lynn M. Harter. "Reflexivity in Practice: Challenges and Potentials of Transnational Organizing." *Management Communication Quarterly* 26, no. 1 (2012): 74–105. https://doi.org/10.1177/0893318911415607.

Parker, Patricia S. *Race, Gender, and Leadership: Re-envisioning Organizational Leadership from the Perspectives of African American Women Executives*. Mahwah, NJ: Lawrence Erlbaum, 2005.

Parkman, Anna. "The Imposter Phenomenon in Higher Education: Incidence and Impact." *Journal of Higher Education Theory and Practice* 16, no. 1 (2016): 51–60.

Reich, Jennifer. "Pregnant with Possibility: Reflections on Embodiment, Access, and Inclusion in Field Research." *Qualitative Sociology* 26, no. 3 (September 2003): 351–367. https://doi.org/10.1093/oxfordhb/9780190842475.013.3.

Richardson, Glenn E. "The Metatheory of Resilience and Resiliency." *Journal of Clinical Psychology* 58, no. 3 (March 2002): 307–321. https://doi.org/10.1002/jclp.10020.

Sutherland, Ian. "Arts-Based Methods in Leadership Development: Affording Aesthetic Workspaces, Reflexivity and Memories with Momentum." *Management Learning* 44, no. 1 (2013): 25–43. https://doi.org/10.1177/1350507612465063.

Turner, Paige K., and Kristen Norwood. "Unbounded Motherhood: Embodying a Good Working Mother Identity." *Management Communication Quarterly* 27, no. 3 (2013): 396–424. https://doi.org/10.1177/0893318913491461.

Wilson, Tanisca M. "Complexities of Female Leadership for the Novice Leader in Higher Education Settings." In *Women as Leaders in Higher Education: Succeeding Despite Inequity, Discrimination, and Other Challenges, Vol. 1*, edited by Jennifer L. Martin, 263–274. Santa Barbara, CA: Praeger, 2011.

Wing, Adrien Katherine. "Lessons from a Portrait: Keep Calm and Carry On." In *Presumed Incompetent: The Intersections of Race and Class for Women in Academia*, edited by Gabriella Gutiérrez y Muhs, Yolanda Flores Niemann, Carmen G. González, and Angela P. Harris, 356–371. Boulder, CO: University Press of Colorado, 2012.

Chapter 7

Communicating Lead(her)ship in the Academy

Navigating a Sea of Organizational Patriarchy

Laura C. Prividera and John W. Howard III

A casual conversation about women leaders is likely to be characterized by an aura of success in the pursuit of equality. References to Hillary Clinton, Sheryl Sandburg, Oprah, and an increasing roster of prominent women leaders have at least some thinking that the hard part is done—equality is simply inevitable. However, the reality lags behind conventional wisdom. According to the 2018 *Catalyst Report*, women hold approximately 40 percent of the management roles in the United States; however, they only hold about 21 percent of senior management roles in the United States and 24 percent of senior management roles globally.[1] Similar reports, such as the *White House Project Report: Benchmarking Women's Leadership* published in 2009, found that while women's representation in other corporate and government leadership positions has increased, there remains a significant difference in the prevalence of female and male leaders.[2]

It is a nearly universal requirement for management and administrative positions that applicants have a college degree. Women are earning a higher proportion of advanced degrees than men. In the academic year 2015/2016, the U.S. Department of Education reported that women earned 57 percent of bachelor degrees, 59 percent of master's degrees, and 53 percent of doctoral degrees.[3] It is through higher education that future organizational members gain access, knowledge, and skills that send them into the upper ranks. Yet, the very organizations charged with enlightening learners and forwarding progress are themselves poor models of the equitable world they aspire for graduates to create as the proportion of women in leadership positions in the academy is not materially different from other settings. As stated in the

White House Project Report, only 23 percent of university presidents are women (14 percent among research institutions), and of governing boards only 30 percent of those seated around the table are women.[4] A similar pattern emerges when examining advances in academic rank. Women comprise approximately 26 percent of full professors, 40 percent of associate professors, 47 percent of assistant professors, and 53 percent of lecturers.[5] That the very institutions most frequently making calls for advancement, progress, and equity are themselves potential examples of the very social stratification their faculty, mission, and vision so often challenge is eye opening indeed.

Even with these disparities, women have entered the middle and upper levels of academic leadership. There is a growing population of women leaders who are established and, arguably, it is the efforts of those women leaders that will have a significant role in changing the gendered face of academic leadership. Susan Madsen argues in the article, "Women and Leadership in Higher Education" that "we need to help prepare (e.g., increase aspirations, develop skills and competencies, obtain mentors and coaches) more women for leadership in higher education."[6] She further argues that more scholarship needs to be done on how programs can prepare female faculty with leadership skills. Like Susan Madsen, Sunny Airini et al. argue that more research is needed on the myriad factors and variables that foster and hinder women's success in university leader positions.[7] This is particularly important to study from a communicative perspective as leadership is as Kathleen Czech and G. L. Forward state "a communication phenomenon."[8]

In this study, we use a grounded theoretical approach to examine the experiences, perceptions, and communication practices of women in leadership positions in the academy. Learning about the experiences of these women leaders and how they conceptualize and enact leadership in the performance of their work is important in understanding the state and future of women as leaders and organizational workers. First, we discuss the gendered culture of organizations that tends to support the masculine leader. Next, we discuss the literature on women, gender, and academic leadership. We then describe our method of in-depth interviews. In our analysis, we discuss three emergent themes: horizontal matriarchy, laboring communication, and eternal work. We conclude with the implications of these themes for women communicating leader(her)ship in the academy.

GENDERED ORGANIZATIONS AND THE MASCULINE LEADER

Examining the nature of organizations in which workers and aspirant leaders participate is essential to contextualizing the experiences of women leaders. Scholars have long argued that organizations are gendered sites that both maintain and reproduce patriarchal ideologies.[9] Rosabeth Moss Kanter observed in her widely cited text, *Men and Women of the Corporation*, that when small numbers of women enter male-dominated corporations they are a highly visible token population.[10] As such, they may experience isolation, stereotyping, and routine scrutiny where sexism and oppression remain normative.[11] Recent work continues to reveal that organizations are gendered sites of meaning construction where social constructions of masculinity and femininity are reaffirmed and patriarchal ideologies prevail.[12]

Of course, one of the most obvious places gender inequity occurs is in wage disparity. Emilio Castilla and Stephen Bernard found in their research that "individuals in managerial positions favor a male employee over an equally qualified female employee by awarding him a larger monetary reward."[13] The material consequence of this is presented in the *White House Project Report* that illustrates women continue to earn 78 cents on the dollar compared to male organizational members.[14] Social relations are also affected by the gendered dimensions of organizational structure. Jeanine Prime, Nancy Carter, and Theresa Welbourne found in their research that "senior managers may be prone to misjudge and/or overestimate the degree to which leader sex and leadership performance are related."[15] Specifically, they found that women were perceived as more effective at caretaking and men more effective at "take charge" behaviors. Male respondents perceived male leaders as outperforming women on problem solving. The authors conclude that such perceptions can impair women's experiences as leaders as well as how they are evaluated.[16] As Marlene Fine argues that "leadership and masculinity" are often viewed as synonymous resulting in the exclusion of women's voices and experiences from discourse on leadership.[17]

Gendered organizations are not simply ordained via policy, they are co-constructed and reproduced during organizational activity. As Joan Acker argues, organizations are gendered through discourse and that discourse is continually (re)negotiated in the social (and therefore organizational) fabric.[18] In Karen Ashcraft and Dennis Mumby's book, *Reworking Gender: A Feminist Communicology of Organization,* they further elaborate on this interplay of organizational and social ideologies as they identify gendered organizations and gendered narratives whereby the social narrative sets gendered expectations that are then applied to and supported by organizational structure and practice.[19] A specific consequence of this is articulated by Annica Kronsell who notes that "institutions largely governed by men have produced and recreated norms and practices associated with masculinity and heterosexuality."[20] As illustrated by Raka Shome, in Western political tradition the ideal, national, state, and governmental representative is framed as masculine and embodies organizational values associated with rationality, the public sphere, and the mind.[21] Thus, "he" is the archetypal leader reified in everyday discourse and promoted to positions of power.

Within organizations, gendered discourse promotes biased decision-making, practices, and policies. The work of scholars Marlene Fine and Patrice Buzzanell, and Joan Acker illustrate how organizational policies and practices generally support men, marginalize women, and embody patriarchal thinking.[22] This is further revealed in the work/family balance and work/life bodies of research.[23] Kirby et al. observe that workplace structures and practices are gendered and privilege work over family, men's careers over women's careers, and work time over family time.[24] More recently scholars are examining how organizational work and one's everyday life impact potential work/life conflicts.[25] Organizational studies also reveal that women experience paradoxical injunctions and double binds that impact their success in masculinized physical and discursive spaces.[26] However, conversations about organizational paradoxes are often discouraged.[27] In sum, a wide range of activities are biased in the patriarchal organizational model.

WOMEN, GENDER, AND ACADEMIC LEADERSHIP

Sharon Bird argues that "while the bulk of the gendered organizations research focuses on work settings other than universities, most of these research findings are relevant also to universities as workplaces."[28] She further asserts that women continue to experience marginalization in the academy through hiring and promotion processes, and within the overarching patriarchal organizational structures.[29] It comes as no surprise that the *White House Project Report* found "when the time comes to advance into tenured positions—the ranks from which top leaders are chosen—women fall behind, especially at the more prestigious institutions."[30]

There is also a patriarchal bias in academic organizational structures. Women faculty are often faced with considering their tenure timeline when making decisions on having children as well as making other life choices regardless of policies that are in place within the workplace.[31] When academic women become mothers, they may experience new challenges regarding balancing work and life responsibilities where the notion of enacting the "ideal worker" is contested.[32] In spite of the challenges posed by disparities in tenure, rank, and administrative advancement, Sharon Bird argues that "women faculty members also perform a disproportionate share of academic departments' care work and emotion labor, and spend more time teaching."[33] Yet, such work, though important in university operations, receives minimal accolades in promotion and tenure processes. The state of women leaders in the academy today is truly a function of leadership as defined by Sherryl

Kleinman and Kenneth Kolb as "a collective process shaped by historical and institutional arrangements."[34]

Janie Fritz[35] and Marlene Fine[36] note that gender is increasingly becoming a primary focus of leadership research. In Alice Eagly, Mary Johannesen-Schmidt, and Marloes van Engen's research, they found that although differences between women and men leaders were small, women tended to have a more "transformational style" and used reward systems in their leadership.[37] Janie Fritz's work highlights that "women and men inhabit somewhat different existential phenomenological worlds" contributing to "different approaches to leadership."[38] In Marlene Fine's scholarly work, she concludes that women's leadership characterizes a more—"collaborative, nurturing and egalitarian" style centered on the importance of communication—an approach at odds with the patriarchal representations of good leadership privileged in discourse.[39]

Effectiveness is a matter of perception in the eyes of those evaluating leaders. People often perceive leaders as having masculine traits making it seem that women are less suited for leadership positions.[40] Yet, research indicates there were relatively few behavioral differences between women and men leaders[41] and they have similar traits.[42] Yet, Alice Eagly and Steven Karau argue that when women's prescribed gender roles are incongruent with their leadership position they are perceived as violations.[43] A material consequence of this is observed by Jennifer Boldry, Wendy Wood, and Deborah Kashy's work that women are disadvantaged in the evaluation process as they are often perceived as lacking in leadership characteristics compared to men.[44]

Alice Eagly and Linda Carli address these double binds by arguing for an approach to leadership that blends masculine and feminine qualities. They further note that one theoretical approach to achieve such goals is through transformative leadership, which is transparent and accountable and suited to today's organizations.[45] Similarly, Alice Eagly states in the foreword to the book *Communicative Understandings of Women's Leadership Development* that "a helpful general template for female leaders contains a mix of more culturally feminine, collaborative behaviors and more culturally masculine, dominant behaviors. With such a repertoire in hand, leaders can . . . respond flexibly."[46]

A Communicative Perspective on Leadership

To address the intersections among leadership, gender, and organizational imperatives, it is important to understand how they emerge and play out in the experiences of leaders. In Gail Fairhurst and Stacey Connaughton's article, "Leadership: A Communication Perspective", they make a compelling argument that communication-centered approaches to leadership have much to offer beyond the existing frames so dominated by traditional psychological approaches.[47] Instead, they suggest that there is no "universal definition of leadership" as it is contested, blurry, and is probably best understood as "a family resemblance among power and influence-oriented language games" in which social actors participate.[48] They organize their discussion around six "value commitments" already evident in the corpus of leadership research:

(a) leadership communication is transmissional *and* meaning-centered; (b) leadership (communication) is relational, neither leader-centric nor follower-centric; (c) influential acts of organizing are the medium and outcome of leadership communication; (d) leadership communication is inherently power-based, a site of contestation about the nature of leadership; (e) leadership (communication) is a diverse, global phenomenon; and (f) leadership communication is alive with the potential for reflexivity, moral accountability, and change.[49]

Their perspective and value commitments are ideally suited for understanding the contested space in which the "woman leader" exists and how she may navigate the challenges, successes, double binds, organizational imperatives, and balance already discussed in the literature.

In summary, Marlene Fine writes "women's voices and experiences are generally absent from the academic discourse on leadership and that absence has profoundly affected theorizing about leadership."[50] Elesha Ruminski and Annette Holba make a call to address this scholarly, social, and organizational disparity. They state "it is evident that women are defining and practicing leadership in extraordinarily diverse ways in our times, despite persistent challenges and constraints; consequently, more expansive metaphoric discourse is needed for this reframing of leadership."[51] As argued in the *White House Project Report*, "the presence—or absence—of female academic leaders can have far-reaching influences not only on the institutions themselves, but beyond that, on the scope of research and knowledge that affects us all."[52] This study responds to these calls.

METHOD

Fourteen female leaders in positions of chair, associate dean, and/or dean participated in this study. Some held interim titles. Participants were located in the Southeastern United States and all were in full-time positions. The majority of participants were White with ages ranging from 41 to 65 and representing disciplines in the arts and sciences and health fields. The majority of women held their current position for less than five years. All had terminal degrees. Nine of the participants had a child or multiple children and more than half were partnered/married during significant portions of their academic careers. It should be noted that the limited diversity of this sample does not capture the full range of leadership experiences of other races, age groups, and ethnicities.

Recalling the argument forwarded by Janie Fritz that women and men emerge from different phenomenological worlds, we employed a grounded approach to analysis.[53] Our data collection and analysis procedures reflect what Thomas Lindlof describes as the "constant comparative method."[54] Two important aspects of this method are that "it specifies the means by which theory grounded in the relationships among data emerges through the management of coding" and "it shows explicitly how to code and conceptualize as field data keep flowing in."[55]

Data were gathered using an in-depth interview format. The ordering of questions varied to preserve the natural flow of conversation and encourage respondents to as Lindlof says, "articulate interests or experiences freely."[56] The data included demographic information, background on the leaders, their aspirations and philosophies, work-family balance, challenges they experienced (including those related to race, gender, and/or rank), what they did and how, their time commitments, communication, and working within the organizational hierarchy. Interviews ranged from one to two hours in duration producing 210 pages of transcripts.

Once our data collection phase was complete, we reviewed interview transcripts multiple times to see how our participants discussed their leadership experiences. Using the process discussed by Anseim Strauss and Juliet Corbin in *Basics of Qualitative Research: Grounded Theory Procedures and Techniques*, we began by documenting topics, expressions, and framings that emerged in each interview.[57] As categories emerged, we began to look across interviews to see if they constituted emerging themes. To emerge as a theme in our analysis, it had to arise in at least half of our interviews. Subsequent coding passes refined and collapsed similar and subthemes as they coalesced around the remaining core themes.

WOMEN LEADERS: EXPERIENCES, PERCEPTIONS, AND COMMUNICATION

The women in this study graciously shared their experiences, perceptions, and communication from the perspective of their academic leader position. Their voices captured the "labyrinth" metaphor noted by Alice Eagly and Linda Carli as their experiences and paths to leadership positions were diverse.[58] Although their experiences were unique, three interconnected themes emerged: horizontal matriarchy, laboring communication, and eternal work.

Horizontal Matriarchy

A coherent and rich frame for leadership quickly emerged from our data. The theme "horizontal matriarchy" captured both the feminine approach to leadership embedded in an organizational hierarchy and the distribution of power in its application. Our participants self-described their leadership as "facilitator," "collaborator," "mentor," "healer," "protector," "mediator," "visionary," and "role model." Collectively their approaches highlighted the importance of change, collaboration, connection, and the well-being of others.

Our participants were motivated by the opportunity and obligation to create "positive change" or to do "good" for the organization and/or its members. Such change was characterized as an opportunity in leading as well as a responsibility of the leader. Patricia states "the role of the leader is . . . creating positive and enduring change." She continues, "I believe I have a responsibility to leave this place better than I found it." Doris thought of "doing good" as foundational to leadership. She observes, "Leaders are anybody who are truly . . . making a difference." Sometimes the positive change simply meant standing on principle or being an advocate. Hillary stated, "If there's something that I think really needs to happen or not happen I will go to bat for or against it no matter what. I think my colleagues know that."

Brenda summarized the importance of creating change at a systemic level. She stated that it is critical to open "people's minds to a broader understanding of what counts as legitimate work . . . so that it's not just this kind of male bean counting so it's really about changing how people think about the discipline and about the university." In sum, positive change is about the community. As noted by Elizabeth "we achieve more if we help other people achieve more—that's a guiding value in my life."

The idea that change is a community experience and leading change is a collective one is reflected by our participants consistently referring to others as "peers" and "colleagues." Even when those labels were not used, the importance of their participation was very clear. Gina sees it as an obligation to involve others as she feels "responsible to try to collaborate." She further states, "I like to work in partnership with people." Beatrice also embraces this approach and states, "I'm very collaborative and seek other people's opinions." Jane notes that leadership is about "empowering faculty and building on their strengths." Rhonda notes that the very process of sending messages to others is constructed with those around her. She states that it is "the team that helps me to take that message to the faculty."

The participants' effort was a collective effort. Consequently, the credit was not for the leader to take alone. As noted by Doris, "I don't want the credit for it. I want the job done." This sentiment was echoed in interview after interview as participants, directly and candidly stated that they had "no ego" in the job. Their main goals were to advance the "discipline" or "the greater good." Patricia stated, "I don't have an ego in this job. . . . There are so many things in the world that need to be done and so many places I could use my interests and expertise." Like Patricia, Brenda states that "even though all this stuff can be really hard and challenging and daunting . . . it's not about me personally. I don't really have any ego . . . I'm always working for the greater good." Elizabeth observes "I try not to be heavily invested in my own perspective." Nora takes the notion a step further as she thinks of her own role: "If someone else could lead us forward in a better way, step right on up."

Collaborating and sharing credit were not only ethical practices for the participants but they also were avenues to connect with and celebrate the achievements of the group. Leadership was about "care."[59] Katherine focuses on care and connection in numerous ways. She states, "I'm really adamant about making sure they are recognized . . . just make people feel like they are heard—that they are part of something." Like Katherine, Jane notes a "simple" way of building connection is sharing good news at the beginning of faculty meetings. She makes it a point to recognize publications and other accomplishments as a part of building community. The role of trust as a community builder was highlighted by Elizabeth who characterized her connection with faculty as follows, "I think it's important that we trust one another." Caroline noted that "when you step into a position like this—it's not about you anymore. It's about everyone else." Success as a leader was defined by positive change in the community. Patricia noted that leadership is about "putting people in the right places so that they can shine." Lara considered it a positive achievement that "faculty seem to know each other a little bit better." Elizabeth summarizes the importance of connection, care, and working as a collectivity. She states that "the part of my leadership that I . . . work the hardest at—is trying to achieve the goals of the institution . . . while also meeting the needs of the people involved."

A specific way cited to support colleagues and create community was through mentoring. Several participants indicated they had little mentorship and the lack of available female mentors was tangible. When referring to specific mentors, numerous participants identified their mothers as having served in that role. Their mothers were strong role models who taught their daughters that anything was possible.

Caroline saw the role of a mentor as critical to the success of female faculty. She states, "We don't do a good job of mentoring and getting our female faculty thru to that higher level to full professor." Doris, who had the benefit of good mentors, concurs, "I'm very passionate about women and helping women to be the next step up. You know—coming after me— somebody greater than me—I really would like to do that." Jane noted that a lot of mentoring actually goes on as a community activity but the name changes based on the relative rank. With peers "we don't call it mentoring we call it just supporting each other whereas if it's junior faculty we call it mentoring." Jane and Patricia saw mentoring as central to advancement and aiding others through the publication process. In some cases mentoring was described as "helping" or even instructive. Hillary recounted an interaction with a job candidate where she walked the candidate through negotiations: "So I said if I were in your shoes, I would ask . . . then I would tell you that I can't . . . so you would then say—well how about you give me . . . more in salary." Mentoring was both an embodiment of caring and fostering success and advancement in the academy.

A more traditional manifestation of our participants' leadership was in the activities they embraced as protective of their colleagues. Many were particularly attuned to the function they served as a buffer or a barrier between the faculty (who did the "work" that makes the academy of value) and the policies and administration (which, although necessary, were frequently seen as complicating faculty work). Consistent with the matriarchal framing, the women leaders recognized the value of all parts involved and saw it as an important activity to mediate or moderate the relationships among the various interests. One thing our participants made clear in their leadership was that it took a significant amount of communicative effort to realize the leadership in practice.

Laboring Communication

Although horizontal matriarchy illustrated an alternative realization of leadership, it was through its communication that organizational and individual resistance to the approach became apparent. Communicating leadership is work. For our participants, that work involved contact time, active listening, perception checking, negotiating, explaining, and justifying not only the "what" but also "how." Both content and process were in play. It is work to successfully lead, and more work for women to successfully lead in ways inconsistent with the patriarchal norm.

Some of the communication labor was straightforward and generally required time more than effort. For example, most of the women in this study had an "open door policy" for faculty, students, and staff and felt "face time" was an important aspect of their job. As Lara stated, "Door's always open . . . I try to have as much contact" with faculty and staff "as I can." The time taken is not without consequence as noted by Katherine, "I speak to everybody and if someone comes in . . . I always stop and I just listen because that's a big part of my job." Brenda noted that she "spends a lot of time observing and listening to people." The effort is not only in processing but in being patient as observed by Doris "I listen well so I have patience. That works in the sense that I will listen to you . . . And then okay—let's get around to what I need to do." Doris's recognition that listening served to validate others as well as learn about issues was echoed by others. Such attention to content and identity not only aided in building relationships but it helped the leaders have a better sense of the organization.

The labor of communication became even more obvious when our participants spoke about how they talked and wrote to others. It is in this context that they "felt" their gender. Specifically, they noted issues of word choice and language and how they consciously navigated the challenges of the system, technology, and perceptions of their femininity. Numerous stories were told of rewriting emails, thinking before speaking at meetings, reflecting on past interactions, and cautiously crafting a response even in interpersonal interactions. These stories illustrated the concerns these leaders had for their communication partners as well as their sensitivity to their own position.

Even more telling were the stories of the leaders who had to change their communication style to fit the role and expectations of others. For participants who characterized themselves as masculine communicators, they found that they needed to engage in communication work so that their communication was perceived in a more supportive, nurturing, and caring manner. Rhonda notes, "I don't have time for emotions in the workplace." Yet, she still does it. Rhonda states, "I have learned to work very hard especially on emails . . . I look at every word. How are people going to perceive that? . . . I spend a lot of time doing that—that I think if I were a male I wouldn't have to . . . it wouldn't be questioned." Like Rhonda, Hillary states, "I'm very direct sometimes too direct and that gets me in trouble." Hillary further states "I actually sometimes have to really check my emails several times before I send something."

The converse occurred for women who had more feminine communication patterns. They found that they often needed to be more assertive and direct in their communication to prevent the perception of weakness. Doris states, "It's something that as a woman I have to be careful of because a collaborative style often can be seen as weak . . . yet most things get done with collaboration . . . and a lot of real strong female leaders of the world have a collaborative style." Doris recognized the perceptions of feminine speech even in how she receives compliments. "The first thing that would be out of my mouth would be—oh I didn't really do it." Yet, she observed those responses undermine credibility. "I've learned that . . . then you're often viewed as that weak non-leader." Regardless of where our participants fell, navigating along the masculine-feminine continuum was necessary for them to be successful in their positions. This consumed time and became a natural part of the work day.

The interpretations of women leaders' communication consistently placed them in a double bind whereby they were not feminine, were not being a good leader, or were not either. Katherine was astutely aware of this in her work. For Katherine, she discussed changing her speech patterns and becoming very direct to get her point across and effect change on an important organizational issue. She said it took her "stepping out of being a woman" to be listened to. She states, "For men it's good leadership and for women, you're a bitch . . . there is a fine line between being a strong leader and then crossing that line between golly, she's so hard to work with." Like Katherine, Elizabeth felt communicative tensions in terms of how women's talk is perceived. She stated "It's like you can either be hard-hitting and in control and authoritative if you are a man but if a woman does that she's a bitch . . . there are situations where that absolutely does happen and . . . and it's up to us to change it." Gina also shared the challenges of the double bind. She discussed how collaboration and democracy were central to her leadership style and decision-making, yet she also shared that such an approach was challenged by some of her colleagues who said leaders should "simply make the decisions." Thus, communicative work occurred in explaining how she chose to lead.

Successfully navigating the liminal space of the "woman leader" required significant effort and skill. Brenda noted that she adapts her style and draws from a wide spectrum of communication tactics "and sometimes I'll be very blunt and forceful . . . and other times I've been much more subtle." Elizabeth echoes the value of adaptability in her own work "I'm really good at dealing with ambiguity and seeing multiple sides."

The labor of communication started even before many of the participants accepted their jobs. The negotiation process itself was labor-intensive and, for many, directly related to their womanhood. Gina discussed her negotiation of salary where she was given a low initial offer and did her homework on others in comparable positions. When asked if the final offer she accepted was fair, she said "I don't think so but it was enough better that I feel satisfied." Nora said of her salary (also perceived as low) "You know it really didn't bother me because I said at the time . . . that I really want opportunities." Hillary notes that although she is not currently underpaid her experience had been otherwise and "I lost an awful lot of emotional time worrying about that and I said I love what I do so I'm just going to deal." Others echoed Nora and Hillary's sentiments as they wanted to be seen as team players and hedged on salary negotiations to not jeopardize their place. Elizabeth couched her experience in terms of time and location. She recalled her long working history "I've seen gender bias and discrimination at so much a worse place."

In sum, laboring communication involves significant investment of time and effort as the participants perform their leadership in a system that does not necessarily value their femininity, departures from that femininity, or their participation as leaders within the system. Yet, not only is the effort significant, it is ongoing and blurs the lines between work and home life.

Eternal Work

In almost all of our conversations, laughter erupted when asked about the work day ending at five or six p.m. Hillary says it best, "Are you kidding me? I'm still here at five and six . . . usually (I work) seven to six here and then I work at home." Doris responded similarly, "The job never ends." Elizabeth confirmed the omnipresent work and simply noted "this place will just simply eat you up. It will consume you if you let it." Several participants identified as "workaholics" while others characterized the amount they worked as a "work ethic" instilled from youth—a work ethic they felt was necessary for the job. Most had a difficult time accounting for all of their work hours as the work/home/life boundary was highly permeable. Thus, we describe this theme as eternal work.

Accountability and expectation were cited as reasons for time spent doing the job. Nora stated, "The loss of autonomy of time when you take on a leadership role in academia it's measurable." Jane noted a similar feeling, "there is an expectation that you do work in the evenings and weekends . . . there is that expectation that you do check your email in the evening. And what's wrong with you if you haven't." Beatrice observes that checking email constantly is "the new culture of what you should do." Beatrice also notes that she does not check all of the time but it means "I don't leave at five." Lara notes "I want to make sure the job gets done," which meant she put in a lot of hours. Gina characterized her efforts in terms of work ethic, "Well I think I am a hard worker. I work a lot. I work long hours. I work a lot of nights. I work a lot of weekends."

The job was also integral to their identities. Elizabeth notes "there's very little definition between me at work and me at home." For Nora, work is "a priority in my life. I try not to make it my entire identity but it means a lot to me." She also confessed, "I like being here and so it's probably by choice." Elizabeth notes, "I think the academy is so much of who we are as people that it's hard to segment those."

The experience of eternal work had significant influence over the family and the work/home/life balance of each participant. Patricia disclosed "I don't believe I have a life" outside of her leadership position. When faced with choices between home and work Lara notes, "The job often wins." Doris notes, "My husband is truly unique . . . he cooks, he cleans, he allows me

... to be the workaholic because he takes care of that stuff." In fact, of the participants who were partnered, nearly all attributed their ability to do their jobs to their partners taking "the second shift" and also lending emotional support. Jane stated her husband "works from home so he's there" for their child "and takes care of the house." She continues, "Most nights now he's cooking." Hillary noted "my husband was a huge support so he did most of the household stuff . . . he was a stay at home dad."

For others it was the absence of family that was salient in making the work time possible. Nora noted "I don't have a spouse, a partner . . . children . . . so I can easily come back [to work]." Rhonda noted "it's just me," so she is able to work long hours.

Some of the participants noted that the growth of their children lifted responsibilities in what is commonly known as "post-primary" caregiving. Beatrice characterizes this as follows, "My children are grown and live away and honestly if . . . my family was any closer it would have been very difficult . . . I have worked in a professional position at another institution—my children were home and it was a real struggle for me." The challenges were immediately recognized by those who were pre-administration and pre-tenure when their children were born or growing up. Hillary called her children "academic babies" as she was allowed more time with them in the summer early on. Gina who also had "academic babies" states, "Now my kids are not home anymore. Of course when they were young I went home earlier." She continues "it's easier now that my kids are grown up." For Caroline, the growth of her children made her work easier and work-home balance is "better now. You know when I was tenure track and my child was a baby it was much more difficult." Caroline questioned how far we have come as she noted that we are talking about the same women's issues now as we were years ago.

A consistent message was that some job efforts impair others. Jane notes, "What I find is my day is so full of meetings and putting out fires . . . I don't have time to do any work." Doris echoes this frustration, "The problem is I'm in meetings all the time. . . . But then there is the job work. The paperwork and things, the emails and so it's hard to do." Patricia and Lara also note with their meeting schedules, they need to work in the evening to get to email. For Brenda, all of the demands make it "more like one and a half jobs than one full-time job."

As suggested above, technology not only defined "work" it was also considered integral to its ongoing nature. Elizabeth specifically indicted technology as a threat to work-home harmony "our immediate access to technology compromises that balance." She continues, "I'm never far from my iPad or my phone." Email was particularly intrusive for our participants. Lara states "I respond to emails day and night. I'm on email 24/7—seriously. If I'm not sleeping, email is open." Patricia notes, "I work all the time ... if I don't keep it moving, I'm going to drown in emails." Jane observes, "Most nights I have to do email ... you just have to." Hillary notes that "my job never ends" and recognizes technology's role "I can't help but check email." Rhonda also felt the immediacy of email but made it a point to prioritize her focus "I draw a line so work I do at home at night is because I choose to do it."

In many cases, the respondents thought of just being away from work as a reward. Patricia says "I try to give myself 'treats' ... Treats are time ... I spent Saturday night [with a friend] and drove home the following day with no computer or email." An equally powerful framing comes from Elizabeth who describes her weekend routine: "I do try to take part of either Saturday or Sunday and not work, work. I'm still going to answer email probably. I'm still going to jot down notes when a good thought occurs to me. I'm still going to be thinking about it ... or I'll devote part of that time to my own writing or professional development." Several of our participants shared these sentiments as evenings were spent on their research or reading student work. The work is valuable, ongoing, and deeply integrated with our leaders' identities.

COMMUNICATING LEAD(HER)SHIP: THE CHALLENGES OF PATRIARCHY

The assembled experiences and perspectives of our participants paint a vivid picture of the tensions experienced by women leaders in patriarchal systems. Past work demonstrates that women are frequently placed in double binds as workforce participants.[60] Our participants experienced double binds through organizational structure, gender, expectations, and communication. The challenges begin with how our participants characterized leadership itself. One of the important observations within horizontal matriarchy is that the collaborative nature of it was largely focused on those lower in the hierarchy. Although they were not discouraged from being collaborative, few of our leaders indicated that their collaborative efforts were embraced at their level or higher. In this sense, "matriarchy" as a form of organizing only trickled down the hierarchy from those who embraced matriarchal principles. Furthermore, there were times when our participants experienced resistance to the distribution of power, voice, and responsibility. Gina and others had faculty who regularly challenged their choice to involve others saying "you are the administrator. You should make the decision." The recognition that collaboration was a potential hotspot was not lost on other participants. Doris observes, "I have to be careful because a collaborative style often can be seen as weak." Yet, collective activity demands work—work that goes undervalued by the system as "getting the job done" is the primary measure of success.

Many of our participants did not see gender as an overt challenge in their work—but they did feel that it was an important variable that impacted their leader experiences. Several questioned how they were approached relative to males at their same level. Rhonda notes that her email efforts may be more intense than her male counterparts "I think if I were a male I wouldn't have to spend any time on it whatsoever and it wouldn't be questioned." She felt the same way when faculty questioned and challenged her on their annual evaluations. Patricia said, "I don't think there is any question that . . . women have to earn, document that they are competent." Not only do women then have to do more for the same recognition they also experience more requests to attend functions or complete tasks. Katherine shares that "I think I get taken advantage of" because she is often the one to complete tasks in a timely manner. She also notes that many of her male colleagues sit back and let her do things because "she'll do it." Others recalled stories where a woman in a gathering expressed an idea only to have a man express it slightly differently and have the man's suggestion taken up for conversation. Beatrice notes that her gender definitely makes a difference but it is difficult to nail down what it is. She states, "I don't really think I'm mistreated . . . just treated differently sometimes." She notes that she encounters small slights that most "wouldn't even pick up on" and it's "not intentional" but after a while it "sinks in."

An even more surprising assessment emerged in the work/home/life balance discussions. Although our participants laughed when asked about the end of the work day/week, which they said "never ended," they saw their lives as fairly balanced. This illustrates the deep connection between our participants' work and identities. In some cases, others complimented the leaders on their ability to balance. Hillary noted a colleague praising her "I can't believe how you balance things—you are a good role model" despite her long hours. Some were not satisfied with how they managed the tensions. Jane states with respect to managing her work and personal time, "I've got to set these days where I'm not going to work and . . . then here's my time and I work." Patricia summed her commitment to the job as "When I'm into it, I'm in to it 100%." Even so, she is reflective on the consequences "I don't want to always put work first." She notes it is the one reason why she may leave the job. Our participants talk about work showed the amount of time they spent on it; eternal work that was perceived as normative.

Research emerged as another dimension of the workload and expectation double bind. A number of our participants cited the effort as part of being a good role model because "if I don't do it, how can I expect my faculty to?" The characterization is simultaneously an embodiment of being a strong role model as a leader and in part a personal drive to achieve rank (for those who were associates). Yet in a surprising an anti-matriarchal expression of leadership some saw the completion of research as justification for challenging faculty as "if I can do it, so can they." Thus, in a subtle move, patriarchy came to colonize participants' framing of eternal work as it transitioned from a personal choice to a group expectation.

CONCLUSION

Lead(her)ship as experienced here is thus betwixt and between—neither completely feminine or feminist nor masculine and patriarchal. It is an approach and practice to organizational participation that is fostered by the leader, devalued by the system, and frequently challenged by organizational members. Our participants' voices revealed the ongoing dialectics of "man-woman" and "leader-follower" as collapsed into the patriarchal "man/leader." It is a patriarchal continuum where male, leader, and autocrat fall on one end and female, follower, cooperator fall on the other. In the middle is the gray region defined by shared effort and responsibility: collaboration. As our participants experiences showed, it is a middle ground but a contested one. Only the dominant gender gets "the pass" to collaborate; the other endures scrutiny.

Leadership itself is a double bind for women leaders who, by definition, experience difficulty in satisfying expectations that make mutually exclusive "woman" and "leader." Unfortunately, without an ideological system that values the blending of styles those who embrace both masculine and feminine style practices become anachronisms. Those who fail in their efforts are defined as not performing gender and/or leader competently. Those who succeed in this approach are understood as idiosyncratic, their work mystified, and their success understood only as somehow innate. It is a sobering reminder of the power of an ideological system that retains patriarchy simply by treating the feminine with neglect.

A more effective way to address the double binds may be to articulate a framework that transcends the bifurcations of "man-woman," "leader-follower," and "strong-weak." This requires deconstructing the patriarchal system and exposing it as a source of the double bind—and capitalizing on a new framing that can supersede the dialectic (e.g., organizational member, instead of leader/follower). As argued by Julia Wood and Charles Conrad, this is the "most realistic means of resolving mystification in the experiences of women" and, in this case, of women leaders.[61]

This research is one step toward better understanding women's forms of leadership in academic contexts. Scholars and practitioners can advance this cause by looking deeply into the very structure of academic organizations that may foster dialectics and double binds. Understanding women leaders and feminine forms of leadership as "leaders" and "leadership" is only one goal. Challenging the eternal work that impinges on personal and family/life time and displacing the double bind that forces the leader to choose work over the personal is critical to reframing what good leadership is in organizations. We must develop realistic expectations for "academics" so that one's life and career are valued without privileging certain groups over others. Such efforts can be used to create opportunities for leadership forms that embrace the care, connectivity, collaboration, and balance appreciated by leaders and followers. One means for this will certainly be to involve more women in academic leadership. As noted in the *White House Project Report*, "increasing women's leadership is an imperative. Advancing women serves us all."[62]

Scholars who are seeking to continue this line of research are urged to investigate and challenge the gendered leader archetype and the academic structures that foster it. Changes in how the academy organizes and leads will not be lost on the leaders or the young minds who learn from them. From there, academics and their institutions can work toward ensuring "that women have equal voice in leadership at all levels of society."[63] It is then that horizontal matriarchy can be fully valued and communication less labor-intensive.

NOTES

1. Catalyst, 2018. *Quick Take: Women in Management.* Retrieved from https://www.catalyst.org/research/women-in-management/.

2. See White House Project. (November, 2009). *The White House Project Report: Benchmarking Women's Leadership.*

3. See U.S. Department of Education. (2018). National Center for Education Statistics, Institute of Education Sciences. Table 318.20 Bachelor's, master's and doctor's degrees conferred by postsecondary institutions, by sex of student and discipline: 2015–2016.

4. White House Project, 10.

5. Ibid.

6. Susan Madsen, "Women and Leadership in Higher Education: Learning and Advancement in Leadership Programs," *Advances in Developing Human Resources* 14, no. 5 (2012): 5. doi: 10.1177/15234223114929668.

7. Sunny Airini et al., "Learning to be Leaders in Higher Education: What Helps or Hinders Women's Advancement as Leaders in Universities," *Educational Management Administration & Leadership* 39, no. 1 (2011): 44–62. doi.org/10.1177/1741143210383896.

8. Kathleen Czech and G. L. Forward, "Leader Communication: Faculty Perceptions of the Department Chair," *Communication Quarterly* 55, no. 4 (2010): 452. doi: 10.1080/01463373.2010.525158.

9. See Joan Acker, "Hierarchies, Jobs, Bodies: A Theory of Gendered Organizations," *Gender and Society* 4, no. 2 (1990). doi.org/10.1177/089124390004002002;

Karen Ashcraft and Dennis Mumby, *Reworking Gender: A Feminist Communicology of Organization* (Thousand Oaks, CA: Sage, 2004).

10. See Rosabeth Moss Kanter, *Men and Women of the Corporation* (New York: Basic Books, 1977).

11. Kanter, *Men and Women of the Corporation*.

12. See Joan Acker, "Inequality Regimes: Gender, Class, and Race in Organizations," *Gender and Society* 20, no. 4 (2006). doi.org/10.1177/0891243206289499; Karen Ashcraft and Dennis Mumby, *Reworking Gender: A Feminist Communicology of Organization* (Thousand Oaks, CA: Sage, 2004); Sharon Bird, "Unsettling Universities' Incongruous, Gendered Bureaucratic Structures: A Case-Study Approach," *Gender, Work & Organization* 18, no. 2 (2011). doi:10.1111/j.1468-0432.2009.00510.x; Marline Fine and Patrice Buzzanell, "Walking the High Wire: Leadership Theorizing, Daily Acts, and Tensions." In Patrice Buzzanell (Ed.), *Rethinking Organizational and Managerial Communication from Feminist Perspectives* (pp. 128–156). Thousand Oaks: Sage, 2000.

13. Emilio Castilla and Stephen Bernard, "The Paradox of Meritocracy in Organizations," *Administrative Science Quarterly* 55, no. 4 (2010): 543. doi.org/10.2189/asqu.2010.55.4.543.

14. White House Project, 14.

15. Jeanine Prime, Nancy Carter, and Theresa Welbourne, "Women 'Take Care,' Men 'Take Charge': Managers' Stereotypic Perceptions of Women and Men Leaders," *The Psychologist-Manager Journal* 12, no. 1 (2009): 44. doi: 101080/10887150802371799.

16. Ibid.

17. Marlene Fine, "Women Leaders' Discursive Constructions of Leadership," *Women Studies in Communication* 32, no. 2 (2009): 182. doi.org/10.1080/07491409.2009.10162386.

18. Acker, "Hierarchies, Jobs, Bodies."

19. Ashcroft and Mumby, *Reworking Gender*.

20. Annica Kronsell, "Gendered Practices in Institutions of Hegemonic Masculinity: Reflections from Feminist Standpoint Theory," *International Feminist Journal of Politics* 7, no. 2 (2005): 281. doi.org/10.1080/14616740500065170.

21. Raka Shome, "White Femininity and the Discourse of the Nation: Re/membering Princess Diana," *Feminist Media Studies* 1, no. 3 (2001): 323–342. doi.org/10.1080/14680770120088927.

22. Acker, "Inequality Regimes"; Fine and Buzzanell, "Walking the High Wire."

23. See Erika Kirby, Annis Golden, Caryn Medved, Jane Jorgenson and Patrice Buzzanell, "An Organizational Communication Challenge to the Discourse of Work and Family Research: From Problematics to Empowerment," *Communication Yearbook* 27, no. 1 (2003): 1–43; Erika Kirby, Stacey Wieland and Chad McBride, "Work-life Conflict." In John Oetzel and StellaTing-Toomey (Eds.), *Handbook of Conflict Communication* (pp. 327–537). Thousand Oaks, CA: Sage, 2006.

24. Kirby et al., "An Organizational Communication Challenge."

25. See Kirby, Wieland and McBride, "Work-life Conflict"; Lisa Wolf-Wendel and Kelly Ward, "Academic Life and Motherhood: Variations by Institutional Type," *Higher Education* 52 no 3 (2006): 487–521. doi: 10.1007/s10734-005-0364-4.

26. See Acker, "Hierarchies, Jobs, Bodies"; Cynthia Stohl and George Cheney, "Participatory Practices/Paradoxical Practices: Communication and the Dilemmas of Organizational Democracy," *Management Communication Quarterly* 14, no. 3 (2001): 349–407. doi.org/10.1177/0893318901143001; Laura Prividera and John Howard, "Paradoxical Injunctions and Double Binds: A Critical Examination of Discourse on Female Soldiers," *Women & Language* 35, no. 2 (2012): 53–73; Ronald Wendt, *The Paradox of Empowerment: Suspended Power and the Possibility of Resistance* (Westport, CT: Praeger, 2001).

27. See Acker, "Hierarchies, Jobs, Bodies"; Wendt, *The Paradox of Empowerment*; Julia Wood and Charles Conrad, "Paradox in the Experiences of Professional Women," *Western Journal of Speech Communication* 47, no 4 (1983). doi.org/10.1080/10570318309374128.

28. Sharon Bird, "Unsettling Universities' Incongruous, Gendered Bureaucratic Structures: A Case-Study Approach," *Gender, Work & Organization* 18, no. 2 (2011): 204. doi:10.1111/j.1468-0432.2009.00510.x.

29. Ibid.

30. White House Project, 19.

31. Bird, "Unsettling Universities"; and Kelly Ward and Lisa Wolf-Wendel, "Academic Motherhood: Managing Complex Roles in Research Universities," *The Review of Higher Education* 27, no 2 (2004): 233–257. doi:10.1353/rhe.2003.0079.

32. Wolf-Wendel and Ward, "Academic Life."

33. Bird, "Unsettling Universities," 204.

34. Sherryl Kleinman and Kenneth Kolb, "Traps on the Path of Analysis," *Symbolic Interaction* 34, no. 4 (2011): 442. doi.org/10.1525/si.2011.34.4.425.

35. Janie Fritz, "Women's Communicative Leadership in Higher Education." In Elesha Ruminski and Annette Holba (Eds.), *Communicative Understandings of Women's Leadership Development: From Ceilings of Glass to Labyrinth Paths* (pp. 19–36). Lanham, MD: Lexington Books, 2012.

36. Marlene Fine, "Women Leaders' Discursive Constructions of Leadership," *Women Studies in Communication* 32, no. 2 (2009): 180–202. doi.org/10.1080/07491409.2009.10162386.

37. Alice Eagly, Mary Johannesen-Schmidt, and Marloes van Engen, "Transformational, Transactional, and Laissez-Faire Leadership Styles: A Meta-Analysis Comparing Women and Men," *Psychological Bulletin* 129, no. 4 (2003): 586. doi:10.1037/0033-2909.129.4.569.

38. Fritz, "Women's Communicative Leadership," 21.

39. Fine, "Women Leaders," 184.

40. See Virginia Schein, "A Global Look at Psychological Barriers to Women's Progress in Management," *Journal of Social Issues* 57, no. 4 (2001): 675–688. doi.org/10.1111/0022-4537.00235.

41. Alice Eagly and Blair Johnson, "Gender and the Emergence of Leaders: A Meta-Analysis," *Psychological Bulletin* 108, no. 2 (1990): 233–256. doi:10.1037/0033-2909108.2.233.

42. Alice Eagly and Linda Carli, *The Truth About How Women Became Leaders* (Boston, MA: Harvard Business School, 2007).

43. Alice Eagly and Steven Karau, "Role Congruity Theory of Prejudice Toward Female Leaders," *Psychological Review* 109, no. 3 (2002): 573–598. doi: 10.1037//0033-295X.109.3.573.

44. Jennifer Boldry, Wendy Wood, and Deborah Kashy, "Gender Stereotypes and the Evaluation of Men and Women in Military Training," *Journal of Social Issues* 57, no. 4 (2001): 689–705. doi.org/10.1111/0022-4537.00236.

45. Eagly and Carli, *Through the Labyrinth: The Truth About How Women Become Leaders*. See also Eagly, Johannesen-Schmidt, and van Engen, "Transformational, Transactional, and Laissez-Faire Leadership Styles."

46. Alice Eagly, "Foreword." In Elesha Ruminski and Annette Holba (Eds.), *Communicative Understandings of Women's Leadership Development* (pp. xi–xii). Lanham, MD: Lexington Books, 2012.

47. Gail Fairhurst and Stacey Connaughton, "Leadership: A Communicative Perspective," *Leadership* 10, no. 1 (2014): 7–35. doi.org/10.1177/1742715013509396.

48. Ibid., 8

49. Ibid., 8

50. Fine, "Women Leaders," 182.

51. Elesha Ruminski and Annette Holba, "Introduction." In Elesha Ruminski and Annette Holba (Eds.), *Communicative Understandings of Women's Leadership Development* (pp. 1–17). Lanham, MD: Lexington Books, 2012.

52. White House Project, 16.

53. Fritz, "Women's Communicative Leadership," 21.

54. Thomas Lindlof, *Qualitative Communication Research Methods* (Thousand Oaks, CA: Sage, 2005), 222.

55. Lindlof, *Qualitative Communication Research Methods*, 222–223.

56. Ibid., 163.

57. Anselm Strauss and Juliet Corbin, *Basics of Qualitative Research: Grounded Theory Procedures and Techniques* (Thousand Oaks, CA: Sage, 1990).

58. Eagly and Carli, *Through the Labyrinth*.

59. See Nel Noddings, "An Ethic of Caring and its Implications for Instructional Arrangements." In Lynda Stone (Ed.), *The Education Feminism Reader* (pp. 171–183). New York, NY: Routledge, 1994.

60. See Acker, "Hierarchies, Jobs, Bodies"; Prividera and Howard, "Paradoxical Injunctions and Double Binds"; Wood and Conrad, "Paradox in Experience."

61. Julia Wood and Charles Conrad, "Paradox in the Experiences of Professional Women," *Western Journal of Speech Communication* 47, no 4 (1983): 316, doi.org/10.1080/10570318309374128.

62. White House Report, 7.

63. Eagly, "Forward," xi.

BIBLIOGRAPHY

Acker, Joan. "Hierarchies, Jobs, Bodies: A Theory of Gendered Organizations." *Gender and Society* 4, no. 2 (1990): 139–158. doi.org/10.1177/089124390004002002.

Acker, Joan. "Inequality Regimes: Gender, Class, and Race in Organizations." *Gender and Society* 20, no. 4 (2006): 441–464. doi.org/10.1177/0891243206289499.

Airini, Sunny, Linsey Conner, Kathryn McPherson, Brenda Midson, and Cheryl Wilson. "Learning to be Leaders in Higher Education: What Helps or Hinders Women's Advancement as Leaders in Universities." *Educational Management Administration & Leadership* 39, no. 1 (2011): 44–62 doi.org/10.1177/1741143210383896.

Ashcraft, Karen, and Dennis Mumby, *Reworking Gender: A Feminist Communicology of Organization*. Thousand Oaks, CA: Sage, 2004.

Bird, Sharon. "Unsettling Universities' Incongruous, Gendered Bureaucratic Structures: A Case-Study Approach." *Gender, Work & Organization* 18, no. 2 (2011): 202–230. doi:10.1111/j.1468-0432.2009.00510.x.

Boldry, Jennifer, Wendy Wood, and Deborah Kashy, "Gender Stereotypes and the Evaluation of Men and Women in Military Training." *Journal of Social Issues* 57, no. 4 (2001): 689–705. doi.org/10.1111/0022-4537.00236.

Castilla, Emilio, and Stephen Bernard. "The Paradox of Meritocracy in Organizations." *Administrative Science Quarterly* 55, no. 4 (2010): 543–676. doi.org/10.2189/asqu.2010.55.4.543.

Catalyst. *Quick Take: Women in Management.* New York, NY. 2018.

Czech, Kathleen, and G.L. Forward. "Leader Communication: Faculty Perceptions of the Department Chair." *Communication Quarterly* 58, no. 4 (2010): 431–457. doi: 10.1080/01463373.2010.525158.

Eagly, Alice. (2012). "Foreword." In Elesha Ruminski and Annette Holba (Eds.), *Communicative Understandings of Women's Leadership Development* (pp. ix–xii). Lanham, MD: Lexington Books, 2012.

Eagly, Alice, and Linda Carli. *Through the Labyrinth: The Truth About How Women Become Leaders.* Boston, MA: Harvard Business School Press, 2007.

Eagly, Alice, Mary Johannesen-Schmidt, and Marloes van Engen. "Transformational, Transactional, and Laissez-Faire Leadership Styles: A Meta-Analysis Comparing Women and Men." *Psychological Bulletin* 129, no. 4 (2003): 569–591. doi: 10.1037/0033-2909.129.4.569.

Eagly, Alice, and Blair Johnson. "Gender and the Emergence of Leaders: A Meta-Analysis." *Psychological Bulletin* 108, no. 2 (1990): 233–256. doi: 10.1037/0033-2909108.2.233.

Eagly, Alice, and Steven Karau. "Role Congruity Theory of Prejudice Toward Female Leaders." *Psychological Review* 109, no. 3 (2002): 573–598. doi: 10.1037//0033-295X.109.3.573.

Fairhurst, Gail, and Stacey Connaughton. "Leadership: A Communicative Perspective." *Leadership* 10, no. 1 (2014): 7–35. doi.org/10.1177/1742715013509396.

Fine, Marlene. "Women Leaders' Discursive Constructions of Leadership." *Women Studies in Communication* 32, no. 2 (2009): 180–202. doi.org/10.1080/07491409.2009.10162386.

Fine, Marlene, and Patrice Buzzanell. "Walking the High Wire: Leadership Theorizing, Daily Acts, and Tensions." In Patrice Buzzanell (Ed.), *Rethinking Organizational and Managerial Communication from Feminist Perspectives* (pp. 128–156). Thousand Oaks, CA: Sage, 2000.

Fritz, Janie. "Women's Communicative Leadership in Higher Education." In Elesha Ruminski and Annette Holba (Eds.), *Communicative Understandings of Women's Leadership Development: From Ceilings of Glass to Labyrinth Paths* (pp. 19–36). Lanham, MD: Lexington Books, 2012.

Kanter, Rosabeth. *Men and Women of the Corporation.* New York, NY: Basic Books, 1977.

Kirby, Erika, Annis Golden, Caryn Medved, Jane Jorgenson, and Patrice Buzzanell. "An Organizational Communication Challenge to the Discourse of Work and Family Research: From Problematics to Empowerment." *Communication Yearbook* 27, no 1 (2003): 1–43. doi.org/10.1080/23808985.2003.11679020.

Kirby, Erika, Stacey Wieland, and Chad McBride. "Work/Life Conflict." In John Oetzel and Stella Ting-Toomey (Eds.), *Handbook of Conflict Communication* (pp. 327–537). Thousand Oaks, CA: Sage, 2006.

Kleinman, Sherryl, and Kenneth Kolb. "Traps on the Path of Analysis." *Symbolic Interaction* 34, no. 4 (2011): 425–446. doi.org/10.1525/si.2011.34.4.425.

Kronsell, Annica. "Gendered Practices in Institutions of Hegemonic Masculinity: Reflections from Feminist Standpoint Theory." *International Feminist Journal of Politics* 7, no. 2 (2005): 280–298. doi.org/10.1080/14616740500065170.

Madsen, Susan. "Women and Leadership in Higher Education: Learning and Advancement in Leadership Programs." *Advances in Developing Human Resources* 14, no. 1 (2012): 3–10. doi: 10.1177/15234223114929668.

Noddings, Nel. "An Ethic of Caring and its Implications for Instructional Arrangements." In Lynda Stone (Ed.), *The Education Feminism Reader* (pp. 171–183). New York, NY: Routledge, 1994.

Prime, Jeanine, Nancy Carter, and Theresa Welbourne. "Women 'Take Care,' Men 'Take Charge:' Managers' Stereotypic Perceptions of Women and Men Leaders." *The Psychologist-Manager Journal* 12, no. 1 (2009): 25–49. doi: 101080/10887150802371799.

Prividera, Laura, and John Howard. "Paradoxical Injunctions and Double Binds: A Critical Examination of Discourse on Female Soldiers." *Women & Language* 35, no. 2 (2012): 53–73.

Ruminski, Elesha, and Annette Holba. "Introduction." In Elesha Ruminski and Annette Holba (Eds.), *Communicative Understandings of Women's Leadership Development* (pp. 1–17). New York, NY: Lexington Books, 2012.

Schein, Virginia. "A Global Look at Psychological Barriers to Women's Progress in Management." *Journal of Social Issues* 57, no. 4 (2001): 675–688. doi.org/10.1111/0022-4537.00235.

Shome, Raka. "White Femininity and the Discourse of the Nation: Re/membering Princess Diana." *Feminist Media Studies* 1, no. 3 (2001): 323–342. doi.org/10.1080/14680770120088927.

Stohl, Cynthia, and George Cheney. "Participatory Practices/Paradoxical Practices: Communication and the Dilemmas of Organizational Democracy." *Management Communication Quarterly* 14, no. 3 (2001): 349–407 doi.org/10.1177/0893318901143001.

Strauss, Anselm, and Juliet Corbin. *Basics of Qualitative Research: Grounded Theory Procedures and Techniques.* Thousand Oaks, CA: Sage, 1990.

The White House Project. (2009, November). *The White House Project Report: Benchmarking Women's Leadership.*

U.S. Department of Education. National Center for Education Statistics, Institute of Education Sciences, 2012.

Ward, Kelly, and Lisa Wolf-Wendel. "Academic Motherhood: Managing Complex Roles in Research Universities." *The Review of Higher Education* 27, no. 2 (2004): 233–257. doi:10.1353/rhe.2003.0079.

Wendt, Ronald. *The Paradox of Empowerment: Suspended Power and the Possibility of Resistance.* Westport, CT: Praeger, 2001.

Wolf-Wendel, Lisa, and Kelly Ward. "Academic Life and Motherhood: Variations by Institutional Type." *Higher Education* 52, no. 3 (2006): 487–521. doi: 10.1007/s10734-005-0364-4.

Wood, Julia, and Charles Conrad. "Paradox in the Experiences of Professional Women." *Western Journal of Speech Communication* 47, no. 4 (1983): 305–322. doi.org/10.1080/10570318309374128.

Chapter 8

No Gentlemen's Agreement Here

Higher Education Reflections on Being Womanist and the Dialectics Present in an African American Woman's Administrative Journey

Jeanetta D. Sims

It was Fall 2003 in Norman, Oklahoma and Dubin's comprehensive book on theory building with Dunnette's postlude on the theory game was required reading.[1] More than fifteen years later, one particular passage from Dunnette's writing stands out, "Let us hope that graduate education, in the years ahead, will become more eclectic and that even the Great Men in our field may adopt a sense of humility when transmitting knowledge to the fledglings of our science."[2]

All students in the late Michael Pfau's Intro to Graduate Studies class in the Department of Communication at the University of Oklahoma (OU) needed to have a copy of Dubin's book. And, the fact that the book was out of print sent graduate students scurrying for a copy from local textbook brokers. Dubin makes a compelling case for propositions as truth statements and for studying hypotheses. Coupled with Chaffee's work on *Explication* as required reading, doctoral students were provided a strong foundation of communication inquiry in the social sciences.[3]

Eventually, I would complete the doctoral program as Pfau's last doctoral student; before being hooded at commencement by a faculty member who wore Pfau's regalia, I would offer words of gratitude and appreciation for his mentorship in his memorial tribute at OU's Burton Hall. Following commencement, I was asked and completed a valuation of his personal library of books donated to OU's Bizzell Library. It was a book collection that included volumes of flagship work in the communication discipline along with a request from Albert Bandura for one of his articles.

Under Pfau's leadership, my doctoral training that began with Dubin and Chaffee has been sufficient to sustain an academic, tenure-track career working across disciplines to apply communication theory in the contexts of marketing, management, public relations, leadership, workforce diversity, higher education, social influence, and persuasion. Now, as the first woman (and thus the first African American female) to serve as dean of the Joe C. Jackson College of Graduate Studies, the timing permits a unique opportunity to consider the tensions, contradictions, and potentialities present in my administrative academic journey. Reflecting on the implications of my leadership in graduate education among great men seems appropriate. It is nestled amid an institutional reality that has taken sixty-five years for the Graduate College to have a female dean, and 129 years for the university to have its first female African American dean.

Drawing from this journey, the purpose of this manuscript is to offer female academicians leadership strategies that are steeped in communication theory and scholarship. Through the lens of intersectionality, of Walker's "womanist" and using a dialectics approach for framing and reframing contradictions present in the academic journey, this chapter serves as a resource for the development of females in higher education.[4] I offer key insights for assisting women in their respective academic journeys whether their aspirations are for faculty or administrative appointments.

WHY BEING WOMANIST IS PREFERRED

The repeated use of "gentlemen" and "men" in classic theory building (e.g., Dubin) and management (e.g., Drucker) texts indicates the prevalent view of men, and most typically, White men, as both architects and recipients of contributions in the Academy.[5] And, what a position of power, privilege, and influence that is. The lineage of my learning and the composition of my academic carriage are supported by this White, male-dominated foundation of inheritance. If other women enjoy a similar academic inheritance, they might find it hard-pressed to "see themselves" as anything other than present in a man's Academy.

The intersectionality of the Black female experience is an even more perplexing presence to consider. Does it matter that females and more specifically that the Black female goes unreferenced in classic texts? At a glimpse, one may regard strong theoretical frameworks and leadership strategies to be the same and applicable regardless of the race/class/gender of the individual or leader; however, claiming and reclaiming my human experience requires a more intersectional framework. "Intersectionality is a way of understanding and analyzing the complexity in the world, in people, and in human experience."[6] While strong theory of a post-positivist perspective can be applicable across contexts, making meaning and gleaning lessons bound in the power relations, contextualization, inequalities, and connectedness of my experience demand a different framework. Indeed, "ordinary people can draw upon intersectionality as an analytic tool when they recognize that they need better frameworks to grapple with the complex discriminations they face."[7] What then does one do with a female Black presence in an Academy that was not designed fully for her presence?

A foremost strategy is to acknowledge that there will be no comfortable journey. She cannot expect to snuggle up under a warm blanket in a cozy spot on the academic sofa; instead, with a hint of audacity, she will need to bring her own chair for a seat at the higher education table. In my case, it is an executive roundtable in a house where no one like me has ever been seated.

Launching a career with this mindset of expecting discomfort better prepares her for what is to come. In the same way that inoculation theory promotes resistance to influence and protects against future attacks, females in the academy need to understand they are most vulnerable to the demands and pressures of higher education when they are least prepared for the attacks that will naturally occur.[8] Prepare in advance to be uncomfortable; this, indeed, is a first attitudinal part of the professional development of women on the academic journey.

To unpack pieces of the experience as a Black female, Walker's view of "womanist" is particularly helpful. This view celebrates the vantage point of both being a woman and of the presence of other people, particularly of other women. "Womanist" is a term associated with Black feminism or feminists of color; it refers to "acting grown up" or wanting to know more and in greater depth than is considered "good" for one.[9] Driven by the need to save one's own female existence, this view sets out with courage and audaciousness to learn more about the challenges, struggles, and connections of women as if speaking with a Black folk expression to female children. In short, a womanist interrogation has great utility. It affords a perspective that can courageously acknowledge the ugly and fearlessly speak with transparency about one's own growth and development—all for aiding others in their personal academic journeys.

Womanist as an approach privileges not a single voice as if the same solo is required among all soloists in the performance; instead, it seeks to hear the entire piece from multiple soloists in an effort to understand the multitude of perspectives present in the same auditorium. Similarly, rather than binary bits (e.g., Black and White; male and female) of comparative differences, the spirit of this chapter seeks to acknowledge the ways in which I have grappled with being originally invisible in academic texts and in leadership at my institution, while simultaneously celebrating the men and women who have contributed to my current presence. Certainly, much exists to unpack about the more mature aspirations of maintaining and thriving in a transdisciplinary tenure-track faculty and administrative career. So, we turn to the dialectics experienced in my administrative academic journey. The hope is that these lessons can support and sustain my own presence as well as the presence of more women.

DIALECTICS AND THE COMPLEXITIES OF MY ADMINISTRATIVE JOURNEY

Prompted by the writings of Bakhtin, relational dialectics theory addresses the complexities of disarray, disorder, and seemingly contradictory elements in human experiences.[10] Within a variety of contexts, dialectics have been used to examine interracial couples' communication, Black men in organizational structures, social networking site communication, the discourse of bereaved parents, and social influence.[11] Among African American females, dialectics have served as explanatory vehicles for scholarship related to understanding their friendships, entrepreneurial efforts, and academic journeys within a Christian institutional context. Identifying dialectical tensions present will enable a more nuanced conversation about the both/and-ness present in my administrative leadership journey.[12]

This section offers three primary dialectics negotiated in my present role with both regret and no shame as well as with mourning and celebration. One never stands alone as if on an island when enjoying accomplishments; from the encouragement of doctoral student colleagues to supportive family members, much of my gratitude and appreciation for others is uncaptured in sharing the complexities discussed. Despite my inability to offer an adequate exhaustive account, the contradictory elements shared of both-and/ness permit a framework to attempt an explanation of both the disgust and the joy in my administrative journey.

The Included/Excluded Dialectic. This tension represents how it is possible for one to be actively included as a leader in contributing oversight and to be graciously welcomed to implement initiatives, while simultaneously being excluded from conversations, meetings, and decisions that directly influence one's ability to accomplish those same contributions.

Through service as a seasoned College of Business faculty member who advanced through business faculty tenure and promotion processes with a PhD in communication, my contributions were certainly included and recognized. From university-level awards in teaching and research to national leadership appointments in five organizations, I have been included and welcomed in a variety of organizations and institutional environments. These collective experiences coupled with professional and academic competencies have prepared me well for making contributions.

In this institutional context, a role as Graduate College dean is a unique type of deanship; this deanship operates in a space of collaboration and integration for graduate studies across, among, and with institutional disciplinary colleges and other offices across campus. The context of collective oversight places graduate faculty as having a home in their respective disciplinary colleges with a shared role of active engagement in the Graduate College. Though I served as interim dean and was an internal dean candidate of graduate studies, I was appointed as dean following a national search. Certainly, then, as the dean of graduate studies my role is acknowledged and included in institutional organizational charts, campus-wide forums, and other forms of formal recognition. As further evidence of inclusionary status, the Graduate College dean attends university-level, executive meetings with other leaders in Academic Affairs, Student Affairs, and the President's Cabinet while working with other associate deans, assistant deans, and staff along with overseeing partnerships, budgets, and additional key campus efforts.

Yet, presence and placement alone is contemporary tokenism when females of color have titles but are neglected from making or not permitted to make institutional contributions. The excluded element of this dialectic has involved me advocating routinely to combat my lack of inclusion in decisions made in the areas connected to my expected contributions. Even as I am included and welcome, this dialectic acknowledges that a need still exists to consistently communicate my intent to retain oversight of or to collaborate with others on job postings, duties and processes, marketing and promotional activities, recruitment and admissions software, and a host of other areas related to graduate studies. This means even as I am included and attend meetings, I also often hear for the first time or learn of next-step decisions in meetings when first steps have already been initiated without my knowledge. Through communicative action, this dialectical tension explains the important role that communication plays in asserting and reasserting one's female presence in one-on-one conversations, luncheons, coffee chats, and meetings to combat exclusionary activities that occur even while one is being included.

The Certain/Uncertain Dialectic. This tension represents the journey as being courageously walked with a knowing confidence while simultaneously traveling in newness and unknowing. Perseverance, grit, and setting out with no retreat are all qualities needed and revered among leaders; these are linked inextricably to success in scaling the administrative academic terrain ahead. The challenge is that uncertainty can exist about knowing *how* to travel the terrain amid the flux of being in a space for the first time. One can expect then to be both certain and uncertain about elements of the administrative journey.

The certain element of this dialectic for me can be seen in the nudges of people and of my heart. People repeatedly appeared certain of my capabilities. I was elected chair of the College of Business Faculty Council, in its second year of existence, and was tapped to provide leadership with the

College's Association to Advance Collegiate Schools of Business (AACSB) accreditation efforts. My role in this AACSB work related to Standard 2 (faculty intellectual contributions), Standard 10 (student–faculty interactions), and Standard 13 (student academic and professional engagement). Also, an appointment to the Peer Corp of the Higher Learning Commission placed me as a member of institutional accreditation efforts through serving on the university's assurance argument writing team. Both college- and university-level accreditation efforts positioned me to work in concert with institutional leaders and cross-campus teams. Both efforts garnered successful outcomes, which further enhanced my interests in administrative work and grew my confidence in my abilities.

An additional nudge of certainty occurred given the timing of an administrative appointment in my career stage. Along with having achieved numerous research awards, teaching recognition, and a full professorship, I had founded an interdisciplinary program of research called Diverse Student Scholars that was in its eleventh year and that represented my contribution to the Academy.[13] To complement the certainty of exposure to administrative tasks, I had labored through the faculty ranks and invested in the development of more than eighty students who received grants, made conference presentations, published as coauthors, and earned top paper awards alongside me on research projects. After a twenty-year span in higher education, I had developed a type of certain, knowing rhythm to my work that was familiar; with knowing certainty, it was likely time for a new and different opportunity.

The uncertain element in the dialectic underscores two important distinctions that are simultaneously present alongside certainty—(1) the doubts associated with never knowing enough and (2) the insecurities from a lack of all-encompassing overlap among a faculty role, prior professional roles, and an academic administrative appointment. This tension acknowledges that one can possess strong doctoral or professional training and scholarly engagement while still lacking sufficient knowledge about key areas of administrative oversight. A great deal of uncertainty exists concerning budget, personalities, relational traps, graduate student recruitment, admissions, enrollment, social capital, networking, campus politics, staffing, and more, even as I have had experience navigating each of those areas in past professional positions. Presumably, easy decisions like going through a day's mail can leave one uncertain about what has importance and what can easily be tossed.

To further chip away at certainty, one's inner critic can be a persistent nag during interactions and times of decision-making. Brady argues that for women the inner critic can wreak havoc with one's own view of herself, her capabilities, and her relationships; the inner critic creates a doubting voice and unnecessary hurdles on bias, clarity, confidence, personal branding, and other areas.[14] Drawing from a space of compassionate center, Brady reveals how effective self-talk can reposition the inner critic from such a central, controlling role in a women's advancement.

Even as I enjoy certain, confident movement, I simultaneously navigate bouts of uncertainty. To address the uncertain, I seek to become more self-aware through paying attention to my affective (e.g., emotional, feeling, etc.) state, through tracking energy-depleting rather than energy-creating interactions, and through noticing triggers that tend to elicit doubts and insecurities. Active self-management is imperative within this dialectic; the female administrator will need to oversee herself and her professional development as supported by a core group of quality girlfriends, mentors, advocates, and champions. This village of support can help a newbie discern whether a single action is likely to have monumental consequences or is just a slight blip in the power and political dynamics of the institutional context.

This dialectical tension underscores why the female academician need never wait for the all-knowing moment to transition to or seek an administrative appointment. Whenever she chooses to begin, the administrative role requires her to assert and reassert her capabilities with knowing confidence, while simultaneously acknowledging a self that is still progressing and learning through uncertainty.

The Self- and Other-Weighted/Self- and Other-Liberated Dialectic. This tension acknowledges both the burden and freedom of serving as the first African American female in a deanship amid the nuances and complexity of change from standpoints of own and other. Through this dialectical tension, I seek to capture the added weight and enlightenment of the administrative appointment with its associated implications for career advancement or derailment, marriage, motherhood, friendships, and self-care. Acknowledging sameness and difference across one's own standpoint and the standpoint of others is inspired from Higgins' self-discrepancy theory.[15] Standpoint juxtaposes a dyadic frame, which makes it possible to consider the female in relationship with others, who are also inspired or impacted by her new role.

The weighted element of this dialectic is multifaceted; it represents the invisible obligation and duty to do well as proof of one's abilities and in honor of one's heritage. As a first-generation college student who matriculated through higher education with the presence of two African American professors and only one fellow African American graduate student, I have intense appreciation for those who persist and share their experiences of being Black in majority White educational institutions.[16] Being a first African American female in an administrative appointment brings to mind both the heritage I enjoy and my desire to make those who sacrificed proud. Such sacrifices in my case were made not only by professors who aided directly or indirectly in my educational journey, but also by family, friends, and colleagues who provided emotional and psychosocial support. The weighted element is both a space of obligation and privilege when one considers the other capable women who were not given the opportunity to serve, to have the position, or to make the contributions that I enjoy.

Irrespective of race/class/gender identity, juggling the time commitment, train of emails, supervision of staff, and overall administrative work schedule while seeking to retain a teacher scholar-mom mental fortitude is perhaps the greatest weight on my administrative self. A most recent scheduling dilemma had me choosing between a love of recognizing Black graduates and a love of appreciating my own Black family as a wife and mother; this occurred on a weekend with university reports and scholarly deadlines looming which were prioritized as unessential for those two weekend days. In a Sunday ceremony dressed in regalia, I could sit as a platform guest to place stoles of kente cloth on the shoulders of all Black graduates in attendance. Or, in a ballpark an hour away from the ceremony, I could sit in a lawn chair cheering for a team with Black men who were coach/husband and player/son.

In this case, I prioritized Sunday worship, watching one ball game, returning to town for the graduation ceremony while missing a second ball game, and driving back for the championship ball game that went into extra innings with a happy ending (at least for our Rangers team). Not all aspects of the juggling act end well or are prioritized appropriately. In womanist vulnerability, I must admit to mistakes in focusing on the unessential and in poor attempts at protecting scheduled time. Some decisions are true sacrifices of hard choice without the ability to assume a dual presence. Even as tough choices involve scheduling conflicts of obligation, having the choice is evidence of the freedom of being in privileged space.

The standpoint of others acknowledges the weightiness and liberation of the role that family, friends, and colleagues have communicated directly to me with intrigue, anticipation, and dissent. From congratulatory emails and impromptu chats to scheduled meetings and celebrations, others sense and appreciate the unique blend of obligation and privilege as well as difficulty and ease associated with the appointment. The inflexibility of my professional schedule and loss of summer months in comparison with the prior faculty appointment has altered friendships and responsibilities as a wife, mother, daughter, and family member; the shift has strained relationships with some who do not understand or who are not willing to tolerate the time commitment or impromptu scheduling changes. Simultaneously, the opportunity has enhanced those same types of relationships as waves of encouragement and pride have more than offset the disappearance of once-supportive people. This particular village of support seems to approve silently and beam with pride; they share in the words spoken to me recently by Black parents of a graduating Diverse Student Scholars research assistant when they learned of my appointment. With broad grins and jubilation, the two parents group hugged me and said, "Congratulations to us!"

Countless more examples of this weighted and liberated dialectic can be offered; these include hiring staff, promoting colleagues, adjusting budgets for pay increases, rebranding academic units, guiding infrastructure risks, and honoring a commitment to followership as well as leadership. These all represent the collective manner in which an administrative role is liberating for self and others, even as others and I have experienced the weightiness of the role.

STRATEGIES FOR THRIVING WHILE STRUGGLING IN YOUR PERSONAL ACADEMIC JOURNEY

Unashamedly, I acknowledge the terrain, especially for women, does not lend itself to being a comfortable administrative journey; there will be struggle. Yet, it is possible to both thrive and struggle as a leader while negotiating the set of dialectical tensions encountered. Women can accelerate their leader identity through using Sims, Cunliff, Sims, and Robertson's emergent model drawn directly from racio-ethnic authentic leaders in higher education.[17] This final section offers additional leadership strategies, gleaned from communication theory, for women to champion themselves and others.

Take Command. Taking command is a communicative act; it is a blend of credibility and professional nonverbal, confident posture exhibited by the speaker. Credibility, as a multidimensional construct, consists of the dimensions of character, competence, and goodwill, and it packs powerful persuasive value.[18] To succeed, women in administrative roles will need to be prepared to display the core dimensions of credibility accompanied with a confident professional posture across multiple situations. They will need to take command in cabinet-level meetings, hosting dinner guests at banquets, facilitating group listening sessions, and having one-on-one meetings with subordinates, superiors, and colleagues. In negotiations for resources and private conversations of concern, women can be most effective not by merely expressing an opinion, but instead by taking command. The manner in which she takes command can be reminiscent of her own personal style, which can be cultivated over time. However, no substitution exists for the lack of having an authoritative and professional advocacy coupled with integrity and concern for others.

Honor People. Amid having an administrative bias for action and taking command, a female administrator can expect to hear key terms such as "collaboration," "strategic goals," and "working together around shared priorities." I have witnessed these key terms being spoken while individuals are simultaneously neglecting the treatment of people or undermining another's area of oversight. In essence, pleasant terms are empty rhetoric, since actions are not supportive of the narrative.

Similar to the dangers of stealth front-group campaigns and corporate spin, nice corporate terms like those shared above can be successful in disguising true interests that detrimentally impact people.[19] In this way, corporate symbols become individual tools of manipulation used to suit administrator aims. An alternative to this type of neglect and manipulation is to affirm, reaffirm, and remind that all organizations perform better when people are treated honorably. A willingness to take command concerning the treatment of people among executive-level leaders serves as a reminder that actions as well as words have influence.

Given the time constraints and added demands placed on her personal life, the female administrator will need to be mindful too of honoring people beyond those in her institution. Nurturing relationships with off-campus colleagues is essential. This group can provide counsel, caution, recommendations, and a listening ear. Another important strategy is not only to honor on-campus and off-campus professional colleagues, but also to avoid neglecting those she loves personally. For women, a true litmus test is to continually evaluate people priorities and values with repeated double-checks on the amount of quality time being devoted to honoring those she loves.

Manage Self, Inspire Others. The female administrator will need to be gentle with herself in recognition that her inner critic can leave her exhausted and cognitively depleted before ever tackling the work at hand. She will need to engage in frequent self-reflection documenting her growth so she can appreciate her own progress. For crafting a vision, developing a personal time map, and prioritizing strategic aims, she will need to manage self before being able to communicate to others about vision, schedules, and institutional aims.

Certainly, administrators oversee people, products, and processes. However, an effective female administrator manages inwardly and inspires outwardly. When turning outwardly toward people, especially those under her oversight and care, she will need to build competent teams where individuals honor, respect, and appreciate one another. Upon hiring and trusting competent people, she enables these individuals to do what she does—manage themselves with guidance, removal of obstacles, and vision casting by her.

In my case, I have left positions vacant for longer than desired to wait patiently for candidates with competencies and cultural fit. I privilege quality, capable people over quick hires who seem ungrateful, reluctant to grow, or unwilling to work in concert with others. People wish to be inspired. This remains a female administrator's greatest communicative act—the ability to use symbols and messages to move other people toward shared desires. Through communication, we help others see a new terrain that yet exists, we call others to action, and we enlist others in the institutional mission. In essence, we manage self so we can inspire others.

CONCLUDING COMMENTS AS COURAGE TO FRAME AND REFRAME COMMUNICATION

Fast-forward fifteen years later from the Fall 2003 Intro to Graduate Studies class to the Summer of 2018 where I was in my first month of transitioning to administration. I had scheduled listening sessions with key leaders across campus and was seated for one of the first chats in an office of an experienced, White male administrator. Following introductory conversation about our respective backgrounds, the colleague proceeded to share how he had enjoyed a "gentlemen's agreement" with my predecessor concerning the roles and responsibilities in our offices; as expressed from his perspective, it was an agreement that placed movements among staff in my office within his purview. I continued listening and expressed appreciation for his time at the end of our conversation.

And, so my 12-month administrative appointment began with the need to cognitively claim that no gentlemen's agreement exists here. The statement itself is steeped in a consensus that denies the presence of women while simultaneously acknowledging her presence as the intended recipient of the message. And, by virtue of her leadership position, she is able to negate the relevance of such an expression since she is not a male.

Female leaders will need to engage in their own communicative acts of framing and reframing as they navigate the intersectionality of power, inequality, connectedness, context, and complexity in their own experiences. Based on a solid foundation of communication theory and diligent mentoring, I have immense gratitude for my doctoral training under Pfau's leadership. From formative coursework with seminal texts to receiving a top dissertation award after Pfau's thoughtful nomination during his illness, I relish my academic lineage of learning. My hope is that this womanist approach, the dialectics discussed, and the strategies offered will empower women as they frame and reframe portions of their experience in an academy that was not originally designed for the fullness of our presence.

NOTES

1. Dubin, Robert. *Theory Building*. New York, NY: The Free Press, 1969; and Dunnette, Marvin D. "Fads, Fashions, and Folderol in Psychology." In *Theory Building*, ed. Robert Dubin (New York, NY: The Free Press, 1969).

2. Dunnette, Marvin D. "Fads, Fashions, and Folderol in Psychology." In *Theory Building*, ed. Robert Dubin (New York, NY: The Free Press, 1969), 268.

3. Chaffee, Steven H. *Explication* (Newbury Park, CA: Sage, 1991), 1.

4. Walker, Alice. *In Search of Our Mother's Gardens* (New York, NY: Houghton Mifflin Harcourt, 1983), xi.

5. Dubin. *Theory Building*, 268; and Drucker, Peter F. *The Effective Executive: The Definitive Guide to Getting the Right Things Done* (New York, NY: Harper, 1967), 1.

6. Collins, Patricia H., and Sirma Bilge. *Intersectionality* (Malden, MA: Polity Press, 2016), 25.

7. Collins and Bilge. *Intersectionality*, 3.

8. Compton, Joshua A., and Michael Pfau. "Inoculation Theory of Resistance to Influence at Maturity: Recent Progress in Theory Development and Application and Suggestions for Future Research." In *Communication Yearbook, 29* (New York, NY: Lawrence Erlbaum, 2005), 97; and Ivanov, Bobi, Sims, Jeanetta D., Compton, Joshua, Miller, Claude, Parker, Kimberly A., Parker, James, Harrison, Kylie, and Joshua M. Averbeck. "The General Content of Post-Inoculation Talk: Recalled Issue Specific Conversations Following Inoculation Treatments." *Western Journal of Communication*, 79, no. 2 (2015): 218.

9. Walker. *In Search of Our Mother's Gardens*, xi.

10. Bakhtin, Mikhail. *The Dialogic Imagination: Four Essays by M. M. Bakhtin.* Translated by Caryl Emerson and Michael Holquist (Austin, TX: University of Texas Press, 1975/1981), 5; Baxter, Leslie A. "Dialectical Contradictions In Relationship Development." *Journal of Social and Personal Relationships*, 7 (1990): 69; Baxter, Leslie. A. "A Tale of Two Voices: Relational Dialectics Theory." *The Journal of Family Communication,* 4, no. 3 (2004a): 181; Baxter, Leslie. A. "Distinguished scholar Article: Relationships as Dialogues." *Personal Relationships*, 11 (2004b): 1; and Baxter, Leslie A., and Barbara M. Montgomery. *Relating: Dialogues and Dialectics* (New York, NY: Guilford, 1996), 6.

11. Baxter, Leslie A., and Carma Bylund. "Social Influence in Close Relationships." In *Perspectives on Persuasion, Social Influence, and Compliance-Gaining*, ed. John S. Seiter and Robert H. Gass (New York, NY: Allyn & Bacon, 2004), 317; Cools, Carine A. "Relational Communication in Intercultural Couples." *Language and Intercultural Communication*, 6 (2006): 262; Hopson, Mark C., and Mark P. Orbe. "Playing the Game: Recalling Dialectical Tensions for Black Men in Oppressive Organizational Structures." *The Howard Journal of Communication*, 18 (2007): 69; Kim, Kyung-Hee, and Haejin Yun. "Cying for Me, Cying For Us: Relational Dialectics in a Korean Social Network Site." *Journal of Computer-Mediated Communication*, 13 (2008): 298; and Toller, Paige W., and Dawn O. Braithwaite. "Grieving together and Apart: Bereaved Parents' Contradictions of Marital Interaction." *Journal of Applied Communication Research*, 37, no. 3 (2009): 257.

12. Goins, Marnel N. "Playing With Dialectics: Black Female Friendship Groups As a Homeplace." *Communication Studies*, 62, no. 5 (2011): 531; Anderson, Peggy, Sims, Jeanetta Davis, Shuff, Jalea, Neese, Sarah, and Atoya Sims. "A Price-Based Approach to the Dialectics in African American Female Entrepreneur Experiences." *Journal of Business Diversity*, 15, no. 2 (2015): 46; and Sims, Jeanetta D. "A Muted Voice on Holy Ground: Reflections on the Dialectics Experienced as an African American Female Professor in a Christian University." In *Still Searching For Our Mothers' Gardens: Experiences of New, Tenure-Track Women of Color at "Majority' Institutions*, ed. Marnel N. Niles and Nickesia S. Gordon (Lanham, MD: University Press, 2011), 21.

13. Scott, Chaunda L., and Jeanetta D. Sims. "Exemplary Models of Faculty Driven Transformative Diversity Education Initiatives: Implications for Metropolitan

universities." Metropolitan Universities, 29, no. 3 (2018): 108; Sims, Jeanetta D., Doré, Anna., Vo, Mindy, Lai, Hung-Lin Lim, and Oon Feng Lim. "Diverse Student Scholars: A Five-Faceted Model of Student Transformation From Embedded Research Mentorship in Marketing Courses." Scholarship and Practice of Undergraduate Research, 2, no. 1 (2018): 33; and Sims, Jeanetta D., Shuff, Jalea, Neese, Sarah, Lai, Hung-Lin, Lim, Oon Feng., and Ashley Neese. "Diverse Student Scholars: How a Faculty Member's Undergraduate Research Program Can Advance Workforce Diversity Learning." In *Expanding Workforce Diversity Programs, Curriculum, And Degrees in Higher Education*, ed. Chaunda L. Scott and Jeanetta D. Sims (Hershey, PA: IGI Global, 2016), 62.

14. Brady, Susan M. *Mastering Your Inner Critic... And 7 Other High Hurdles To Advancement: How The Best Women Leaders Practice Self-Awareness To Change What Really Matters* (New York, NY: McGraw-Hill, 2019), 11.

15. Higgins, E. Tory. "Self-Discrepancy: A Theory Relating Self and Affect." *Psychological Review*, 94, no. 3 (1987): 322; and Higgins, E. Tory. "Self-Discrepancy Theory: What Patterns of Self-Beliefs Cause People to Suffer." *Advances in Experimental Social Psychology*, 22 (1989): 93.

16. Daniel, Jack L. Negotiating a Historically White University While Black (Seattle, WA: Amazon Publishing, 2019), 103; and Sims, "A Muted Voice on Holy Ground," 36.

17. Sims, Jeanetta D., Cunliff, Ed, Sims, Atoya, and Kristi Robertson. "Probing Leadership from Racio-Ethnic Perspectives in Higher Education: An Emergent Model of Accelerating Leader Identity" In *Global and Culturally Diverse Leaders and Leadership: New Dimensions and Challenges for Business, Education, and Society*, ed. Jean L. Chin, Joseph E. Trimble, and Joseph E. Garcia (Bingley, UK: Emerald Publishing, 2018), 183.

18. McCroskey, James. C. "Scales for the Measurement of Ethos." *Speech Monographs*, 33 (1966): 65; McCroskey, James. C., and Jason J. Teven. "Goodwill: A Reexamination of the Construct and its Measurement." *Communication Monographs*, 66 (1999): 90; and McCroskey, James C., and Thomas J. Young. "Ethos and Credibility: The Construct and its Measurement After Three Decades." *Central States Speech Journal*, 32 (1981): 24.

19. Pfau, Michael, Haigh, Michel M., Sims, Jeanetta D., and Shelley Wigley. "The Influence of Corporate Front-Group Stealth Campaigns." *Communication Research*, 34 (2007): 73; and Sims, Jeanetta D., and Rod Carveth. "Corporate Spin." In *Encyclopedia of Deception*, ed. Timothy Levine (Thousand Oaks, CA: Sage, 2014), 862.

BIBLIOGRAPHY

Anderson, Peggy, Jeanetta Davis Sims, Jalea Shuff, Sarah Neese, and Atoya Sims. "A Price-Based Approach to the Dialectics in African American Female Entrepreneur Experiences." *Journal of Business Diversity* 15, no. 2 (2015): 46–59. Retrieved from http://www.na-businesspress.com/jbdopen.html.

Bakhtin, Mikhail. *The Dialogic Imagination: Four Essays by M. M. Bakhtin*. Translated by Caryl Emerson and Michael Holquist. Austin, TX: University of Texas Press, 1975/1981.

Baxter, Leslie A. "Dialectical Contradictions in Relationship Development." *Journal of Social and Personal Relationships* 7 (1990): 69–88. doi: 10.1177/0265407590071004.

Baxter, Leslie A. "A Tale of Two Voices: Relational Dialectics Theory." *The Journal of Family Communication* 4, no. 3 (2004a): 181–192. doi: 10.1080/15267431.2004.9670130.

Baxter, Leslie A. "Distinguished Scholar Article: Relationships as Dialogues." *Personal Relationships* 11 (2004b): 1–22. doi:10.1080/15267431.2004.9670130.

Baxter, Leslie A. and Carma Bylund. "Social Influence in Close Relationships." In *Perspectives on Persuasion, Social Influence, and Compliance-Gaining*, edited by John S. Seiter and Robert H. Gass, 317–336. New York, NY: Allyn & Bacon, 2004.

Baxter, Leslie A., and Barbara M. Montgomery. *Relating: Dialogues and Dialectics*. New York, NY: Guilford, 1996.

Brady, Susan M. *Mastering Your Inner Critic... and 7 Other High Hurdles to Advancement: How the Best Women Leaders Practice Self-Awareness to Change What Really Matters*. New York, NY: McGraw-Hill, 2019.

Chaffee, Steven H. *Explication*. Newbury Park, CA: Sage, 1991.

Collins, Patricia H., and Sirma Bilge. *Intersectionality*. Malden, MA: Polity Press, 2016.

Compton, Joshua A., and Michael Pfau. "Inoculation Theory of Resistance to Influence at Maturity: Recent Progress." in *Theory Development and Application and Suggestions for Future Research*. In *Communication Yearbook 29*, 97–145. New York, NY: Lawrence Erlbaum, 2005.

Cools, Carine A. "Relational communication in intercultural couples." *Language and Intercultural Communication* 6 (2006): 262–274. doi: 10.2167/laic253.0.

Daniel, Jack L. *Negotiating a Historically White University While Black*. Seattle, WA: Amazon Publishing, 2019.

Drucker, Peter F. *The Effective Executive: The Definitive Guide to Getting the Right Things Done*. New York, NY: Harper, 1967.

Dubin, Robert. *Theory Building*. New York, NY: The Free Press, 1969.

Dunnette, Marvin D. "Fads, Fashions, and Folderol in Psychology." In *Theory Building*, edited by Robert Dubin, 268–280. New York, NY: The Free Press, 1969.

Goins, Marnel N. "Playing with Dialectics: Black Female Friendship Groups as a Homeplace." *Communication Studies* 62, no. 5 (2011): 531–546. doi: 10.1080/10510974.2011.584934.

Higgins, E. Tory. "Self-Discrepancy: A Theory Relating Self and Affect." *Psychological Review* 94, no. 3 (1987): 322–323. doi: 10.1037/0033-295X.94.3.319.

Higgins, E. Tory. "Self-Discrepancy Theory: What Patterns of Self-Beliefs Cause People to Suffer." *Advances in Experimental Social Psychology* 22 (1989): 93–136. doi:10.1016/S0065-2601(08)60306-8.

Hopson, Mark C., and Mark P. Orbe. "Playing the Game: Recalling Dialectical Tensions for Black Men in Oppressive Organizational Structures." *The Howard Journal of Communication* 18, (2007): 69–86. doi: 10.1080/10646170601147481.

Ivanov, Bobi, Sims, Jeanetta D., Compton, Joshua, Miller, Claude, Parker, Kimberly A., Parker, James, Harrison, Kylie, and Joshua M. Averbeck. "The General Content of Post-Inoculation Talk: Recalled Issue-Specific Conversations Following

Inoculation Treatments." *Western Journal of Communication* 79, no. 2 (2015): 218–238. doi: 10.1080/10570314.2014.943423.

Kim, Kyung-Hee, and Haejin Yun. "Cying For Me, Cying For Us: Relational Dialectics in a Korean Social Network Site." *Journal of Computer-Mediated Communication* 13 (2008): 298–318. doi: 10.1111/j.1083-6101.2007.00397.x.

McCroskey, James. C. "Scales for the Measurement of Ethos." *Speech Monographs* 33 (1966): 65–72. doi: 10.1080/03637756609375482.

McCroskey, James C., and Jason J. Teven. "Goodwill: A Reexamination of the Construct and its Measurement." *Communication Monographs* 66 (1999): 90–103. doi: 10.1080/03637759909376464.

McCroskey, James C., and Thomas J. Young. "Ethos and Credibility: The Construct and its Measurement After Three Decades." *Central States Speech Journal* 32 (1981): 24–34. doi:10.1080/10510978109368075.

Pfau, Michael, Haigh, Michel M., Sims, Jeanetta D., and Shelley Wigley. "The Influence of Corporate Front-Group Stealth Campaigns." *Communication Research* 34 (2007): 73–99. doi: 10.1177/0093650206296083.

Scott, Chaunda L., and Jeanetta D. Sims. "Exemplary Models of Faculty-Driven Transformative Diversity Education Initiatives: Implications for Metropolitan Universities." *Metropolitan Universities* 29, no. 3 (2018): 108–122. doi: 10.18060/21491.

Sims, Jeanetta D. "A Muted Voice on Holy Ground: Reflections on the Dialectics Experienced as an African American Female Professor in a Christian University." In *Still Searching For Our Mothers' Gardens: Experiences of New, Tenure-Track Women of Color at 'Majority' Institutions*, edited by Marnel N. Niles and Nickesia S. Gordon, 21–40. Lanham, MD: University Press, 2011.

Sims, Jeanetta D., and Rod Carveth. "Corporate Spin." In *Encyclopedia of Deception*, edited by Timothy Levine, 862–865. Thousand Oaks, CA: Sage, 2014.

Sims, Jeanetta D., Ed Cunliff, Atoya Sims, and Kristi Robertson. "Probing Leadership from Racio-Ethnic Perspectives in Higher Education: An Emergent Model of Accelerating Leader Identity." In *Global and Culturally Diverse Leaders and Leadership: New Dimensions and Challenges for Business, Education, and Society*, edited by Jean L. Chin, Joseph E. Trimble, and Joseph E. Garcia, 183–210. Bingley, UK: Emerald Publishing, 2018.

Sims, Jeanetta D., Anna Doré, Mindy Vo, Hung-Lin Lim Lai, and Oon Feng Lim. "Diverse Student Scholars: A Five-Faceted Model of Student Transformation from Embedded Research Mentorship in Marketing Courses." *Scholarship and Practice of Undergraduate Research* 2, no. 1 (2018): 33–42. doi: 10.18833/spur/2/8.

Sims, Jeanetta D., Sarah Neese, Atoya Sims, and Peggy Anderson. "Notions in Their Heads: Exploring the Discrepant Selves of African-American Female Entrepreneurs." *The Florida Communication Journal* 43, no. 1 (2015): 41–54. Retrieved from http://www.flcom.org/journal.asp.

Sims, Jeanetta D., Jalea Shuff, Sarah Neese, Hung-Lin Lai, Oon Feng Lim, and Ashley Neese. "Diverse Student Scholars: How a Faculty Member's Undergraduate Research Program Can Advance Workforce Diversity Learning." In *Expanding Workforce Diversity Programs, Curriculum, and Degrees in Higher Education*, edited by Chaunda L. Scott and Jeanetta D. Sims, 62–73. Hershey, PA: IGI Global, 2016.

Toller, Paige W., and Dawn O. Braithwaite. "Grieving Together and Apart: Bereaved Parents' Contradictions of Marital Interaction." *Journal of Applied Communication Research* 37, no. 3 (2009): 257–277. doi: 10.1080/00909880903025887.

Walker, Alice. *In Search of Our Mother's Gardens*. New York, NY: Houghton Mifflin Harcourt, 1983.

Chapter 9

Enacting a Feminist Ecological Ethos of Leadership at a Christian Liberal Arts College

Sarah Stone Watt

The well-established antagonism between Christianity and feminism in the United States makes it unsurprising that at a Christian college, even one with a student body that is more than 50 percent female, questions of women in leadership are complicated.[1] Christian colleges are not alone in facing barriers to women in leadership—the problem persists across academia—but when the academic mission of the institution is closely bound to the Christian mission of a particular denomination, the complications are magnified.[2]

This chapter examines the ways that establishing a Committee on Women Faculty at one Christian institution addressed some of the complexities and expanded women's formal and informal leadership roles. Focusing on ethos, I analyze three of the moves that the Committee made, which created the conditions for leaders to emerge as a natural outgrowth of the Christian mission that blends "the highest standards of academic excellence and Christian values, where students are strengthened for lives of purpose, service, and leadership."[3] I contend that by communicating that their inclusion is integral to the college's shared Christian values, female faculty developed an ecological *ethē* or "dwelling place" that fosters partnership with stakeholders at multiple levels of the university to advance the mission and vision of the institution.[4]

This analysis of three of the Committee's primary actions seeks to demonstrate how they succeeded in interrupting tradition to "advocate for themselves and others in transformative ways, and relate to others, both powerful and powerless" and to create a supportive environment that nurtures women's careers, especially in the area of leadership.[5] I begin by explaining the interpretations of ethos that ground this analysis. Then, I discuss the conditions for the creation of the Committee, followed by an analysis of strategies the

Committee enacted in its first few years to change the climate surrounding women in leadership on campus: policy advocacy, mentorship, and honoring past and present leaders.

ECOLOGICAL ETHOS, DWELLING PLACE

This chapter takes as its starting point two interpretations of *ethos* that challenge traditional applications of the term as character or credibility. Neither interpretation denies the importance of character and credibility as elements of *ethos*, but both demonstrate that there is more at work in the concept. Michael J. Hyde has called on rhetorical scholars to attend to "the *ethos* of rhetoric" to consider the ways that "discourse is used to transform space and time into 'dwelling places' (*ethos*; pl. *ethea*) where people can deliberate and 'know together' (*con-scientia*) some matter of interest."[6] Hyde's interpretation of ethos shifts the focus from a singular individual to a communal relationship. Similarly, Kathleen Ryan, Nancy Myers, and Rebecca Jones have argued that rhetors who fall outside of the norm in a given community "face countless challenges in constructing an authoritative Aristotelian ethos."[7] They call instead for a "feminist ecological *ethē*" that seeks to understand the ways women specifically attend to the interconnections between "time, contexts, and different relationships" in the construction of their ethos.[8] Taken together, these perspectives demonstrate how marginalized rhetors foster change by attending to the ways that members of a community relate to one another and performing relationships that alter what the group perceives to be normal.

Aristotle, and the substantial body of rhetorical scholarship based on his work, conceives of ethos as "an artistic accomplishment" whereby the rhetor wins audience trust in their ability to reason.[9] However, Hyde demonstrates that this artistic accomplishment is only possible because it is always already grounded in the past as well as "ongoing communal existence: the 'places,' 'habitats,' and 'haunts' (*ethea*) wherein people dwell and bond together."[10] This means that a rhetor's moral character or credibility is bound up in their way of being with others. In order to fully grasp this interpretation of ethos, it is important to move away from simple speaker-audience models of rhetoric that focus on how one individual moves an audience through the use of specific symbols. Instead, rhetoric is an ongoing interaction in which humans negotiate ways of being together.[11] Thinking of ethos as dwelling place helps to understand how some members of a group may change the communal way of being by convincing other members to dwell with them. In this way, ethos is less about how a community understands the rhetor, and more about how the community understands itself and its relationship to public affairs.[12]

Coretta Pittman has demonstrated how thinking of ethos as "good sense, good moral character, and good will" is further flawed because it ignores rhetors who are positioned outside of the power structure that would affirm their choices as moral or credible.[13] Focusing on Black women writers in the United States during and after the period of enslavement, she points out that they were rarely assumed to have good moral character and the choices they made to protect themselves and their children magnified indictments of their virtue. These rhetors had to formulate alternative models of ethos within existing sociopolitical boundaries. The women Pittman describes used slave narratives and autobiography to establish ethos, while other marginalized women have had to find different means of crafting ethos within their existing boundaries. Ryan, Myers, and Jones propose the feminist ecological approach as a way of understanding a multiplicity of rhetors, situations, and strategies.

The feminist ecological approach to ethos is derived from Lorraine Code's work on ecology, which entails examination of the "physical and social" ways in which "people endeavor to live well together."[14] The approach requires consideration not only of the ways that rhetors speak or write in order to persuade, but how they live in and relate with all of the elements of the rhetorical situation. Ryan, Myers, and Jones argue that traditional concepts of ethos tend to cover over difference and oppression with a presumption that everyone shares a single definition of credibility.[15] However, rhetors or groups that fall outside of the normative definition must attend to "the multiple, nonlinear relations operating among rhetors, audiences, things, and contexts (i.e., ideological, metaphorical, geographical)" and view "all elements in any rhetorical situation as shifting and morphing in response to others (persons, places, things)."[16] Thus, in any rhetorical situation, there may exist "a variety and plurality of ethos, or ethē."[17] Practices of interrupting, advocating, and relating in women's rhetorical strategies are some of the ways that Ryan, Myers, and Jones contend these marginalized rhetors "construct new ethē" to "alter ecosystems."[18] This analysis centers on how the Committee used those rhetorical strategies to reconfigure their institutional ecosystem and create a dwelling place in which community members increasingly see female leaders as normal, even as they remain a numerical minority.

INSTITUTIONAL NORMS

In 2011, the Association of American Colleges and Universities (AAC&U) celebrated the advancements that women have made in enrollment and graduation rates at the graduate and undergraduate levels from the 1970s to the 2000s.[19] At that time, the numbers of female faculty had also more than doubled.[20] Women have been appointed to senior academic leadership positions, including the presidency—most notably at Harvard in 2007—though in far fewer numbers than their male colleagues. Despite these advances in higher education generally, women still have not moved into the highest levels of the faculty and into leadership positions in great numbers, and women from racially and ethnically minoritized groups are almost nonexistent in academic leadership.[21] Most advancements in women's leadership in higher education seemed to stall in the 2000s. The White House Project noted that women remain underrepresented on college boards.[22] Institutions have not made any progress in closing the gender gap between male and female faculty salaries. In fact, women are actually making slightly less than they were in comparison with male counterparts in the 1970s.[23]

Although many factors influence whether and how different groups advance into leadership roles, Vice President of the American Council on Education Claire Van Ummersen points out that these inequities remain embedded in the culture of academic institutions.[24] At religious colleges and universities, the institutional culture tends to be influenced by both historical and theological assumptions about who can lead and how. Karen A. Longman and Patricia S. Anderson studied trends in gendered leadership among member institutions of the Council for Christian Colleges and Universities over twelve years. They concluded that "both institutional and denominational understandings of gender roles for those working in Christian institutions can add complexity to the leadership journeys of women," even on campuses that are making efforts to increase the diversity and well-being of their communities.[25]

Pepperdine University began as a liberal arts college in the tradition of the Churches of Christ, a diverse group of individual churches focused on adherence to the Bible rather than denominational rules or traditions.[26] The Churches of Christ emerged out of the American Restoration Movement of the early nineteenth century. The movement sought to heal protestant denominational divisions by uniting Christians around "the simple faith proclaimed in the biblical text," and moving away from clerical or denominational authority over the interpretation of the text.[27] Like any religious tradition, the Churches of Christ have evolved and changed over time. For example, in the early nineteenth century, the tradition's textual focus led many to see the Bible as "a legal blueprint for the restoration of the ancient church." But, from the 1960s to the 1990s, Richard Hughes explains that "many Churches of Christ began to view Scripture as a theological document, revealing transcendent truths about God and His relationship with humankind, and an ethical document, defining the kinds of lives Christians should live in response to God's love and grace."[28] The lack of accountability to a denominational authority means that different Churches of Christ may hold very different biblical interpretations. The diversity of viewpoints, ability to change, and the tradition's commitment to the pursuit of truth have offered both challenges and opportunities to those seeking change in the tradition, particularly in the area of women's leadership.

Historically, the Churches of Christ have viewed leadership as a male domain. As in many social contexts, gender roles in the church are "carefully defined, though usually unspoken."[29] The roles of pastor and elder have long been reserved for men in the Churches of Christ along with many other Christian denominations. While some denominations, permit women to occupy these roles, they are rarely seen as the primary leader of their congregation.[30] Still, some congregations within the Churches of Christ tradition are making changes. Women continue to perform traditionally female tasks, such as teaching children in Sunday school and preparing food for church events, but they are also slowly finding their way into more prominent leadership roles. Women are moving into traditionally male roles leading prayer and worship, serving communion, and in some cases, even preaching or serving as elders.[31] The change has come as some Church of Christ congregations become convinced, both by biblical scholarship and recognition of their own denominational history, that there is not a biblical basis for the limitations on women's leadership.[32] Some congregations continue to see a biblical justification for limiting leadership roles on the basis of sex, while others do not. Even as churches change their views on women's ability to lead, change can be slow as many churches avoid making changes that they fear their congregants are not ready to accept.[33]

Church of Christ women have found both opportunities and constraints on their leadership at Pepperdine. The university appointed its first chaplain in 2001, a woman named D'Esta Love, who had previously served as Dean of Students and an adjunct professor in both Humanities and Religion.[34] Pepperdine's Seaver College was the first college affiliated with the Churches of Christ to tenure a female professor in its religion division.[35] However, male faculty still outnumber female faculty and the university has a dearth of female faculty at the rank of full professor and in the higher levels of administrative leadership.[36]

ESTABLISHING THE COMMITTEE ON WOMEN FACULTY

The gender disparities at Pepperdine are similar to other institutions, but the institution's response to the disparities has not always mirrored other institutions. In 2009, a group of faculty and staff examined the university's peer and aspirational schools' responses to gender disparities on their campuses. They found that all of the university's aspirational schools had established

Women's Centers.[37] This group developed a proposal to establish a Women's Resource Office at Pepperdine with a mission "to empower, educate, and serve both local and global communities on issues pertinent to women, their faith, and personal development."[38] They proposed to serve faculty, staff, students, and the broader community in a variety of areas including everything from scholarship to life and career skills. As they waited to see whether the proposal would gain traction with higher administration and potential donors, they looked for smaller ways to address the gender gap, particularly at Seaver College.[39]

Seaver College is Pepperdine's undergraduate residential liberal art college. As the "flagship college of Pepperdine University's five schools," Seaver strives to maintain a close connection to Churches of Christ and their religious traditions.[40] One of the primary ways that the college fosters its relationship with the church is through employment of faculty and recruitment of students who identify as members of a Church of Christ.[41] Although faculty and students recognize differences between women's roles in the church and in educational environments, women in the institution have shared experiences that indicate church norms do cloud their experiences on campus. For example, female faculty note students attempting to compliment them by commenting that the faculty member reminds them of their Sunday school teacher. Recognizing that women faculty face these and other, more problematic but often unspoken, barriers to their success, the Seaver Faculty Association approved the creation of an ad hoc Committee on Women Faculty.

The Committee was not designed to promote women in leadership. The initial proposal was for an "Ad Hoc Committee on Women's Issues" to focus on "recruitment, retention, and promotion of women faculty," as well as "resources and support"—namely mentoring—and "education and enrichment on issues related to women faculty."[42] The women who proposed the ad hoc committee chose the name "Committee on Women's Issues" to preempt concerns that some of their colleagues may feel threatened by other possible titles such as "Committee for the Advancement of Women Faculty."[43] The Seaver Faculty Association's Executive Committee instead received comments about the pejorative implications of the phrase "women's issues," and approved the title "Ad Hoc Committee on Women Faculty." They also added a mandate that the committee specifically address issues of "quality of life and work-life balance." It is worth noting that although it did not become the official title of the Committee, the group was referred to as the "Women's Issues Committee" by faculty, both male and female, including some committee members and the dean of Seaver College for many years, even after it shifted from an ad hoc to a standing committee.[44] It took more than formal recognition of the committee for its pejorative nickname to fade away. References to "women's issues" faded over time as the Committee shifted its ethos by successfully advocating for changes to the college's family leave policy, establishing a mentoring program, and cultivating support for an annual celebration honoring women's excellence in leadership at the university. These moves interrupted tradition to advocate for change while also celebrating shared values across the institution and enhancing the community's way of being together.

POLICY ADVOCACY

In its early years, the Committee found it easy to catalog the challenges facing women in academia broadly and at Seaver College specifically. However, it proved more difficult to determine those areas of concern in which they might have agency to foster positive change. The Committee addressed issues of equal pay as the college considered implementing a merit pay system, they advocated for gender equity in the makeup of faculty committees, and established a women's caucus that invited all faculty to gather on a regular basis to raise and discuss issues relevant to women in academia. The Committee's most effective advocacy effort was aimed at revising the college's family leave policy.

In academia, women disproportionately bear the consequences of the outdated assumption that faculty are either single or have a partner that stays home with the children.[45] Francesca Dominici, Linda Freid, and Scott Zeger explain "the timing of tenure decisions often coincides with the optimal childbearing years, requiring women to resolve individually the conflicts between biological and career clocks."[46] This timing is likely to influence whether and when women seek romantic partners and/or attempt to become pregnant. For example, they see the fact "that tenured women in academic science are twice as likely as tenured men to be single" as one possible manifestation of the concern. They also point out that "women academics who have children still shoulder the majority of domestic responsibilities, and those with children of prekindergarten age are less likely to be in a tenure-track job than their male counterparts."[47] Mary Ann Mason and Marc Goulden used the Survey of Doctoral Recipients' longitudinal data on the life course of more than 160,000 PhD recipients across all disciplines to examine choices regarding marriage, family, and career. They determined that

> Only one in three women who takes a fast-track university job before having a child ever becomes a mother. Women who achieve tenure are more than twice as likely as their male counterparts to be single twelve years after earning the Ph.D. And, . . . women who are married when they begin their faculty careers are much more likely than men in the same position to divorce or separate from

their spouses. Women, it seems, cannot have it all—tenure and a family—while men can.[48]

Some universities have responded to this research with more family-friendly policies. They have adjusted the tenure clock or allowed for "flexible workload or job sharing" to signal to women that they are valued members of the organization.[49]

Seaver College signals that it values families in a variety of ways. Due to the high cost of living in Malibu, California, the college offers a limited number of lower cost condominiums on campus designed for families. This move not only enables the university to recruit and retain faculty members who might not otherwise be able to afford the cost of living, it also fosters community by placing multiple families and their children in close proximity to one another and the campus. Similarly, the institution recruits families to travel with students and live in their study abroad programs where the faculty family is encouraged to build community with students through practices such as shared meals and hosting Bible study, or "house church." Seaver also makes funds available for faculty to host students for a meal in their home each semester if they choose. While each of these moves demonstrates that the institution values families, some also tend to perpetuate the assumption that a faculty member is married to a partner who stays home with the children. For example, the duration of the study abroad program makes it impossible for a two-income household to participate unless the spouse leaves their job or is able to arrange long-term remote work. The program funding meals in the home does not make the same money available for the faculty member to host students at a restaurant, assuming that either the faculty member or a spouse will be available to cook the meal. Female faculty have shared that they experience this double-edged sword in other ways, such as having their division arrange work schedules in such a way that parents are able to navigate child care concerns, but also having colleagues tell them that they should not take a leadership role in the division until their smaller children are grown.

At the time that the Committee on Women Faculty was established, Pepperdine had a family leave policy that not only complied with California's generous (compared to many other states) paid family leave policy, but also subsidized a faculty member's leave so that she was able to take an entire semester off after giving birth while still earning her regular salary. Many faculty agreed that the compensation provided by the policy was generous. However, they complained that the policy was vague, leading to differing interpretations for different faculty members, or preventing some women from pursuing the benefits they needed for fear of asking for too much. Additionally, the policy suffered from the problem of benevolent sexism.[50] In an attempt to protect women from potential setbacks to their research agenda and a decrease in time spent improving their classroom teaching, the policy allowed the faculty member to stop their tenure clock while on family leave. While some supervisors interpreted the policy as providing the option to stop the tenure clock, others advised faculty that the stop was mandatory. So, for many women having a child automatically meant extending their time toward tenure, whether they deemed the extension beneficial or not. Similarly, while most faculty understood the policy to be an all or nothing leave, some faculty successfully negotiated alternative arrangements. For example, a woman giving birth in the summer may choose to return to work in the fall and remain on a reduced load throughout the academic year.

As the Committee began to sort through the confusion surrounding the policy, they administered a survey to gauge faculty awareness, understanding, and perception of the policy. They found that in addition to the confusion women were experiencing, men were confused about whether and how the policy provided for paternity leave. The Committee worked closely with the Dean's Office to clarify the policy to the benefit of all Seaver faculty.

The revised Seaver College Faculty Parental Leave Policy provided much needed clarity that benefitted female and male faculty. The new policy clarified that female faculty may choose between being fully "released from all teaching, scholarly and service responsibilities for a period equal in length to the FMLA/CFRA [Family and Medical Leave Act/California Family Rights Act] leave period and for no less than one academic semester (or its equivalent)."[51] Alternatively, she "may choose a modified schedule leave allowing for a reduced teaching load over a period not exceeding two academic terms."[52] The policy also provides male faculty and/or adoptive parents the choice of "a two course reduction for one term or a one course reduction over two terms."[53] The policy continues the practice of providing faculty members with their full salary and benefits during the leave period. Importantly, the revised policy clarified how leave would affect both the tenure clock and sabbatical eligibility. With regard to tenure, the policy indicates that "Faculty members granted faculty parental leave may request to extend their tenure and promotion period by one year," and it outlines the process for pursuing that request.[54] Further, it specifies exactly which tenure and promotion processes are affected by the stoppage so that faculty can make an informed decision and implementation is no longer left up to individual supervisors. Finally, the policy clarifies that "The faculty parental leave period is considered a continuous service period with respect to eligibility for sabbatical leave."[55] After careful collaboration with the Committee, the Dean circulated the revisions for faculty review and comment before they were added to the revised faculty handbook.

The Seaver College community responded positively to the revisions. They appreciated both the clarity of the new policy and the conversation it sparked surrounding family leave. Clarifying the policy not only made it easier to use, it also seemed to decrease the perceived stigma surrounding issues of family leave for both women and men.

Advocating for a clarification of the family leave policy required the Committee carefully negotiate their relationship to the community. Ryan, Myers, and Jensen acknowledge that advocacy can create a "dilemma" for rhetors as they seek to establish their authority to speak on an issue while simultaneously "negotiating the complexity of speaking for others."[56] Traditional assumptions about motherhood and the central place of mothers in the family, particularly within Christian communities, provided Committee members with some presumed authority over the family leave policy. Yet, the Committee was constantly aware that not all women on campus were, could be, or desired to be mothers. They had to be careful to demonstrate the importance of a clear family leave policy to the benefit of the community as a whole, not just to women who intended to have children. Doing so required members to be "critically reflective of [their] own and others' participation, leadership and agency in creating positive and healthy work environments."[57] By integrating both Christian and feminist values, they were able to effectively advocate for the needs of multiple community members.

As they worked on the family leave revision, the Committee encountered a variety of related issues. Faculty raised concerns that the policy only pertained to those in tenured and tenure-track positions. They also recognized that family needs extended far beyond the first year after birth and adoption. Notably, they cited concerns regarding childcare and elder care that prevented faculty from attending professional conferences that are necessary for advancing scholarly research agendas.

Through their policy advocacy, the Committee took responsibility for the betterment of the community. Rather than conceiving of motherhood as an "individualized location" that women faculty may occupy and need accommodation for, they worked to improve conditions for a variety of intersecting family formulations and needs.[58] Their advocacy bridged the personal and political, the religious and academic, positioning the Committee to lead. Although the Committee was not able to affect policy change for every concern, namely those regarding non-tenure-track faculty in the leave policy, they were successful in meeting a variety of other needs that the community expressed to them during or after the successful revision of the policy. For example, they went on to negotiate how the policy was applied in some cases where women experienced miscarriage. They secured university funding for childcare during the graduation ceremony so that faculty were able to attend, and they continue to advocate for more permanent childcare on campus. Most significantly, they secured funding for faculty to use in caring for children and elderly dependents as they travel to academic conferences. The Faculty Dependent Care Travel Initiative, funded by the provost, helps offset the cost of additional care or travel for the dependent and/or caregiver to accompany the faculty member attending a professional conference or other professional development opportunity.[59] Advocating for the provost to sponsor this program extended benefits beyond Seaver College, altering the broader Pepperdine ecosystem. In doing so, the Committee altered community members' way of being such that scholars, male and female, with all manner of family configurations could flourish.

MENTORING

Feminist ecological thinking prompts constant communication between community members through an ethical orientation toward fostering communal well-being.[60] An important part of the Committee's work in this regard was the creation of a mentoring program focused on the concerns women must address as they advance through their academic career. The college has long provided mentoring for first-year faculty members in the form of monthly breakfasts and pairings of new faculty with a pre-assigned senior faculty member from a different academic division of the college who could answer questions and provide guidance in navigating the institution. While the college's mentoring program was helpful for faculty in their first year, the pairs rarely kept up meeting together after the year ended due to time constraints or the mismatch of interests between mentor and mentee. The end to formal mentoring efforts left faculty to establish their own informal connections to help them navigate the university. Unfortunately, in their study of barriers to women's leadership, Dominici, Fried, and Zeger found that "male faculty members are more likely to build substantive collegial relationships with other men than women, often leaving newly appointed women to fend for themselves because the majority of senior faculty are men."[61] This finding was consistent with the anecdotal evidence the Committee had heard at Seaver College. Male faculty seemed to easily form friendships with senior male colleagues both at school and at church. Even when those involved saw these relationships as primarily social, they provided informal mentoring by exposing the newer male faculty to the experiences of the senior male faculty, a benefit that most newer female faculty did not have.

To respond to this concern, the Committee reviewed existing research into gender and mentorship as well as best practices for successful mentoring programs. They found that it was common for women to desire mentoring, but fail to find it, and that insufficient mentorship was one of the most common obstacles women cited for failing to reach goals on their path toward career advancement.[62] They also found that faculty goals for mentoring change as women progress through their academic career and as their family situations change.⁶³ Furthermore, mentoring matches involving members of the same gender, ethnicity, or research goals had higher levels of success.⁶⁴ In reviewing best practices, they determined that a network or "constellation" of mentoring opportunities was preferable to a one-on-one grooming relationship with a seasoned mentor an early career mentee.⁶⁵ Mentoring constellations proved useful because they created "a more flexible network of support," by removing the expectation that any one mentor should have all of the expertise necessary to help someone navigate all of the layers of academic life.⁶⁶

In response to their research, the Committee sought to establish a program that would not merely provide guidance in normative paths for career advancement and thus reinforce existing power dynamics. Instead, they aimed to foster a communal shift that recognized the multiple maneuvers women make as they seek to achieve career goals.⁶⁷ The Committee created mentorship pods comprised of all female faculty from different divisions within the college with at least one member at the rank of professor, at least one associate professor, and an evenly distributed number of assistant professors. This allowed members to network with colleagues at all levels and give and receive a diversity of advice that spanned multiple stages of career advancement. The design intentionally distributed power across the group. They asked one member of each group to volunteer to be the facilitator. That person was not the leader of the group. They were responsible for logistics—finding times for the pod to meet and sending reminders about discussion topics and resources. Taking volunteers created an opportunity for faculty to determine whether the facilitator role was something that they would be good at or want to do, rather than something they were assigned by virtue of their rank or age.

Establishing a facilitator was important to the committee to address the difficulty of finding time to meet, which appeared in the research and had challenged the established mentoring program at the college.⁶⁸ Since mentoring requires trusting relationships, it was necessary for the pods to meet regularly over an extended period.⁶⁹ The Committee determined that the program would run for three semesters (spring-fall-spring). This allowed for recruitment in the fall, relationship building in the first spring, and extension of deeper conversations into the following year. Then, the Committee took a year to assess and regroup before running the program a second time with minor alterations to timing and composition of pod members.⁷⁰

At the start and end of each iteration of the program, the Committee hosted a half-day retreat. The kickoff took place at the university's beach house, which removed people from the typical academic setting and provided space to foster personal and spiritual connections. They took time for a devotional, prayer, and reflection that prompted participants to consider the needs they brought to the program and how the connections they were establishing could enrich their lives. They ate breakfast and lunch together, conducted a brief survey to help assess the program, and allowed pods to meet in an informal setting and get to know one another. Participants specifically outlined their challenges and questions with regard to the four major goals of the program:

1. To promote successful professional development in the areas of teaching, scholarship, and service
2. To develop institutional awareness
3. To encourage self-advocacy
4. To facilitate discussion on work-life balance issues.[71]

Providing dedicated time and space to reflect on these areas of development and to rest, pray, reflect, and converse enabled participants to foster strong initial connections and set the groundwork for trusting mentoring relationships. At the end of the program, they came together again to do similar activities, but with the goal of reflecting on what they had gained from the program and how they could sustain those benefits. At the end of each iteration of the program, participants reported improvements in many of the program goals, including in establishing "a support system" for professional and personal development. At the end of the first iteration of the program, all participants agreed or strongly agreed with the statement "I have found colleagues at Pepperdine with whom I can discuss work-life balance issues."[72] I highlight this finding because it speaks to the way the program advanced professional goals by enriching women faculty's ability to thrive in community with their colleagues.

The success of the program was due, I think, in large part to the Committee's care in providing intentional, research-focused, guidance to pods with regard to topics of conversation. In between the kickoff and closing retreats, the Committee arranged for pods to discuss material related to one of each of the program goals per meeting and provided readings to ground the conversations. Pods began by sharing their Faculty Data Form (FDF). The FDF is a detailed report faculty members submit for all major benchmarks in the tenure and promotion process—pre-tenure, tenure, and five-year reviews. Since the form offers more detail regarding their thinking on teaching, research, and service than a CV (*curriculum vitae* or "course of life," i.e., an overview of someone's work history) and it evolves as the faculty member revises it to reflect their thinking at each stage of the review process, it provides insight into both the individual and their interactions with institutional norms and expectations. Pod members who had not yet reached the pre-tenure review submitted their CV to the group and then gained the benefit of seeing how different faculty constructed their FDF based on discipline, rank, and individual preference. The exchange of CV/FDF offered a basis on which pods could then discuss the many aspects of one another's professional life while also opening the door to conversations about why each person has taken their particular path. These insights allowed pod members to bond over shared experiences, ask questions, and discuss ways of productively navigating challenges, laying the groundwork for a conversation about institutional awareness and self-advocacy in the second semester and work-life integration in the third.

Nadine M. Bean, Lisa Lucas, and Lauri L. Hyers state that "mentoring humanizes the workplace by building relationships of the head, heart, and soul."[73] The Committee on Women Faculty sought to enact these relationships by providing space and resources for women to negotiate gaps between themselves and others.[74] The relationships they established in the pods provided one layer of ethos, while the relationships that pods enabled by fostering institutional awareness and work-life integration were another. The pods fostered reflection on participants' own subjectivity and helped them to become more mindful of others.[75] This type of relating is different from the traditional model of grooming mentorship because it strips away some of the problematic power dynamics. The typical mentoring relationship endows the mentor with power to determine what topics of conversation are most important for the mentee's growth and allows them to choose which power dynamics to highlight and which they prefer to avoid. This practice "risks a blindness to ways of life other than one's own" and can be counterproductive, or even violent as it fosters disidentification.[76] Instead, the pods allowed all participants to occupy the mentor and mentee role simultaneously, encouraging them to explore where each person comes from and what they bring to the group. The structure expanded each participant's professional network at the same time that it invited conversations about difference and commonality, offering pods opportunities to consider the ways that working together could improve their communal existence. While the assessment indicates that the interactions were generally positive, pods could not fully eliminate power dynamics or bridge all potential gaps in power or identity. However, coming together regularly to explore their individual and communal existence fostered bonds for many women that enabled them to better navigate the institution and their own career choices.

Fostering an ethos of relating within their pods translated to ways participants could also relate to others at the university. In discussions about institutional awareness, pod members brought insights into their areas of the university enabling other members to consider ways they might relate to previously unfamiliar colleagues and power structures. Conversations focused on everything from who to talk to for different needs, to when and how to raise personal concerns with supervisors or navigate difficult conversations with colleagues. Increasing institutional awareness, equipping participants with strategies for self-advocacy, and later sharing strategies for work-life integration fostered healthier community engagement for women who were previously suffering in silence as they took on too much work for fear of seeming incompetent, or who had brewing resentment toward power structures they did not know how to navigate. Dean et al. contend that for women to advance in leadership, it is vital to "maintain vigilant awareness of campus work life and environment and question what we define and accept as normal."[77] The pods not only prompted consideration of campus norms but also equipped participants with the tools to effectively alter the community's established ways of relating to one another.

CELEBRATING ESTABLISHED LEADERS

The Committee on Women Faculty was designed to review campus policies, advocate for necessary changes, and create mentoring relationships that would improve the climate of gender equity on campus. These are important goals, especially in light of the research indicating that across academia "women do not become tenured and promoted at the same rates as men" and that "this lower tenure and promotion rate is part of the explanation for why there are fewer female than male administrators at the level of dean or above."[78] Policy advocacy and mentorship are critical strategies for rhetorically contesting and constructing space for women to succeed.[79] However, tenure and promotion are only some of the elements necessary for women to advance into leadership positions, and women are needed in these positions.

Department heads, deans, and higher-level administrators have more opportunities to make institutional change and "diversify the academy" by "encouraging new approaches."[80] However, women have lower representation in these roles than in the highest ranks of the professoriate. Even when women do occupy these leadership roles, they tend not to earn the same rewards for their work as male leaders and they tend to discourage younger women from following in their footsteps.[81]

It is not enough to simply give women tools to advance, Dean, Bracken, and Allen contend that we must reflect on what we and our campuses identify as the traits and behaviors of effective leadership and question what leadership traits we accept and reward."[82] Pepperdine's mission focuses on the values of purpose, service, and leadership. Pepperdine encourages students and faculty to consider these values through the lens of vocation, or calling. Each first-year student at Seaver College is encouraged to read and reflect on an essay about vocation. The essay combines scripture and biblical scholarship to encourage readers to find the intersection between their career and the gifts God has equipped them with that can help to meet people's needs. It demonstrates Pepperdine's view that vocation is a journey that requires self-awareness, mentorship, and the ability to stretch to serve others. Pepperdine encourages faculty to consider how their position at the institution is part of their own vocational journey. At the end of the first year of tenure-track employment, faculty go on a retreat to one of the school's study abroad locations where they have time to read and think together about their vocation and the integration of faith and learning.

While the institution encourages faculty to consider their vocation, particularly in terms of the intersection between their faith and their teaching, research, and service, there is less prompting to consider whether they are called to lead. In an environment where the majority of leaders have historically been male, which is ingrained in a faith tradition undergoing debate about whether women can be called into leadership positions and/or whether people are ready for them to lead if called, it can be difficult for women to embrace a vocational calling to leadership. The Committee on Women Faculty recognized that if they were going to truly advance equity on campus, the community needed to be able to see leadership as a calling for women, just as much as for men.

The lack of women in leadership at the university was not the result of a policy prohibition or a lack of mentorship. Much like gender roles in the church, gender roles in higher education leadership are unspoken, yet clearly defined. There were women in leadership, but they were not the norm. To change that norm, the Committee had to foster a competing narrative. They did so by establishing an award to honor the women's excellence in formal leadership roles within the institution. The award came with an honorarium and was presented at an evening banquet, funded by both the Pepperdine Provost's Office and the Seaver College Dean's Office.

The Committee invited nominations of women who met the following criteria:

> Women who have had a faculty role (present or past) at Pepperdine University, have been employed by the University for ten or more years, and are role models for academic leaders. Potential areas of leadership could include but are not limited to: administration at the university, school, and division levels; offices in professional organizations and academic societies; leadership in civic and service organizations; and leadership in the areas of scholarship, teaching, and university service.[83]

This process defined qualities of a good academic leader—experience as a faculty member, longevity in the community, and occupation of a formal leadership role. It prompted community members to consider who might meet these qualifications. The Committee was particularly interested in inviting the community to consider formal leadership roles because that required consideration of where and how women were occupying these roles at the institution and outside of it. The process also called on the community to define what they valued in a leader by asking them to offer reasons for their nomination. Nominations came from faculty, staff, and administrators, all highlighting the influence women's leadership had on their own career at the institution.

Once the Committee selected a recipient, they invited faculty and administrators to "an evening banquet celebrating Women in Leadership at Pepperdine."[84] The evening banquet and award, as well as specific reference to "generous funding provided" by the provost and dean signaled the significance of the event. The Committee also included a brief note about the award recipient. In the first year, they indicated that the banquet would honor "D'Esta Love for her outstanding contribution to the University as a teacher, a leader and a role model." The announcement also indicated that the recipient would give a keynote address. Love titled her address, "Called to Courage."

The creation and promotion of the dinner and award raised awareness that there were women in important leadership roles at Pepperdine and conveyed that the community valued their contributions. Some people attended the dinner to signal their shared value for women in leadership, some were there to support an individual honoree, still others came out of curiosity, a love of free food, or a perceived obligation to attend events sponsored by the upper administration. Whatever their motivation for attending, faculty and administrators engaged in a communal celebration of women in leadership that featured an autobiographical account of one woman's journey as a leader at Pepperdine. Starting with Love, each year attendees have encountered a new story that evidences the path for women in leadership at Pepperdine.

It is significant that Love, as the first honoree, focused on calling. As Chaplain Emerita, it was fitting for Love to draw on Pepperdine's integration of faith and learning. Love traced her vocational journey from office work to academics and wove a beautiful picture of the winding journey that Pepperdine prizes in the aforementioned essay on calling. She did not shy away from discussing challenges she faced, but she also celebrated allies and champions who supported her along the way. Her talk, like the ones that came after it, displayed Pepperdine's values and its challenges. These keynote addresses evidence the belief that women are called by God to lead and when they answer the call, they enrich the community. In subsequent years, the committee has honored women with a variety of leadership positions—deans, directors, and more. Each one has provided an autobiographical account of her journey and advice for continuing to advance women in leadership at the institution. Some talks have been more academic, others more personal. Some have focused on the elements of good leadership, while others have focused on elements of a good life. Each year, the community adds to the story of excellence in women's leadership at Pepperdine and reshapes its understanding of what is possible. In this way, the award reconceives the ethos of women in leadership at Pepperdine each year by highlighting another example of how the community flourishes when women lead.

RECONSTITUTING THE BOUNDARIES OF WOMEN'S LEADERSHIP

The Committee's work highlights the "ethical and communal dimensions involved in building and performing credibility."[85] They address barriers to women's informal and formal leadership by creating partnerships on issues that benefit the broader university ecosystem. Through their dynamic practices of interrupting tradition, advocating for policy change, relating to one another and the community, and celebrating women leaders, the Committee helps members of the institution "deliberate and 'know together'" what changes may foster communal flourishing.[86] In this way, the Committee does not need to engage questions of credibility directly, particularly questions concerning whether and how women should lead. Instead, they construct an ethos within the existing ideological and institutional boundaries that invites the community to see women lead well. As the community responds to that invitation, the institution becomes a more hospitable dwelling place for everyone.

The Committee has received some pushback, mainly from women concerned that creating a separate space for female faculty fosters division and may impede advancement. While those concerns are understandable, I contend that the rhetorical maneuvers featured in this chapter demonstrate how the Committee foregrounds women's professional success while attending to the ways that advancement is dependent on how the community understands itself. Their policy advocacy and leadership award banquet invite the community to consider how changes to institutional norms benefit everyone. While the mentoring program is for women only, it equips those women to improve their engagement with all members of the community. The Committee's work enables that community to negotiate healthier ways of living out their Christian mission together.

There is always more to do, but in the years since it was created as an ad hoc committee, this group has made great strides in shifting community norms and creating the conditions for leaders to emerge as a natural outgrowth of the Christian mission. Their work to interrupt some traditions while bolstering others has shifted the ethos of women in leadership on campus by demonstrating that women's inclusion enriches the community in a variety of ways.

Dean et al. caution against focusing on identifying problems and looking for others to provide solutions. While this process is often necessary, they also encourage women to "become solution seekers, asking ourselves what are the best practices for developing and practicing academic leadership, and what more may be achieved on our own campuses."[87] The Committee on Women Faculty not only identified challenges but they also actively sought productive solutions.

Michael Hyde explains that "the meaning of ethos points to an essential relationship that exists among the self, communal existence, discourse, Being, and, perhaps, God."[88] The Committee's feminist ecological approach attended to each of these elements as they worked to alter the community and find better ways for people to exist together across differences. Their rhetorical moves attended to existing divisions while simultaneously establishing ground on which to connect and celebrate one another. Their efforts provide one model for bridging the gender gap that persists in academia, particularly on campuses where institutional norms and values make the chasm seem insurmountable.

NOTES

1. Valerie Hobbs, "Characterizations of Feminism in Reformed Christian Online Media." *Journal of Media and Religion* 14, no. 21 (2015): 211–229; Sally K. Gallagher, "Where Are the Antifeminist Evangelicals? Evangelical Identity, Subcultural Location, and Attitudes toward Feminism." *Gender & Society* 18, no. 4 (2004): 451–472; Nicola Hoggard Creegan and Christine D. Pohl, *Living on the Boundaries: Evangelical Women, Feminism, and Theological Academy* (Dawman's Grove, IL: InterVarsity Press, 2005).

2. For challenges in academia broadly, see Kirsti Cole and Holly Hassel, *Surviving Sexism in Academia: Strategies for Feminist Leadership* (New York, NY: Routledge, 2017); and Susan R. Madsen, "Women and Leadership in Higher Education: Current Realities, Challenges, and Future Directions." *Advances in Developing Human Resources* 14, no. 2 (2012): 131–139. For the importance of mission, see: Karen A. Longman and Patricia S. Anderson, "Gender Trends in Senior-Level Leadership: A 12-Year Analysis of the CCCU U.S. Member Institutions." *Christian Higher Education* 10 (2011): 1–22.

3. "Welcome to Pepperdine." Pepperdine University, 2019. https://www.pepperdine.edu/.

4. For shared values, see E. Bruce Harrison and Judith Mühlberg, *Leadership Communication: How Leaders Communicate and How Communicators Lead in Today's Global Enterprise* (Business Experts Press, 2014). For ecological ethos, see Kathleen J. Ryan, Nancy Myers, and Rebecca Jones, *Rethinking Ethos: A Feminist Ecological Approach to Rhetoric* (Carbondale, IL: Southern Illinois University Press, 2016). For dwelling place, see Michael J. Hyde, *The Ethos of Rhetoric* (Columbia, SC: University of South Carolina Press, 2004).

5. Ryan, Myers, and Jones, *Rethinking Ethos*, 3.

6. Hyde, *The Ethos of Rhetoric*, xiii.
7. Ryan, Myers, and Jones, *Rethinking Ethos*, vii.
8. Ibid, 2.
9. Hyde, *The Ethos of Rhetoric*, xvi.
10. Ibid.
11. Thomas W. Benson, "Rhetoric as a Way of Being," in *American Rhetoric: Context and Criticism*, edited by Thomas W. Benson (Carbondale, IL: Southern Illinois University Press, 1989): 293–322.
12. Jansen B. Werner, "Building a Dwelling Place for Justice: Ethos Reinvention in Martin Luther King Jr.'s "Where Do We Go from Here?" *Rhetoric & Public Affairs* 20, no. 1 (2017): 110.
13. Coretta Pittman, "Black Women Writers and the Trouble with *Ethos*: Harriet Jacobs, Billie Holiday, and Sister Souljah." *Rhetoric Society Quarterly* 37, no. 1 (2007): 47.
14. Lorraine Code, *Ecological Thinking: The Politics of Epistemic Location* (New York, NY: Oxford University Press, 2006): 25.
15. Ryan, Myers, and Jones, *Rethinking Ethos*, 5.
16. Ibid., 3.
17. Ibid.
18. Ibid.
19. Association of American Colleges and Universities, "Forty Years of Change: Highlights from the Data." *On Campus with Women* 39, no. 3. Retrieved from: http://archive.aacu.org/ocww/volume39_3/contents.cfm.
20. Madsen, "Women and Leadership in Higher Education."
21. Claire Van Ummersen, "Foreword," in *Women in Academic Leadership: Professional Strategies, Personal Choices*, edited by Diane R. Dean, Susan J. Bracken, and Jeanie K. Allen (Sterling, VA: Stylus, 2009): ix–xii.; Alice H. Eagly and Jean Lau Chin, "Diversity and Leadership in a Changing World." *American Psychologist* 65, no. 3 (2010): 216–224.
22. The White House Project, *The White House Project Report: Benchmarking Women's Leadership* (The White House Project, 2009): 10.
23. The White House Project, *The White House Project Report*.
24. Van Ummersen, "Foreword," ix–xii.
25. Longman and Anderson, "Gender Trends in Senior Level Leadership," 6.
26. Richard T. Hughes, "What Can the Church of Christ Contribute to Higher Education," in *Scholarship, Pepperdine University, and the Legacy of the Churches of Christ: A Primer for Faculty, Staff, and Students*, edited by Richard T. Hughes and Thomas H. Olbricht (Pepperdine University Center for Faith and Learning, 2004): 30.
27. Richard T. Hughes, "Who are the Churches of Christ?" in *Scholarship, Pepperdine University, and the Legacy of the Churches of Christ: A Primer for Faculty, Staff, and Students*, edited by Richard T. Hughes and Thomas H. Olbricht (Pepperdine University Center for Faith and Learning, 2004): 3.
28. Hughes, "Who are the Churches of Christ?" 9–10.
29. Jan Hughes, "Hear My Voice," in *Finding Their Voices: Sermons by Women in the Churches of Christ*, edited by D'Esta Love (Abilene, TX: Abilene Christian University Press, 2015): 15–18.

30. Carol Kuruvilla, "These are the Religious Denominations that Ordain Women." *Huffington Post*, September 26, 2014, https://www.huffpost.com/entry/religion-ordain-women_n_5826422

31. See, for example, Sheila Bost et al., "Women in Roles of Congregational Leadership." *Harbor: Pepperdine Bible Lectures*, April 30–May 3, 2019, https://engage.pepperdine.edu/s/lt-event?id=a2n610000002XCDAA2#Schedule

32. Lindsey Sullivan, "SCEWP Elevates Women to Lead." *Pepperdine University Graphic*, September 5, 2018, http://pepperdine-graphic.com/scewp-elevates-women-to-lead/.

33. Sullivan, "SCEWP Elevates Women to Lead."

34. Pepperdine University, "History of the First University Chaplain." Chaplain Archives, 2019, https://www.pepperdine.edu/spiritual-life/chaplain/about/archives/.

35. Sullivan, "SCEWP Elevates Women to Lead."

36. Maria Valente, "Pepperdine Women Pave the Road of Leadership and Equality." *Pepperdine University Graphic*, February 7, 2018, http://pepperdine-graphic.com/pepperdine-women-pave-road-of-leadership-and-equality/; Office of Institutional Effectiveness, "Fall Semester Census." Pepperdine University, 2017, https://www.pepperdine.edu/oie/institutional-research/page_facultyallinone.htm. The patterns at Pepperdine mirror the national trends described earlier in this chapter.

37. Maire Mullins et al., "Women's Resource Office Proposal." Unpublished. 2009.

38. Ibid., 1.

39. The Women's Resource Office did not ultimately gain traction with administration and donors. Seaver College still does not have anything along these lines. However, Pepperdine did establish a Center for Women in Leadership at its Graziadio Business School. This is an advancement, for sure, but due to the university structure, the influence this center has on students, staff, and faculty at Seaver College is limited.

40. Pepperdine University, "Seaver College," 2019, https://www.pepperdine.edu/academics/schools/seaver/.

41. Over the past five-years 30–40 percent of Seaver College Faculty have identified as members of the Churches of Christ. While faculty at Pepperdine's graduate schools tend to come from other, still mostly Christian, traditions. Office of Institutional Effectiveness, "Fall Semester Census."

42. Maire Mullins, Email. August 27, 2009.

43. Ibid.

44. Committee on Women Faculty, "Meeting Minutes," Meeting of September 18, 2013; Email to the author, February 27, 2014.

45. Catherine D. Clark, and Janeen M. Hill, "Reconciling the Tension Between the Tenure and Biological Clocks to Increase the Recruitment and Retention of Women in Academia." *The Forum on Public Policy*, 2010: 3; Ummersen, "Foreword," ix.

46. Francesca Dominici, Linda P. Fried, and Scott L. Zeger, "So Few Women Leaders: It's No Longer a Pipeline Problem, So What Are the Root Causes?" *Academe* (2009) https://www.aaup.org/article/so-few-women-leaders#.XHcoH3JKhaS.

47. Dominici, Fried, and Zeger, "So Few Women Leaders."

48. Mary Ann Mason, and Marc Goulden, "Do Babies Matter (Part III)?" *Academe* 90, no. 6 (2004).

49. Longman and Anderson, "Gender Trends in Senior Level Leadership," 18.

50. Benevolent sexism is a "subjectively positive orientation toward women that adopts a chivalrous or paternalistic lens." Heather Maldonado and John Draeger, "Surviving Sexism in Academia: Identifying, Understanding, and Responding to Sexism in Academia," in *Surviving Sexism in Academia: Strategies for Feminist Leadership*, edited by Kirsti Cole and Holly Hassel (New York, NY: Routledge, 2016): 6.

51. Seaver College, "Faculty Parental Leave Policy." *Seaver College Faculty Handbook* https://seaver.pepperdine.edu/about/administration/dean/content/faculty/handbook/benefits/faculty-parental-leave-policy.pdf.

52. Seaver College, "Faculty Parental Leave Policy."

53. Ibid.

54. Ibid.

55. Ibid.

56. Ryan, Myers, and Jones. *Rethinking Ethos,* 111.

57. Dean, Bracken, and Allen, *Women in Academic Leadership,* 6.

58. Ryan, Myers, and Jones. *Rethinking Ethos,* 9–13. Ryan, Myers, and Jones rely on Aimee Carillo Rowe's work on feminist alliances to argue that feminist ecological thinking relies on a shift from location to relation-based politics that considers how one group's actions may affect others and works for everyone to flourish.

59. Pepperdine University, "Faculty Dependent Care Travel Initiative," Last modified 2018, https://www.pepperdine.edu/academics/research/facultydependenttravelinitiativepage.htm; Seaver Faculty Association, "Meeting Minutes," Meeting of April 20, 2016, https://community.pepperdine.edu/seaver/sfa/content/sfa-minutes2016-04-20.pdf.

60. Ryan, Myers, and Jones, *Rethinking Ethos,* 9–13.

61. Dominici, Fried, and Zeger, "So Few Women Leaders."

62. Ibid.

63. Emily Blood et al., "Academic Women Faculty: Are They Getting the Mentoring They Need?" *Journal of Women's Health* 21, no. 11 (2012). https://doi.org/10.1089/jwh.2012.3529.

64. Howard Waitzkin et al., "Mentoring Partnerships for Minority Faculty and Graduate Students in Mental Health Services Research." *Academic Psychiatry* 30, no. 3 (2006): 205–217, https://www.ncbi.nlm.nih.gov/pmc/articles/PMC2965353/.

65. Nadine M. Bean, Lisa Lucas, and Lauri Hyers, "Mentoring in Higher Education Should be the Norm to Assure Success: Lessons Learned from the Faculty Mentoring Program, West Chester University, 2008–2011." *Mentoring & Tutoring: Partnership in Learning* 22, no. 1 (2014): 56–73; Mara H. Wasburn, "Mentoring Women Faculty: An Instrumental Case Study of Strategic Collaboration." *Mentoring & Tutoring: Partnership in Learning* 15, no. 1 (2007): 57–72.

66. Mary Dean Sorcinelli, and Jung Yun, "From Mentor to Mentoring Networks: Mentoring in the New Academy." *Change: The Magazine of Higher Learning* 39, no. 6 (2007): 58–61.

67. See Ryan, Myers, and Jones, *Rethinking Ethos,* 12, for more on the connection between Kendall Phillips' work on rhetorical maneuvers and their formulation of a feminist ecological ethos.

68. Bean, Lucas, and Hyers, "Mentoring in Higher Education should be the Norm."

69. Ibid., 58.

70. The assessments revealed that most faculty had experience in one-on-one mentoring prior to joining the program, with varying levels of success. Women came to the pods looking for improvement in all areas—teaching, research, service, institutional awareness, and work-life balance. In the end, most participants showed improvement in these areas and valued the experience. They indicated that they would appreciate a slightly shorter duration for the program and more intentionality in the composition of pod members. Regan Shaffer, and Kendra Killpatrick, "Survey on Mentoring Results," Unpublished, 2015–2016.

71. Kendra Killpatrick, "Committee on Women Faculty 2015 Report," Unpublished, 2015.

72. Regan Shaffer, and Kendra Killpatrick, "Survey on Mentoring Results," Unpublished, 2016.

73. Bean, Lucas, and Hyers, "Mentoring in Higher Education should be the Norm," 58.

74. Ryan, Myers, and Jones, *Rethinking Ethos*, 196.

75. Ibid., 195.

76. Krista Ratcliffe, *Rhetorical Listening: Identification, Gender, Whiteness* (Southern Illinois University Press, 1996): 58–62.

77. Dean, Bracken, and Allen, *Women in Academic Leadership*, 5.

78. Athena Perrakis and Cynthia Martinez, "In Pursuit of Sustainable Leadership: How Female Academic Department Chairs with Children Negotiate Personal and Professional Roles." *Advances in Developing Human Resources* 14, no. 2 (2012): 207.

79. Sarah Hallenbeck and Michelle Smith. "Mapping Topoi in the Rhetorical Gendering of Work." *Peitho Journal* 17, no. 2 (2015): 201.

80. Dominici, Fried, and Zeger, "So Few Women Leaders."

81. Ibid.

82. Dean, Bracken, and Allen, *Women in Academic Leadership*, 5–6.

83. Office of the Provost, email to Seaver Faculty "Nominations for Award for Women in Leadership," October 3, 2017.

84. Andrew Yuengert, email, "Women in Leadership Dinner," February 14, 2014.

85. Kendall Leon and Stacey Pigg, "Conocimiento as a Path to Ethos: Gloria Anzaldúa's Networked Rhetoric," in *Rethinking Ethos: A Feminist Ecological Approach to Rhetoric*, edited by Rebecca Jones, Nancy Myers, and Kathleen J. Ryan (Carbondale, IL: Southern Illinois University Press, 2016): 259.

86. Hyde, *The Ethos of Rhetoric*, xiii.

87. Dean, Bracken, and Allen, *Women in Academic Leadership*, 6.

88. Hyde, *The Ethos of Rhetoric*, xiiv.

BIBLIOGRAPHY

Association of American Colleges and Universities. "Forty Years of Change: Highlights from the Data." *On Campus with Women* 39, no. 3. Retrieved from: http://archive.aacu.org/ocww/volume39_3/contents.cfm.

Bean, Nadine M., Lisa Lucas, and Lauri Hyers. "Mentoring in Higher Education Should be the Norm to Assure Success: Lessons Learned from the Faculty Mentoring Program, West Chester University, 2008–2011." *Mentoring & Tutoring: Partnership in Learning* 22, no. 1 (2014): 56–73. doi: 10.1080/13611267.2014.882606.

Benson, Thomas W. "Rhetoric as a Way of Being." In *American Rhetoric: Context and Criticism*, edited by Thomas W. Benson, 293–322. Carbondale, IL: Southern Illinois University Press, 1989.

Blood, Emily, Nicole J. Ullrich, Dina R. Hirshfeld-Becker, Ellen W. Seely, Maureen T. Connelly, Carol A. Warfield, and S. Jean Emans. "Academic Women Faculty: Are They Getting the Mentoring They Need?" *Journal of Women's Health* 21, no. 11 (2012). https://doi.org/10.1089/jwh.2012.3529.

Bost, Sheila, Amy Bost Henegar, Thomas Robinson, and Elizabeth Smith. "Women in Roles of Congregational Leadership." *Harbor: Pepperdine Bible Lectures*, April 30–May 3, 2019. https://engage.pepperdine.edu/s/lt-event?id=a2n610000002XCDAA2#Schedule.

Code, Lorraine. *Ecological thinking: The Politics of Epistemic Location*. New York, NY: Oxford University Press, 2006.

Cole, Kirsti, and Holly Hassel. *Surviving Sexism in Academia: Strategies for Feminist Leadership*. New York, NY: Routledge, 2017.

Creegan, Nicola Hoggard, and Christine D. Pohl. *Living on the Boundaries: Evangelical Women, Feminism, and the Theological Academy*. Downers Grove, IL: InterVarsity Press, 2005.

Dean, Diane R., Susan J. Bracken, and Jeanie K. Allen. *Women in Academic Leadership: Professional Strategies, Personal Choice*. Sterling, VA: Stylus, 2009.

Dominici, Francesca, Linda P. Fried, and Scott L. Zeger. "So Few Women Leaders: It's No Longer a Pipeline Problem, So What Are the Root Causes?" *Academe* (2009) https://www.aaup.org/article/so-few-women-leaders#.XHcoH3JKhaS.

Eagly, Alice H., and Jean Lau Chin. "Diversity and Leadership in a Changing World." *American Psychologist* 65, no. 3 (2010): 216–224. doi: 10.1037/a0018957.

Gallagher, Sally K. "Where are the Antifeminist Evangelicals? Evangelical Identity, Subcultural Location, and Attitudes toward Feminism." *Gender & Society* 18, no. 4 (2004): 451–472. https://doi.org/10.1177%2F0891243204266157.

Hallenbeck, Sarah, and Michelle Smith. "Mapping Topoi in the Rhetorical Gendering of Work." *Peitho Journal* 17, no. 2 (2015): 200–225. http://peitho.cwshrc.org/files/2015/09/17HallenbeckSmith.pdf.

Harrison, E. Bruce, and Judith Mühlberg. *Leadership Communication: How Leaders Communicate and How Communicators Lead in Today's Global Enterprise*. New York, NY: Business Expert Press, 2014.

Hobbs, Valerie. "Characterizations of Feminism in Reformed Christian Online Media." *Journal of Media and Religion* 14, no. 21 (2015): 211–229. doi: 10.1080/15348423.2015.1116267.

Hughes, Jan. "Hear My Voice." In *Finding Their Voices: Sermons by Women in the Churches of Christ*, edited by D'Esta Love, 15–18. Abilene, TX: Abilene Christian University Press, 2015.

Hughes, Richard T., and Thomas H. Olbricht. *Scholarship, Pepperdine University, and the Legacy of Churches of Christ.* Malibu, CA: Pepperdine Center for Faith and Learning, 2004.

Hyde, Michael J. *The Ethos of Rhetoric.* Columbia, SC: University of South Carolina Press, 2004.

Kuruvilla, Carol. "These are the Religious Denominations that Ordain Women." *Huffington Post,* September 26, 2014. https://www.huffpost.com/entry/religion-ordain-women_n_5826422.

Longman, Karen A., and Patricia S. Anderson. "Gender Trends in Senior-Level Leadership: A 12-Year Analysis of the CCCU U.S. Member Institutions." *Christian Higher Education* 10 (2011): 1–22. doi: 10.1080/15363759.2011.559874.

Madsen, Susan R. "Women and Leadership in Higher Education: Current Realities, Challenges, and Future Directions." *Advances in Developing Human Resources* 14, no. 2 (2012): 131–139. doi: 10.1177/1523422311436299.

Maldonado, Heather, and John Draeger. "Surviving Sexism in Academia: Identifying, Understanding, and Responding to Sexism in Academia." In *Surviving Sexism in Academia: Strategies for Feminist Leadership,* edited by Kirsti Cole and Holly Hassel. New York, NY: Routledge, 2017, 5–12.

Mason, Mary Ann, and Marc Goulden. "Do Babies Matter (Part III)?" *Academe* 90, no. 6 (2004). http://www.jstor.org/stable/40252699?origin=JSTOR-pdf.

Mullins, Maire, Larissa Hamada, Jeff Banks, and Andrea Harris. "Women's Resource Office Proposal." Unpublished, 2009.

Office of Institutional Effectiveness. "Fall Semester Census." Pepperdine University, 2017. https://www.pepperdine.edu/oie/institutional-research/page_facultyallinone.htm.

Pepperdine University. "History of the First University Chaplain." Chaplain Archives, 2019. https://www.pepperdine.edu/spiritual-life/chaplain/about/archives/.

Pepperdine University. "Seaver College." Last modified 2019. https://www.pepperdine.edu/academics/schools/seaver/.

Pepperdine University. "Welcome to Pepperdine." Last modified 2019. https://www.pepperdine.edu/.

Perrakis, Athena, and Cynthia Martinez. "In Pursuit of Sustainable Leadership: How Female Academic Department Chairs with Children Negotiate Personal and Professional Roles." *Advances in Developing Human Resources* 14, no. 2 (2012): 205–220. https://doi.org/10.1177%2F1523422312436417.

Pittman, Coretta. "Black Women Writers and the Trouble with *Ethos*: Harriet Jacobs, Billie Holiday, and Sister Souljah." *Rhetoric Society Quarterly* 37, no. 1 (2007): 43–70. https://doi.org/10.1080/02773940600860074.

Ratcliffe, Krista. *Rhetorical Listening: Identification, Gender, Whiteness.* Carbondale, IL: Southern Illinois University Press, 2005.

Ryan, Kathleen J., Nancy Myers, and Rebecca Jones. *Rethinking Ethos: A Feminist Ecological Approach to Rhetoric.* Carbondale, IL: Southern Illinois University Press, 2016.

Seaver College. "Faculty Parental Leave Policy." *Seaver College Faculty Handbook.* https://seaver.pepperdine.edu/about/administration/dean/content/faculty/handbook/benefits/faculty-parental-leave-policy.pdf.

Selby, Gary. "Finding Your Heart's True Calling," *Exploring Vocation.* Pepperdine Center for Faith and Learning.

Sorcinelli, Mary Dean, and Jung Yun. "From Mentor to Mentoring Networks: Mentoring in the New Academy." *Change: The Magazine of Higher Learning* 39, no. 6 (2007): 58–61.

Sullivan, Lindsey. "SCEWP Elevates Women to Lead." *Pepperdine University Graphic*, September 5, 2018. http://pepperdine-graphic.com/scewp-elevates-women-to-lead/.

Valente, Maria. "Pepperdine Women Pave the Road of Leadership and Equality." *Pepperdine University Graphic*, February 7, 2018. http://pepperdine-graphic.com/pepperdine-women-pave-road-of-leadership-and-equality/.

Van Ummersen, Claire. "Foreword." In *Women in Academic Leadership: Professional Strategies, Personal Choices*, edited by Diane R. Dean, Susan J. Bracken, and Jeanie K. Allen. Sterling, VA: Stylus, 2009: ix–xii.

Waitzkin, Howard, Joel Yager, Tassy Parker, and Bonnie Duran. "Mentoring Partnerships for Minority Faculty and Graduate Students in Mental Health Services Research." *Academic Psychiatry* 30, no. 3 (2006): 205–217. https://www.ncbi.nlm.nih.gov/pmc/articles/PMC2965353/.

Wasburn, Mara H. "Mentoring Women Faculty: An Instrumental Case Study of Strategic Collaboration." *Mentoring & Tutoring: Partnership in Learning* 15, no. 1 (2007): 57–72. https://doi.org/10.1080/13611260601037389.

Werner, Jansen B. "Building a Dwelling Place for Justice: Ethos Reinvention in Martin Luther King Jr.'s 'Where Do We Go from Here'?" *Rhetoric & Public Affairs* 20, no. 1 (2017): 109–132. doi: 10.14321/rhetpublaffa.20.1.0109.

The White House Project. *The White House Project Report: Benchmarking Women's Leadership.* Washington DC: The White House Project, 2009.

Chapter 10

Contemplating Leadership
Struggles, Transformation, and Transcendence
Mary E. Wildner-Bassett

The goal of this paper is to incite awareness, contemplative inquiry, and experiential reflection about leadership, gender, and power in academic settings. The means for achieving this goal are to understand the processes used by women for living the challenges of leadership for women in the academy. The objective is to revisit the ways of knowing, of narrative, and of being that women bring to leadership positions. While several chapters in this volume address both the barriers and the successes of women in leadership, I base my paradigm on exploring and understanding some responses to the question of "why?" on those who have published various kinds of excellent analyses before me.[1]

What I hope to add here is a new synthesis of approaches to leadership development for women in academic settings. This synthesis is based on several sources.[2] First, I will explore the life pathways of women in academe and in alternative academic contexts who primarily hail from the "silent generation," those born from 1928 to 1945, who are seventy years old or more at this writing.[3] These in-depth explorations include acknowledging the various ways these women broke through or transgressed many boundaries as they reveal their stories—perhaps even more boundaries than women today must face. They were and are effective leaders, sociable, assertive individuals who are to this day open to new ideas and who are conscientious, honest, and trustworthy.[4] The larger project includes summaries of reflections, pathways for understanding, even wisdom ways of knowing, all informed by life stories and struggles of women who have amazing life journeys. What we learn from these women and their lives lies in their insights and perseverance as they transcend their challenges, pain, and struggles. We also learn a lot about how creating their own, unexpected journeys can be the best pathway to leadership and to creating a fulfilling life. In addition to their own versions of true success, these women embody joy, fun, wisdom, and depths of spirituality, commitment, and emotion that are beacons of light and living. Rather than thinking about various theories of leadership in general, as important as they are, we will make this exploration one where we can integrate the "heart, head, and hands" of women's lives and leadership.[5]

There were and are, of course, also barriers and struggles to overcome. The project's process is to elicit rich descriptions from individual women's narratives and interpretations of their own personal experience and life stories. This gives us the opportunity to learn directly from these women about their various approaches to the practice and experience of leadership in many different areas of professional life.[6]

In addition, their own descriptions of their personal approaches and practices of leadership include a deep focus on layers of "transcendence" that are revealed in their narratives. Applying this deeper understanding, along with various characteristics of contemplative inquiry, supports the discovery of possible responses to this "why?" question. Features of this paradigm may give rise to new ways of knowing, researching, and being. They can thus enhance our understanding of some responses to the "why?" questions surrounding women's lives and leadership.[7]

Furthermore, it became clear during the process of this inquiry that addressing some insights about transcendence revealed in the narratives could lead to an interpretation based on "transcendent realism."[8] This approach includes important paradigmatic ideals such as: (1) *Ontology (what is real?):* the possibility of an objective reality . . . that transcends our discovered, constructed, interpreted, and/or transformed understandings of this reality which could be defined in terms suggesting spirit or energy. (2) *Epistemology (how do we know?):* can be revealed as well as discovered and constructed and can include an acceptance of what is seemingly nonrational, that is, not having direct cause-effect connections, or could be apparently or temporarily mysterious as indicative of transcendence. (3) *Methodology (how do we find out?):* here we note that researcher practice transcends cognitive activity to include embodied and/or emotional knowledge centers; willingness to receive revealed knowledge or intuitive insights; co-constructed with peers and with [the] transcendent. . . (4) *Axiology (what does it mean and ethical limits?):* Research findings used as a tool for immediate and apparent ends [such as improving various contexts of and pathways to women's leadership], as well as for ends that transcend this time and space.[9]

This is, then, an example of *contemplative inquiry* used to explore and interpret the richness of the stories of women's pathways and lives in leadership and transcendence. This transcendence is based on possibilities rather than certainties, and a paradigm that is flexible enough to explore principles of contemplative inquiry from multiple perspectives.[10] Drawing connections among women's lives and leadership, transcendence, and what we so often refer to, in various understandings and applications, as active "wisdom."[11] In these ways, we can explore what can be learned with this research paradigm to begin further reenvisioning education for leadership. That education may include the necessity of "embodied pathways" to and inspired by wisdom that can lead to further social transformation.[12]

"BOSSY DAMES": LEADERSHIP AND GENDER IN ACADEME

Leadership has often been described as synonymous with meaning-making and as the "management of meaning."[13] In addition, all leadership communication is essentially intercultural.[14] Each of us, in any organization or any interaction where meaning is created and managed, engages in collaboration that relies on both predictable and unpredictable connections to contexts/cultures of meaning. These are intrapersonal, interpersonal, social, organizational, and transcultural.

It is very common in almost any context to assume that those in leadership positions have power. The old saw that "with great power comes great responsibility" is, though, much more about responsibility than any glories of power. In institutions of higher education, generally, there is usually great responsibility attached to a very questionable level of the ability to make changes that are connected to the institutional levels beyond our immediate context. Again, there are contexts and cultures of leadership responsibility that are connected to leadership positions and at the same time beyond their influence in intrapersonal, interpersonal, social, organizational, and transcultural ways.

These general ideas concerning leadership lead us to remember that some issues concerned with leadership in academe also lead to separate and not-always-equal thoughts about gendered leadership in academe. In the 2018 Convention of the Modern Language Association (MLA), a panel was organized under the title of "Bossy Dames," and I borrow that title, with the intent of eliciting a smile from our readers, as well as underscoring the awareness that is the focus of this entire volume: communication with and about women in leadership positions. More importantly, we want to discuss how best to develop leadership goals and accomplishments for those women, especially, who might be contemplating these possibilities. As mentioned in the introduction, these discussions are also generally informed by the interviews described there, and by ethnographic/auto-ethnographic analyses of them.

It is helpful to describe women's and others' contexts in the academy in terms of gender and power by beginning with a definition of power as related to control and ascendancy. The claim is that while many academics would claim little or no interested in such an authoritarian view of power, as one scholar has described it, that "all academics inhabit institutions shaped by the hierarchies of professor and student, tenured and untenured."[15] She goes on to explain how our academic structures equate authority with superiority, and she points out that the ranks of full professors, college presidents, deans, and provosts are dominantly filled with White males. Her point is that "everyone belonging to that group, no matter their actual level of achievement, starts to have superiority attributed to them."[16]

If we look at leadership theory for a moment, authentic leaders are those whose talk and actions are as consistent with their beliefs and values as possible. Authentic women leaders in academe, then, or we "bossy dames," will most often have an applied theory of leadership that strives to be consistent with our beliefs and values. At the same time, as we learned in the interview project and from our own experience, it is most likely that women leaders' beliefs and values may be at odds with some or even most of the common assumptions about power and leadership in academic and other contexts. Our first experiences of facing being "at odds" is the fact that we are female. The effects of this simple fact of being female mean that "we know that women academics sometimes face unique challenges to their entry and advancement in the academic profession, among them inequities in salary and promotion rates, sexual harassment, and discriminatory treatment."[17]

I'll return to these points about "bossy dames" and the overall context below, in the segment on the importance of both sharing and critical analysis of narrative knowledge.

SEXUALITY, GENDER, AND POWER IN ACADEME

I proceed here with another quote from a recent article in the *Chronicle of Higher Education* series "The Awakening: Women and Power in Academe," cited above. Maggie Doherty wrote the following there:

> When it comes to "women and power in the academy," my first thought is: "We have none." This has been clear to me for the last 10 years, since the day I entered a doctoral program in English. At the time, the department had only a few female tenured faculty members. I was 22, fresh from undergrad, and, as a child of the "girl power" 1990s, entirely unused to the idea that anyone would take me less seriously simply because I was not a man.[18]

Power can mean getting things done. Women do very well with that kind of power. Power can also mean strength and capacity, which tend to grow when one's achievements are recognized and valued. By this definition, women in the academy aren't doing so well. As has been documented in abundance, female faculty receive lower pay, fewer promotions, and fewer honors than their male counterparts. Yet, everyone seems to know how to find a female academic when it comes to requesting a letter of recommendation, finding an adviser, or seeking advice. Just at the beginning of October 2018, Donna Strickland, University of Waterloo, Canada, was one of the three people to receive the Nobel Prize in Physics. She is an associate professor there. Strickland's job title struck many observers as further evidence of the inequality of career paths walked by men and women in the academy. In other words, some have commented, even a Nobel Prize isn't enough to allow a woman to ascend to academe's highest level of job descriptions.

One thing my colleagues and I have been thinking about lately is the importance of realizing that some of us have power over others, even when it doesn't seem or feel that way. This is pertinent both to those who are powerless in some or even many relationships, and yet they might not realize that they have power in other situations or relationships. This idea might also seem moot or illusory to those who have been removed from any actual experience of relative powerlessness for a long time, so it doesn't occur to them to acknowledge power relations as a real and present background issue in nearly every interaction.

I would like to include here the comments of an advanced graduate student to give voice to this issue from another perspective. Her comments also connect to my next segment about sexual or gender harassment and academe. I have her permission to use these comments. They were made in an online discussion in our PAH-SLAT (Public and Applied Humanities-Second Language Acquisition and Teaching) 570 course on program leadership in postsecondary institutions. Her name is Emily Jo Schwaller.

> After reading through the *Awakening* articles, there were various themes I began to recognize: . . . intersectionality is something we continually need to address in academia; . . . and micro-aggressions are present, real and foster uncomfortable cultures in higher education, [often] leading to macro-aggressions.
> The hardest piece for me to swallow in these narratives was Dreger's piece "Power Is Hot, Let's Admit It." . . . Her point about attraction and taking ownership over the body is important but I also think she misses moments of intersectionality when she doesn't discuss the able body or the vulnerability of graduate students. . . . I think our continual avoidance of uncomfortable topics does a disservice—but also not allowing people to be uncomfortable . . . does a disservice. I am constantly sexualized as a woman who is small and "cute" (according to my Teacher Evaluations), and . . . I feel deeply manipulated by those in power. I wonder if power would feel so sexy if we were the ones who actually had it. What would it look like if people of color or other under-represented groups had

power? Would the attraction still be there? Would we, after years of oppression, feel entitled in the same way as men? I don't think the constant sexualization of humans is necessary or . . . appropriate. . . . I think being aware of power dynamics and sexuality is important. . . . Part of owning your sexuality is defining who gets to be in charge of it and I hate the idea that just by existing in an [academic] space I am up for grabs (pun intended).

She continues, "This entire semester I have been overwhelmed with the sudden realization of what it means to be a woman in academia, and further what it has meant in the past. I am now starting to reflect back on some of the horrifying inequalities that have shaped my education and thus my person." Thank you, Ms. Schwaller.

SEXUAL OR GENDER HARASSMENT AND NARRATIVE KNOWING

In the fall of 2018, the country took part, willingly or unwillingly, in an experience of national trauma with the details of the concerns about Brett Kavanaugh's appointment to the U.S. Supreme Court. For the first time, a whole nation of women, and many men, were triggered about a narrative of sexual abuse or even assault, and many found themselves not afraid to speak up with their own narratives. As reported in the *New York Times*,[19]

> Twitter exploded on September 21, 2018, with tweets tagged #WhyIDidntReport. The tweeters—mostly women—shared intimate stories of assault and harassment, and detailed why they had not reported the incidents to the police or other law-enforcement authorities. Advocates for victims of sexual assault say they choose not to report for myriad reasons, especially on a college campus, where official procedures and social life often add new layers of complicated concerns about reporting. As cited in the same article, several different studies suggest that as many as 20 percent of women who attend residential campuses are victims of sexual assault, and the vast majority don't report the experience.
>
> Alternative approaches to traditional reporting start with the offender admitting responsibility and agreeing to repair the harm. This can appeal to some students who aren't interested in seeing someone suspended or expelled. Proponents see alternative resolution agreements as a way to cut down on Title IX investigations, save colleges money, and potentially be fairer to the accused. But skeptics worry students will feel pressured to bypass a formal investigation and will regret it later on if offenders get off too easily. And asking a student to sit down with an assailant and work out an agreement is not only unrealistic, they argue, but possibly retraumatizing.

Here at the University of Arizona, some of us have learned from victims we know that even after reporting, there are many hurdles and many instances of potential retraumatizing. I have heard from those involved that a student who had been raped had found some resources here on campus, but that it was and is very difficult to navigate and even get information about where and how to report and get help. For example, the victim must come up with her (or his) own cash to co-pay for pay or some medical or psychological therapeutic care and especially STD testing, even in the campus health center. Many don't report because they have heard stories of those who are retraumatized in this and many other ways.

As these and other reports indicate, though, one way of transcending or living beyond these extremely difficult experiences and the difficulties of their aftermath is to tell the stories. The #MeToo movement and the more recent #WhyIDidntReport responses to the details surrounding the Kavanaugh case have begun to create cultural and even global changes in our respect for the healing power of narrating our experiences as women in leadership positions. Narrative ways of knowing add to our abilities to understand our individual and collective experiences. They help us to transcend or heal at least some of the most traumatic residue and, with time, to engage with the experiences as meaning-making in our lives. This kind of engagement with meaningfulness is also an essential attribute for developing and honing leadership skills, especially for women who are so often subject to negative or even traumatic experiences in the workplace and beyond. As we've seen, academic settings are no exception.

#METOO AND ACADEME, ESPECIALLY AVITAL RONELL, JUDITH BUTLER, AND THE MLA

In May of 2018, an article in the *Washington Post* reported that a growing number of former students and faculty colleagues had stepped forward in recent months to accuse tenured professors of sexual harassment and, in some cases, sexual assault. These women are now demanding a reckoning for long-hidden incidents they say left them scared, scarred, and disillusioned. Some of these accounts targeted eminent faculty members at Harvard University, the University of Virginia, and other prominent schools. One recent case, though, is both high profile and unusual: Avital Ronell, a world-renowned female professor of German and Comparative Literature at New York University, was found responsible for sexually harassing a male former graduate student, Nimrod Reitman. After its investigation, the university found that Ronell's conduct was "sufficiently pervasive to alter the terms and conditions of Mr. Reitman's learning environment" and suspended her for the upcoming academic year.[20]

Coming in the middle of the #MeToo movement's accounting about sexual misconduct, it raised a challenge for some—how to respond when a woman behaved badly. And the response extended through many parts of academia. Among those who publicly came to Ronell's defense were a number of well-known academics, led by Judith Butler. In a draft letter, which was ultimately published in draft form, the professors admitted that they did not know all details of the case.

In an apology published on in the *Chronicle of Higher Education*, the author writes the following:[21]

> The letter was written in haste and the following are my current regrets about it. First, we ought not to have attributed motives to the complainant, even though some signatories had strong views on this matter. The claims of sexual harassment have too often been dismissed by discrediting the complainant, and that nefarious tactic has stopped legitimate claims from going forward and exacerbated the injustice. When and where such a claim proves to be illegitimate, it should be demonstrated on the basis of the evidence alone.
>
> Second, we should not have used language that implied that Ronell's status and reputation earn her differential treatment of any kind. Status ought to have no bearing on the adjudication of sexual harassment. All faculty should be treated the same under Title IX protocols, that is, subject to the same rules and, where justified, sanctions.
>
> Immediately after the confidential draft letter was published online, "I [Judith Butler] was in direct communication with the MLA officers (the executive director, the president and the first vice president) to apologize for the listing of my position within the organization after my name. I acknowledged that I should not have allowed the MLA affiliation to go forward with my name." Paula Krebs, executive director of the MLA, has previously confirmed that the organization accepted her apology. The MLA recognizes the "power disparity between faculty members and graduate students, and we affirm our strong commitment to graduate student rights and welfare and to academic professional rights and responsibilities. Those commitments will not change."

TELLING OUR STORIES

The statement that follows has been very influential both on this contribution and on my larger project described in the introduction of this chapter: "The significance of creating strategies for women from diverse backgrounds to give birth to their own voices, to hear and learn from each other, and to learn how to be heard by all, including by coworkers and by those in the seats of power who might not be listening."[22] This approach shows us all how vital it is to let all of our voices flourish, to hear and learn from each other, and to explore some best practices for being heard. In fact, these goals are the reason for this collection of essays on the theme that is its title, in addition to the book-length project by this author.

Encouraging and expanding narrative knowledge is one essential part of what we do in the humanities, the social sciences, and in many other fields.

In discussing what is characterized as the "narrative turn" in research, Butler-Kisber outlines an increasing dissatisfaction with reality being seen as purely dominated by "scientific" law and facts.[23] She notes that "Researchers demanded that the human element in their work warranted recognition,"[24] a tension that extends throughout the development of modern science. Within the broad parameters of qualitative research, the various approaches to narrative are appreciated as providing more detail of complex human situations and of the fine distinctions that can be made between situational factors.[25]

In this discussion, intended as a contribution to the body of work about developing women leaders in the academy through enhanced communication strategies, I want to emphasize and give a few examples of narrative knowledge here.[26] These comments are intended to explicate the relationships between leadership development, communication, and especially narrative knowledge as an important possibility for giving meaning and meaningfulness to experiences of women in academe. Just as important is encouraging us all to use the narrative knowledge gained in leadership development:[27]

Leaders' life stories are organized around the themes [that include] . . . leadership development as a natural process . . . ; leadership development out of struggle—enduring a crucible experience or by overcoming challenges; leadership development as finding a cause—often through relating one's own challenges to wider social needs or injustice; leadership development as learning from experience—from failures or role models.[28]

This integrative spiral theory of leadership development is the one I embrace because, among its many positive contributions, it also best describes my own story. It includes surprises of many kinds, upward and downward spirals, and feelings of both incompetence and hard-earned competence in specific areas over time. I use my own narrative as one of many similar illustrations of women's work in academe and our often nonlinear movement to leadership positions. The communication strategies, both failed and successful, that accompany these movements, will follow my description of the spiral I traveled as it masquerades as an apparently linear outline in the mode of a simplest academic CV.

My story includes, in the shortest sense, my progress along these curves in the spiral refers to:[29]

- Beginnings as an assistant professor and at the same time becoming a mother of three children in four and a half years

- Promotion to associate professor after regular tenure-track time—youngest child was 3 years old then
- Work with several other women to establish a still thriving interdisciplinary PhD program in Second Language Acquisition and Teaching (SLAT) in its earliest years
- Becoming director of graduate studies for that program, with sixty PhD students at the time
- Asked to be a department chair—served in that role for four years
- Establishing, with the department, a transcultural PhD program during my service as department chair
- Asked to be interim dean of a College of Humanities in a large, land-grant, Research I University
- Transitioning to an appointment as permanent dean of the College of Humanities (COH) for a total of eight years
- Stepping down from the deanship at my own initiative, and back to full-time professor position
- Engaging in the recovery phase of post-deanship.

This is my CV-level story. Several important narrative landmarks and directional changes are missing there, though. It leaves out the harassment and conscious or unconscious misogyny by many colleagues and superiors that accompanied me throughout this journey. Even as dean, one of five female deans among a group of seventeen deans on our large campus, there were harassment-level comments and actions by many colleagues and upper administrators, by both men and women in those roles. The other women deans experienced similar or worse anti-female dean commentary and actions, including lower pay, comments about clothing choices, negative comparisons including some about an alleged "Hillary Clinton complex," sometimes brutal bullying, or "mansplaining" to us about how to run our colleges by some who had never served as department heads or deans. We women deans created our own mutual support group to share our stories and strategies.

My goal for this narrative is to reiterate the importance of both the sharing and a critical analysis of narrative knowledge. Stories are about power. They demand that we ask questions like these: Whose story counts? Who owns the story? What voices or stories go unheard? Do these stories silence other stories? Which ones? Are there stories from marginalized communities? Are there stories that challenge the social or institutional power structures? How do we best communicate our stories, and other, to have the best opportunities for those narratives to be heard and to contribute to new or deeper ways of knowing?[30]

One response to those many questions is this: a key is developing leaders by encouraging and practicing the skills of simultaneously listening to multiple levels of narratives—the individual and the social, the personal and the institutional. This is a set of necessary communication strategies for us to develop if we are to engage with the social and political underpinnings of leadership in academe and of narrative acts about leadership. This can enhance our abilities to think about our responsibilities in both telling and witnessing narratives from the margins. Topics concerning gender and power in academe and beyond are rife with opportunities to ask and respond to these and other questions.

TRANSCENDENCE

Not only in my own narrative, but also in many of the stories from those women leaders whom I have interviewed, our struggles most often included some suffering and recovery. Transcendence—above and beyond disregard, shaming, disbelief in our skills and fortitude, and various versions of what we still call a "glass ceiling" or even a "glass cage"—was part of all of our journeys, too. These struggles are still very present. The pathways to leadership are convoluted and complex. There were many moments of being surprised by these labyrinthine pathways as we made our way to a place of leadership that often transcended all expectations. These are the themes that women leaders return to often when they are asked to describe their path to a particular leadership position in academia or in "alt-ac" (alternatives to academia) contexts.

My own evolving focus on the complex spiral of "composing a life" and a "further life [in] the age of active wisdom" development gradually became a primary metaphor for individual narratives and the ensuing analyses and discussions.[31] These included the complex dynamic systems that are related to leadership by women in various contexts, to the way that we center our understandings and experiences in language and reflection, and the additional layers of complexity that relate to contemplative inquiry and transcendence for each of the individuals involved as we move toward an "age of wisdom."[32] All three descriptors are important: *dynamic* as not-static and not occurring just one time, but iterative at different levels and types of development for different aspects and different ways of knowing; *nonlinear* in that the developments and additions of narrative ways of knowing for different times of life and opportunities for leadership and transcendence are spiraled and complex; and *systematic*, in that even what seems chaotic or overwhelming or garbled, at any one phase or time frame, will move out of chaos into newly organized levels and ways of knowing and being.

Throughout the experiential engagement with the individual narratives, each aspect of the process included inquiry that we understood, implicitly or explicitly, to be contemplative, reflexive, and always already emergent. The processes are self-organizing and based on different ways of knowing brought to the process by individuals in local relationships. The contexts were embedded in ever-changing external environments that were always colored by gendered interactional constraints, and thus influenced by positive or negative feedback that had amplifying or dampening effects.[33]

All of us who were participants in this project included in our narratives many instances of "narratively structured, liminal, existential spaces" in our recounting of the compositions of our lives and leadership experiences in their many iterations. We all reflected on and shared in the narratives the way that the liminal and often existential spaces we recalled and storied led to transcendence of a particular situation, mind-set, or more. That transcendence very often led, in dynamic, nonlinear ways, to leadership situations. Reflecting, individually and then together, on these moments of dynamic, nonlinear transcendence from a stance of contemplative inquiry, led us to see how these results came about. By virtue of this collaborative, contemplative inquiry, we can cocreate new and deeper narrative ways of knowing. We know now that these compositions of leadership in the world where women of maturity were rarely seen in such roles were unexpectedly *systematic*. What seemed chaotic, overwhelming, or garbled at any one phase or time frame for any one individual had in fact moved out of chaos into newly organized levels and ways of knowing and being.

TRANSCENDING, THE LIMINAL, AND WISDOM

In the spirit, then, of exploring and understanding the question of wisdom and its relation to the focus of this chapter, it is worthwhile to engage in a short explication of what we pursued together in this collaborative contemplative inquiry. This effort is certainly not the first one to want to dig deeper into what wisdom, life experience, and the pathways walked by those in the "age of active wisdom" might have to teach the next group walking similar pathways.[34] There is a focus on women's pathways to leadership positions as follows:

> [We] invoke a labyrinth metaphor throughout the book to symbolize the situations that women face as leaders and potential leaders . . . the labyrinth conveys the idea of a complex journey that entails challenges and offers a goal worth striving for. Passage through a labyrinth is not simple or direct, but requires persistence, awareness of one's progress, and a careful analysis of the puzzles that lie ahead . . . passing through a labyrinth is more demanding than traveling a straight path. Thus, the labyrinth provides an encouraging metaphor for aspiring women and recognition of the challenges that these women face.[35]

The "wisdom way of knowing" is a foundational work that contributes the insight that focuses on life pathways that can increase "our receptivity to higher meaning" and a "way of knowing that goes beyond one's mind, one's rational understanding, and embraces the whole of a person: mind, heart, and body."[36] There is a "study not of old age or even of late adulthood but rather of the ways in which the extended period of health and activity achieved by modern science fits into a lifetime, and of the potential contributions that period can make to human society," where "wisdom is combined with activity and often with activism for the common good."[37]

All of these authors write important and foundational contributions to our understanding of the question that is wisdom.[38] What this project seeks to expand on is connected to all of these contributions and many others, and with it we hope to add to some emergent understandings of wisdom for women in leadership by making some further connections. In the larger study, we explore how contemplative and collaborative auto-ethnography can deepen and further help us understand the wisdom questions posed by women, especially women leaders in academic or alternative academic careers from the "silent generation" mentioned above. We delve further into wisdom ways of knowing by an additional contemplative focus on transcending limits or transgressing boundaries that time, place, race, and gender imposed on these women. We acknowledge throughout the discussion that this contemplative inquiry is taking place in a complex tapestry of raced and gendered histories and practices, and that we are transcending and transgressing even as we engage in the "mutual construction of otherness in social and self-formation."[39] We explore how these boundaries, and the transcending of them, defined these women's labyrinthine progress along the pathways they followed to leadership and to transcendent and wisdom ways of knowing.

In order to expand into that deeper investigation of wisdom ways of knowing, another kind of transcending or transgressing of boundaries of research into the question of women's pathways to leadership is necessary. Here is an explanation of the transgressions and transcending of more typical research paradigms and investigative processes as follows:[40]

> [I recommend] . . . a holistic model and set of approaches to conducting humanities research and in interpreting reality that also typically include both quantitative and qualitative methods. [This approach] . . . is also open to include individual experience and perception as tools for cognizing and interpreting the world. The term "inner awareness" refers . . . to knowledge about oneself that is not limited to one's physical, mental, or emotional dimensions, but comes about as one's inner consciousness awakens. It involves a more holistic concept and approach that incorporates conscious awareness of oneself as a unique individual, but also as a being in relationship with all other forms of existence. . . . Ultimately, the more preconceptions one carries into the investigative process,

the less one is likely to actually expand one's overall awareness or awaken one's consciousness of the more essential aspects of reality.[41]

So the process of transcending boundaries and entering a liminal space for contemplative inquiry using collaborative auto-ethnographic approaches involved letting go of as many preconceptions as possible. We have a goal of maintaining overall awareness and even of awakening our individual and mutual consciousness to more essential aspects of wisdom ways of knowing and women's lives in leadership and service. This kind of research approach can inhabit liminal space.[42] His description is indeed an apt one for the process of the in-depth auto-ethnographic explorations we all undertook as this work evolved and grew.

> [Our intention is] . . . to include an openness to utilizing and integrating additional methods of learning and experience found within diverse subjects of study as well as approaches that inspire conscious expansion of the researcher as part of the process . . . those using a spiritual research paradigm are typically open to, or even seeking, personal inner growth as integral to the process. . . . What is relevant is that the researcher seeks to move beyond passively observing the world being studied and *instead seeks to experientially cognize it and grow from the process*.[43]

This description of contemplative inquiry echoes what was written more than a decade before in the description of the wisdom way of knowing already referenced above.[44] There, the author discussed the liminal space of transcending a more limited cognitive center for knowing by moving into what she refers to as three-centered knowing.[45] She describes the center of intellectual or cognitive intelligence, the "moving center" or physical, embodied intelligence that carries and expresses knowledge not always directly accessible by rational cognition, and the emotional center. She goes on to show the ways that a mature emotional center can express a "reconciling" force: "It serves as a bridge between the mind and the body and also between our usual physical world and [the transcendent]. When properly attuned, the emotional center's most striking capacity, lacking in the mind alone, is the ability to comprehend the language of paradox."[46]

CONCLUSION

It is my proposal, then, to encourage women who are developing skills, approaches, and communication strategies for leadership positions in academe to consciously and contemplatively enter a liminal space of multiple approaches to understanding the questions of leadership wisdom. My own experience and narrative, as well as those of the women I interviewed, were grounded in contemplative inquiry of women's pathways toward leadership. Paradox and some mystery involved with transcending and especially transgressing previously held perceptions, boundaries, and beliefs about women's lives and pathways are essential aspects of this approach to developing women's leadership skills, communication strategies, and opportunities in academic settings. In addition, narrative knowledge and wisdom ways of knowing can be developed across the individual and then collaborative narratives by those who feel called to or find themselves walking, or sometimes even stumbling, along the pathways toward leadership in academia. We need to make our own stories count and own them so we can pass on our narrative knowledge to those following us. We need to do our best so that no voices or stories go unheard or are silenced. More and more stories from marginalized communities need to be included, and especially those narratives that challenge the social or institutional power structures. Most important, and the reason why the project of this volume is itself so important, is providing the spaces for us all to communicate our own and others' stories, to create the best opportunities for those narratives to be heard and to contribute to new or deeper ways of knowing more about leadership and about communication about it.

My sincere thanks and acknowledgement for the help in developing this bibliography by the graduate students in a graduate course on "Program Leadership: Institutional Contexts," especially Stefan Vogel and Mariia Khorosheva.

NOTES

1. Anne Anderson, "Out of the Everywhere into Here: Rhetoricity and Transcendence as Common Ground for Spiritual Research," in *Toward a Spiritual Research Paradigm*, ed. J. Lin, R. L. Oxford and T. Culham (Charlotte, NC: Information Age Publishing, Inc., 2016), 25–53; Heewon Chang, *Autoethnography as Method* (Walnut Creek, CA: Left Coast Press, 2008); Heewon Chang, Faith Ngunjiri, and Kathy-Ann C. Hernandez, *Collaborative Autoethnography* (Walnut Creek, CA: Left Coast Press, 2013); Michael Dyson, "My Story in a Profession of Stories: Auto Ethnography—An Empowering Methodology for Educators," *Australian Journal of Teacher Education* 32, no. 1 (2007): 35–48; Alice Hendrickson Eagly and Linda L. Carli, *Through the Labyrinth: The Truth about How Women Become Leaders* (Harvard Business Press, 2007); Oren Ergas, "Knowing the Unknown: Transcending the Educational Narrative of the Kantian Paradigm through Contemplative Inquiry," in *Toward a Spiritual Research Paradigm*, ed. J. Lin, R. L. Oxford and T. Culham (Charlotte, NC: Information Age Publishing, Inc., 2016), 1–23; Ramdas Lamb, "Using a Spiritual Research Paradigm for Research and Teaching," in *Toward a Spiritual Research Paradigm*, ed.

J. Lin, R. L. Oxford and T. Culham (Charlotte, NC: Information Age Publishing, Inc., 2016), 55–75; Jing Lin, Rebecca L. Oxford, and Edward J. Brantmeier, *Re-envisioning Higher Education: Embodied Pathways to Wisdom and Social Transformation* (Charlotte, NC: Information Age Publishing, Inc., 2013); Cara Meixner, "Locating Self by Serving Others," in *Re-envisioning Higher Education:Embodied Pathways to Wisdom and Social Transformation,* ed. J. Lin, R. L. Oxford, and E. J. Brantmeier (Charlotte, NC: Information Age Publishing, Inc., 2013), 317–334.

2. Mary Wildner-Bassett, *The Unbreakable Place Inside: The Courage, Grit, and Wisdom of Women's Leadership in Academic/Alternative Contexts* (In preparation, n.d.).

3. Wendy Wang, "Women and Leadership: Public Says Women Are Equally Qualified, but Barriers Persist," Pew Research Center-Social and Demographic Trends, last modified January 14, 2015, https://www.pewsocialtrends.org/2015/01/14/women-and-leadership/.

4. Eagly and Carli, *Through the Labyrinth: The Truth about How Women Become Leaders.*

5. Barbara Crosby, *Teaching Leadership: An Integrative Approach* (New York, NY: Taylor Francis, 2016).

6. Mike Pedler, "Leadership, Risk and the Imposter Syndrome," *Action Learning: Research and Practice* 8, no. 2 (2011): 89–91.

7. Jing Lin, Rebecca L. Oxford, and Tom E. Culham, *Toward a Spiritual Research Paradigm: Exploring New Ways of Knowing, Researching and Being* (Charlotte, NC: Information Age Publishing, Inc., 2016).

8. Anderson, "Out of the Everywhere into Here," 25–53.

9. Ibid., 25–53.

10. Ibid., 25–53.

11. Mary Catherine Bateson, *Composing a Life* (Grove Press, 1989); Andrew Zuckerman, *Wisdom* (Auckland, New Zealand: PQ Blackwell Ltd., 2008); Cynthia Bourgeault, *The Wisdom Way of Knowing: Reclaiming an Ancient Tradition to Awaken the Heart* (San Francisco, CA: Jossey-Bass, Wiley Imprint, 2003).

12. Jing Lin, Rebecca L. Oxford, and Edward J. Brantmeier, *Re-Envisioning Higher Education: Embodied Pathways to Wisdom and Social Transformation* (Charlotte, NC: Information Age Publishing, Inc., 2013).

13. Linda Smircich and Gareth Morgan, "Leadership: The Management of Meaning," *Journal of Applied Behavioral Science* 18, no. 3 (1982): 257–273.

14. Brent D. Ruben, Richard De Lisi, and Ralph A. Gigliotti, *A Guide for Leaders in Higher Education: Core Concepts, Competencies, and Tools* (Stylus Publishing: LLC, 2016).

15. Sharon Marcus, "We're Not Even Close," *Chronicle of Higher Education*, last modified 2018, https://www.chronicle.com/interactives/the-awakening.

16. Marcus, "We're Not Even Close."

17. Mary W. Gray, "The AAUP and Women," *Academe* 101, no. 1 (2015): 46–53.

18. Maggie Doherty, "Something Has to Give," *Chronicle of Higher Education*, last modified 2018, https://www.chronicle.com/interactives/the-awakening.

19. L. Salzillo, "Thousands of American Women and Men Repudiate Trump with Personal Stories of #WhyIDidntReport." *Dailydos.com.* September 21, 2018, https

://www.dailykos.com/stories/2018/9/21/1797539/-Hashtag-WhyIDidn-tReport-begins-to-explode-on-Twitter-by-women-and-men.

20. Zoe Greenburg, "What Happens to #MeToo When a Feminist Is Accused?" *New York Times*, August 13, 2018, https://www.nytimes.com/2018/08/13/nyregion/sexual-harassment-nyu-female-professor.html.

21. Judith Butler, "Judith Butler Explains Letter in Support of Avital Ronell," *Chronicle of Higher Education*, August 20, 2018, https://www.chronicle.com/blogs/letters/judith-butler-explains-letter-in-support-of-avital-ronell/.

22. Lisa J. Brown, "Forward," in *Gender, Communication, and the Leadership Gap. Women and Leadership: Research, Theory, and Practice*, ed. Carolyn Cunningham, Heather M. Crandall, and Alexa MacKellar Dare (Charlotte, NC: Information Age Publishing, 2017).

23. Lynn Butler-Kisber, *Qualitative Inquiry: Thematic, Narrative and Arts-Informed Perspectives* (London, UK: Sage, 2010).

24. Butler-Kisber, *Qualitative Inquiry*, 64.

25. Neil Hooley, "Critical Narrative Inquiry: Respecting Australian Indigenous Knowledge in the Regular Classroom," Paper presented at the British Educational Research Association Annual Conference, University of Warwick, 1–4 September 2010.

26. Crosby, *Teaching Leadership*.

27. Ibid.

28. Ibid., 25.

29. Ibid.

30. Sayantani DasGupta, "Listening as Freedom: Narrative, Health, and Social Justice," in *Health Humanities Reader,* ed. T. Jones, D. Wear and L. Friedman (Piscataway, NJ: Rutgers University Press, 2014).

31. Bateson, *Composing a Life*; Mary Catherine Bateson, *Composing a Further Life: The Age of active Wisdom* (New York, NY: Vintage Books, Division of Random House, Inc., 2010).

32. Bateson, *Composing a Further Life*.

33. Mary Uhl-Bien, Russ Marion and Bill McKelvey, "Complexity Leadership Theory: Shifting Leadership from the Industrial Age to the Knowledge Era," *The Leadership Quarterly* 18, no. 4 (2007): 298–318.

34. Bateson, *Composing a Further Life*.

35. Eagly and Carli, *Through the Labyrinth*, 68–76.

36. Bourgeault, *The Wisdom Way of Knowing*, 355–358.

37. Bateson, *Composing a Life*; Bateson, *Composing a Further Life*, 233.

38. Chip Conley, *Wisdom At Work: The Making of a Modern Elder* (New York, NY: Penguin Random House Currency, 2018).

39. J. Watson, "Autoethnography," in *Encyclopedia of Life Writing: Autobiographical and Biographical Forms,* ed. M. Jolly (London, UK: Fitzroy Dearborn Publishers, 2001).

40. Lamb, "Using a Spiritual Research Paradigm for Research and Teaching."

41. Ibid., 57–58.

42. Ibid.

43. Ibid., 65.

44. Bourgeault, *The Wisdom Way of Knowing*.
45. Ibid., 360–361.
46. Ibid., 426–427.

BIBLIOGRAPHY

AAUP. 2016. "Women in the Academic Profession." AAUP Issues. Updated November 19, 2017. https://www.aaup.org/issues/women-academic-profession.
Anderson, Anne W. "Out of the Everywhere into Here: Rhetoricity and Transcendence as Common Ground for Spiritual Research." In *Toward a Spiritual Research Paradigm*, edited by Jing Lin, Rebecca Oxford, and Tom Culham, 25–53. Charlotte, NC: Information Age Publishing, 2016.
Astin, Alexander. W. *Leadership Reconsidered: Engaging Higher Education in Social Change*. Battle Creek, MI: Kellogg Foundation, 2000.
Bateson, Mary Catherine. *Composing a Life*. New York, NY: Grove Press, 1989.
Bateson, Mary Catherine. *Composing a Further Life: The Age of Active Wisdom*. New York, NY: Vintage Books, Division of Random House, 2010.
Bolden, Richard, Georgy Petrov, and Jonathan Gosling. "Distributed Leadership in Higher Education: Rhetoric and Reality." *Educational Management Administration and Leadership*, 37, no. 2 (2009): 257–277.
Bolman, Lee G., and Joan V. Gallos. *Reframing Academic Leadership*. San Francisco, CA: Jossey-Bass, 2011.
Bourgeault, Cynthia. *The Wisdom Way of Knowing: Reclaiming an Ancient Tradition to Awaken The Heart*. San Francisco, CA: Jossey-Bass, Wiley Imprint, 2003.
Brown, Lisa J. "Forward." In *Gender, Communication, and the Leadership Gap*, edited by Carolyn Cunningham, Heather M. Crandall, and Alexa M. Dare. Charlotte, NC: Information Age Publishing, 2017.
Bryman, Alan. "Effective Leadership in Higher Education: A Literature Review." *Studies in Higher Education*, 32, no. 6 (2007): 693–710.
Chang, Heewon. *Autoethnography as Method*. Walnut Creek, CA: Left Coast Press, 2008.
Chang, Heewon, Faith W. Ngunjiri, and Kathy Ann Hernandez. *Collaborative Autoethnography*. Walnut Creek, CA: Left Coast Press, 2013.
Chronicle of Higher Education Series. 2018. "The Awakening: Women and Power in Academe." Chronicle.com. Updated March 13, 2019. https:/www.chronicle.com/interactives/the-awakening.
Conley, Chip. *Wisdom At Work: The Making of a Modern Elder*. New York, NY: Penguin Random House Currency, 2018.
Crosby, Barbara C. *Teaching Leadership: An Integrative Approach*. New York, NY: Taylor Francis, 2016.
Cunningham, Carolyn, Heather Crandall, and Alexa Dare, eds. *Gender, Communication, and the Leadership Gap*. Charlotte, NC: Information Age Publishing, 2017.
DasGupta, Sayantani. "Listening as Freedom: Narrative, Health, and Social Justice." In *Health Humanities Reader*, edited by Therese Jones, Delese Wear and Lester Friedman, 251–260. Piscataway, NJ: Rutgers University Press, 2014.

de Bot, Kees, Wander Lowie, and Marjolijn Verspoor. "A Dynamic Systems Theory Approach to Second Language Acquisition." *Bilingualism, Language and Cognition*, 10, no. 1 (2007): 7–21.

Denzin, Norman K. *Interpretive Autoethnography*. Los Angeles, CA: Sage, 2014.

Doherty, Maggie. "Something Has to Give." *Chronicle of Higher Education*, 2018. Updated March 18, 2019. https://www.chronicle.com/interactives/the-awakening.

Dooley, Kevin J. "A Complex Adaptive Systems Model of Organization Change." *Nonlinear Dynamics, Psychology, and Life Sciences* 7 (1997): 2–10.

Drath, Wilfred, and Charles Palus. *Making Common Sense: Leadership as Meaning-Making in a Community of Practice*. CCL Report No. 156, Center for Creative Leadership, 1994.

Dyson, Michael. "My Story in a Profession of Stories: Autoethnography: An Empowering Methodology for Educators." *Australian Journal of Teacher Education*, 32, no. 1 (2007): 35–48.

Eagly, Alice H., and Linda L. Carli. *Through the Labyrinth: The Truth About How Women Become Leaders*. Boston, MA: Harvard Business School Press, 2007.

Ergas, Oren. 2016. "Knowing the Unknown: Transcending the Educational Narrative of the Kantian Paradigm through Contemplative Inquiry." In *Toward a Spiritual Research Paradigm*, edited by J. Lin, R. L. Oxford and T. Culham, 1–23. Charlotte, NC: Information Age Publishing.

Field, Andy T. "How 3 Colleges Changed their Sexual-Assault Practices in Response to a National Survey." *Chronicle of Higher Education*, October 11, 2018. Updated October 26, 2018. https://www.chronicle.com/article/How-3-Colleges-Changed-Their/244777.

Gray, Mary. "The AAUP and Women." *Academe*, 101, no. 1 (2015): 46–52.

Greenberg, Zoe. 2018. "What Happens to #MeToo When a Feminist is Accused?" *New York Times*, August 13, 2018. Updated August 18, 2018. https://www.nytimes.com/2018/08/13/nyregion/sexual-harassment-nyu-female-professor.html.

Gzemski, Sarah. "An Interview with Rita Dove." *University of Arizona Poetry Center*, October 26, 2016. Updated November 17, 2017. http://poetry.arizona.edu/blog/interview-rita-dove.

Hooley, Neil. "Critical Narrative Inquiry: Respecting Australian Indigenous Knowledge in the Regular Classroom." *Paper Presented at the British Educational Research Association Annual Conference*. Warwick, UK: British Educational Research Association, September 3, 2010.

Jones, Sandra, Geraldine Lefoe, Marina Harvey, and Kevin Ryland. "Distributed Leadership: A Collaborative Framework for Academics, Executives, and Professionals in Higher Education." *Journal of Higher Education Policy and Management*, 34, no. 1 (2012): 67–78.

Kafka, Alexander. "Are Students Learning Anything about Love Here?" *Chronicle of Higher Education*. November 20, 2016. Updated October 8, 2018. https://www.chronicle.com/article/Are-Students-Learning/238449.

Kezar, Adriana, and Jaime Lester. "Supporting Faculty Grassroots Leadership." *Research in Higher Education*, 50, no. 7 (2009): 715–740.

Kezar, Adriana, and Cecile Sam. 2010. "Special Issues: Understanding the New Majority of Non-Tenure Track Faculty in Higher Education: Demographics, Experiences, and Plans of Action." *ASHE Higher Education Report*, 36, no. 4 (2010): 1–133.

Lamb, Ramada's. "Using a Spiritual Research Paradigm for Research and Teaching." In *Toward a Spiritual Research Paradigm*, edited by Jing Lin, Rebecca L. Oxford and Tom Culham, 55–75. Charlotte, NC: Information Age Publishing, 2016.

Larsen-Freeman, Diane. "Complex Dynamic Systems: A New Transdisciplinary Theme for Applied Linguistics." *Language Teaching*, 45, (2012): 202–214.

Larsen-Freeman, Diane, and Lynne Cameron. *Complex Systems and Applied Linguistics*. Oxford, UK: Oxford University Press, 2008.

Leiter, Brian. "Blaming the Victim is Apparently OK When The Accused in a Title IX Proceeding is a Feminist Literary Theorist." *Leiter Reports: A Philosophy Blog*, June 10, 2018. Updated June 20, 2018. https://leiterreports.typepad.com/blog/2018/06/blaming-the-victim-is-apparently-ok-when-the-accused-is-a-feminist-literary-theorist.html.

Lichtenstein, Benjamin B., Mary Uhl-Bien, Russ Marion, Anson Seers, James Douglas Orton, and Craig Schreiber. "Complexity Leadership Theory: An Interactive Perspective on Leading in Complex Adaptive Systems." *Emergence: Complexity and Organization*, 8, no. 4 (2006): 2–12.

Lin, Jing, Rebecca L. Oxford, and Edward J. Brantmeier, eds. *Re-envisioning Higher Education: Embodied Pathways to Wisdom and Social Transformation*. Charlotte, NC: Information Age Publishing, 2013.

Lin, Jing, Rebecca L. Oxford, and Tom Culham, eds. *Toward a Spiritual Research Paradigm: Exploring New Ways of Knowing, Researching, and Being*. Charlotte, NC: Information Age Publishing, 2016.

Marcus, Sharon. "We're Not Even Close." *Chronicle of Higher Education: The Awakening: Women and Power in the Academy*, 2018. Updated August 18, 2018. https:// www.chronicle.com/interactives/the-awakening.

Marshall, Steven J., Janice Orrell, Alison Cameron, Agnes Bosanquet, and Sue Thomas. "Leading and Managing Learning and Teaching in Higher Education." *Higher Education Research and Development*, 30, no. 2 (2011): 87–103.

Meixner, Cara. "Locating Self by Serving Others." In *Re-envisioning Higher Education: Embodied Pathways to Wisdom and Social Transformation*, edited by Jing Lin, Rebecca L. Oxford and Edward J. Brantmeier, 317–334. Charlotte, NC: Information Age Publishing, 2013.

Pedler, Mike. "Leadership, Risk, and the Imposter Syndrome." *Action Learning: Research and Practice*, 8, no. 2 (2011): 89–91.

Ruben, Brent, Richard De Lisi, and Ralph A. Gigliotti. *A Guide for Leaders in Higher Education: Core Concepts, Competencies, and Tools*. Sterling, VA: Stylus Publishing, LLC, 2017.

Salzillo, Leslie. "Thousands of American Women and Men Repudiate Trump with Personal Stories of #WhyIDidntReport." Dailydos.com, September 21, 2018. Updated October 6, 2018. https://www.dailykos.com/stories/2018/9/21/1797539/-Hashtag-WhyIDidn-tReport-begins-to-explode-on-Twitter-by-women-and-men.

Savonick, Danika, and Cathy N. Davidson. "Gender Bias in Academe. An Annotated Bibliography of Important Recent Studies." *hastac.org*, January 26, 2015. Updated May 1, 2018. https://www.hastac.org/blogs/superadmin/2015/01/26/gender-bias-academe-annotated-bibliography-important-recent-studies.

Simkins, Tim. "Leadership in Education: 'What Works' or 'What Makes Sense'?" *Educational Management Administration and Leadership*, 33, no. 1 (2005): 9–26.

Smircich, Linda, and Gareth L. Morgan. "Leadership: The Management of Meaning." *Journal of Applied Behavioral Science*, 18, no. 3 (1982): 257–273.

Uhl-Bien, Mary, Russ Marion, and Bill McKelvey. "Complexity Leadership Theory: Shifting Leadership from the Industrial Age to the Knowledge Era." *The Leadership Quarterly*, 18, no. 4 (2007): 298–318.

van Ameijde, Jitse D., Patrick C. Nelson, Jon Bilsberry, and Nathalie van Meurs. "Improving Leadership In Higher Education Institutions." *Higher Education*, 58, no. 6 (2009): 763–779.

Wang, Wendy, et al. "Women and Leadership: Public Says Women are Equally Qualified, but Barriers Persist." pewsocialtrends.org, January 14, 2015. Updated October 10, 2018. http://www.pewsocialtrends.org/2015/01/14/women-and-leadership/.

Warrell, Margie. "Glass Ceiling or Glass Cage? Breaking Through the Big- gest Barrier Holding Women Back." *Forbes.com*, August 4, 2013. Updated September 29, 2018. https://www.forbes.com/sites/margiewarrell/2013/08/04/glass-ceiling-or-glass-cage-breaking-through-the-biggest-barrier-holding-women-back/#56ad70a53101.

Watson, Julia. "Autoethnography." In *Encyclopedia of Life Writing: Autobio- graphical and Biographical Forms*, edited by Margaretta Jolly. London, UK: Fitzroy Dearborn, 2001.

Wildner-Bassett, Mary. n.d. *The Unbreakable Place Inside: The Courage, Grit, and Wisdom of Women's Leadership in Academic/Alternative Contexts*. In Preparation.

Zajonc, Arthur. *Meditation as Contemplative Inquiry: When Knowing Becomes Love*. Great Barrington, MA: Lindisfarne Books, 2010.

Zuckerman, Andrew. *Wisdom*. Auckland, NZ: PQ Blackwell, Ltd., 2008.

Index

advice, 44, 46, 61, 75, 76, 77, 79, 80, 83, 84, 87, 91, 131, 138, 202, 207, 221; ad hoc, 146; maternity leave;82, 77–80, 93; messages, 85, 86, 90, 92, 93; professional, 61
alternative logics, 133, 135
Amoah, Jewel, 108
assertive accommodation, 17
assertive communication, 17
authoethnographic, 136

Bakhtin, Mikhail, 178
Bass, Bernard M., 56, 57
benevolent sexism, 198
Black feminism, 32, 104, 107, 109, 110, 111, 112, 113, 120, 121, 177
Black feminist epistemology, 38
Black feminist theory, 108, 109
Black feminist thought, 107, 108, 110, 113
Black intelligentsia, 116, 117; Black women's intelligentsia, 112, 113, 114, 115, 117, 118
Black public sphere, 112, 113
Black women, 2, 3, 5, 38, 41, 42, 44, 45–49, 55, 64–66, 103–5, 107–21
Black women in academia, 105, 107, 109, 110, 112, 117
bounded reality, 17

bullying, 138, 139, 140, 226
Buzzanell, Patrice, 135, 154
bystander interpersonal communication, 17

certain/uncertain dialectic, 179
Chaffee, Steven, 175, 176
Christian, 178, 191, 194, 200, 208
#Cite Black Women, 118
#Cite Black Women Sunday, 118
collaborative communication, 17
communicative messages, 90
community colleges, 4, 53, 54, 55, 59, 62, 64, 67, 68
complex dynamic systems, 227
constant comparative analysis (CCA), 84
contemplative inquiry, 217–19, 227–31
Cooper, Anna Julia, Project on Gender, Race & Politics in the South, 104–7, 118, 124
credibility, 10, 43, 66, 85, 119, 120, 161, 183, 192, 208

department chair, 38, 39, 43, 76, 79, 89, 226
dialogue, 13, 38, 48, 118
discursive positioning theory, 81
double-bind, 162–68

double-bindedness, 5, 10, 28
Dubin, Robert, 175, 176
dwelling place, 6, 191, 192, 193, 208

ecology, 193
emotion, 218
emotional dimensions, 229
emotional intelligence, 63
emotional investment, 140
emotional knowledge center, 218, 230
emotional labor, 154
emotional support, 83, 164, 182
emotional time, 162
eternal work, 5, 152, 158, 163, 166, 167, 168
ethos, 191, 192, 193, 196, 204, 208
explication, 175

faculty members, 39, 76, 78, 81, 87, 139, 198, 199, 203, 224; eminent, 223; first-year, 201; male, 45; older, 47; women, 83, 88, 154, 220
family leave, 61, 75, 80, 197–200
Family Medical Leave Act (FMLA), 5, 75, 76, 137, 199
feminist ecological ethos, 6; approach, 193, 209; ethē, 192
feminist organizational communication, 133
feminist theory, 132. See also Black feminist theory
friendship, 4, 38, 47–50, 113, 138

gender and leadership, 2, 14, 15, 17, 20, 27, 28, 38, 43, 46, 62, 142, 152, 153, 162, 167, 168, 194, 205, 217, 219, 220, 225, 228, 229. See also women leaders
gendered status quo, 18
GIF (graphics interchange format), 38
grounded theory, 5, 157

harassment, gender-based, 133, 222, 226; sexual, 61, 220, 221, 222, 223, 224
Harré, Rom, 82, 90

Harris Perry, Melissa, 103–7, 116. See also MHP
higher education, 12, 15, 16, 24, 48, 49, 54, 55, 60, 64, 65, 67, 133, 138, 144, 151, 152, 176, 177, 180, 181, 194, 206, 219, 221; Black women in, 116; leadership pipeline in, 11; women in, 131
Hill Collins, Patricia, 107, 112, 113, 117, 119, 121
historically Black colleges and universities (HBCUs), 3, 4, 10, 12, 13, 14, 18, 19, 20, 22, 24–29, 37, 39, 47, 48, 49, 111
honor people, 183
horizontal matriarchy, 5, 152, 158, 160, 165, 168
humor, 17, 38; sense of, 28

implicit bias, 61, 62
included/excluded dialectic, 178
inclusive communication, 17
industrial-organizational psychology, 53, 55, 57, 58, 59
inoculation theory, 177
inspire others, 184
institutional awareness, 203, 204
intellectual activism, 108, 112
internalized oppression, 10, 27
intersectionality, 108, 118, 133, 143, 176, 177, 185, 223

laboring communication, 152, 158, 163, 168
labyrinth as metaphor, 157
Langenhove, Luk, V., 82
leadership, 55; church, 196; executive, 61; higher ed, 64, 152; ladder, 61
leadership, and gender. See gendered leadership
leadership, and women, 152
leadership development, 68, 114, 217, 225
leadership style(s): affiliative, 24; coaching, 24; commanding, 24;

democratic, 24; pacesetting, 24; visionary, 24
liminality, 6, 22, 162

MacGregor Burns, James, 56
manage self, 184
maternity, 4, 76–78, 93, 136, 137
maternity leave, 4, 76–93, 136, 137
maternity leave policy, 82, 83, 88
mediated communication, 48; computer mediated, 249
mentoring, 4, 10, 11, 23, 25, 26, 28, 38, 39, 46, 48, 65, 79, 87, 109, 158, 160, 185, 196, 197, 201, 202, 203, 204, 205, 208
microaggression(s), 17, 51, 221
microassaults, 17
microinsults, 17
microinvalidations, 17
MHP, 103. *See also* Melissa Harris Perry
Moses, Yolanda, 15, 110, 111
multiple ways of knowing, 230

narrative, 6, 15, 108–10, 193, 206, 221, 222, 227, 231; gendered, 153; knowledge, 220, 225; language, 226; lived, 117; personal, 39, 80, 81, 83, 84, 90, 92, 93, 133, 135, 139, 140, 143; sharing, 104, 107
narrative knowledge, 220, 225
#Nerdland, 106
#NerdlandForever, 106
network(s), 5, 48, 49, 54, 60, 61, 64, 76, 83, 135, 202, 204; Black women's, 120, 121; old boy, 15, 135, 202, 204; personal, professional, support, 143, 144; on social networking sites, 178, 181
networking, 28, 46
nonlinear developmental experiences, 227, 228

parental leave policy, 136, 199; Seaver college faculty, 199

personal narrative, 38, 133
Pfau, Michael, 175, 176, 185
predominately White institutions (PWIs), 11, 13, 16, 26
pregnancy, 75, 76, 79, 85, 87, 89–92, 138; disruption of, 138
project implicit, 62

reflexivity, 5, 132, 134, 137, 143, 144
relational dialectics, 178
resilience, 5, 27, 88, 91, 93, 132, 135, 140, 143, 144
role models, 13, 62, 84, 89, 225

self-advocacy, 203, 204
self-and other-weighted/self-and other-liberated dialectic, 181
sensemaking, 81, 83, 91, 92, 132, 133, 134, 135, 136, 144
sensemaking theory, 91, 92, 132, 133, 176, 178, 200, 206, 226; and positioning, 134–36, 144

take command, 183, 184
tenure, 11, 16, 51, 60, 63, 76, 78, 79, 83, 85, 87, 90, 92, 154, 195; clock, 198, 199; decisions, 197; post-tenure, pre-tenure, 137, 104, 164, 203; tenured, 39, 104, 154, 205, 220; tenured professors, 223; tenure track, 136, 164, 176; untenured, 44
theological assumptions, 194
theories of leadership, 218
think manager-think male model, 16
top management team (TMT), 20
transcendence, 6, 218, 219, 227, 228
transformational executive leadership, 53, 55, 59, 60, 65; at community colleges, 59
transformational leadership, 54, 56, 57; communication styles, 66; transformative style, 155
transformational leadership theory, 56
transgression, 140, 229
Twitter, 103, 118, 222

unconscious bias, 16, 61
upper echelon(s) theory, 5, 9, 14, 19, 20, 27, 60

Walker, Alice, 58; Walker's, Alice, womanist theory, 176. *See also* womanist theory
womanism, 55, 58
womanist, 5, 58, 176, 177, 182; approach, 185; educators, 59
womanist theory, 6, 53, 55, 58, 59
women leaders, 60. *See also* gendered leadership
women of color, 4, 10, 15–18, 28, 40, 54, 60–62, 64–66, 105–7, 110, 133
work-life balance, 75–77, 79–84, 86–89, 91, 92, 93, 119, 163, 196, 203
work-life integration, 204

About the Editor

Jayne Cubbage (PhD, Howard University) is an assistant professor in the Department of Communications at Bowie State University where she teaches courses in the Graduate Program in Organizational Communication. In addition to earning a doctorate in mass communication and media studies from Howard University, she also holds an MA in liberal arts from the University of Pennsylvania, an MS in journalism from the Columbia University Graduate School of Journalism and a BA in communications/broadcast journalism from Temple University. After working for a number of years as a journalist in various news outlets, she entered the academy where she has previously taught graduate level courses in broadcast journalism and mass communication including media literacy, broadcast news writing, mass communication theory, and television production. Her research interests include media audiences of color, media literacy, news literacy, and the impact of social networking on society. She has published numerous journal articles and book chapters on these topics in various publications. In addition to this work, she has also served as editor for the volume, *Handbook of Research on Media Literacy in Higher Education Environments* (IGI Global, 2018), and she will author the upcoming work on journalism and news literacy education titled, *Business As Usual?: Examining the Need to Reshape News Literacy for Effective Academic and Industry Outcomes* (Lexington Books, 2020). She also serves as reviewer for the *Journal of Media Literacy Education* and the *Howard Journal of Communication*, and she is the current vice chair of the African American Communication and Culture Division of the National Communication Association. She has also served as president of the Maryland Communication Association.

About the Contributors

L. Simone Byrd (PhD, Howard University) is the chair and an associate professor of public relations in the Department of Communications at Alabama State University, where she teaches public relations/advertising, media entrepreneurship, and strategic social media courses. She has completed fellowships through the Tow-Knight Center for Entrepreneurial Journalism's Disruptive Educators program (CUNY Graduate School of Journalism) and the Scripps Howard Entrepreneurial Journalism Institute in the Walter Cronkite School of Journalism and Mass Communication at Arizona State University. She has also participated in the Advertising Education Foundation's (AEF) Visiting Professors' program at Havas Worldwide and Cake Group New York, as well as in the Corporate Communications division at Regions Financial Corporation in Birmingham, Alabama through the University of Alabama's Plank Center for Leadership in Public Relations' Educator Fellowship program. Previously, she has received grants for entrepreneurial programs from the Downtown Business Association (DBA) and the Alabama Press Association. Currently, she is the editor of the forthcoming book, *Advancing Journalism Education through Social Entrepreneurship Cultivation*, which is scheduled for release by IGI Global in early 2020.

Nicole Files-Thompson (PhD, Howard University) is the chair and an associate professor of communications in the Department of Communications at Lincoln University in Pennsylvania. In addition to her doctorate, she holds an MA in moving image studies from Georgia State University and a BA in film production from Howard University. Dr. Files-Thompson's research engages the theory, practice, and epistemology of marginalized groups through interdisciplinary paradigms and the scholarship of teaching and learning. She focuses on constituting, touring, and empowering marginalized identities, via the critical questions: What constitutes marginalized identities? How do spaces (touring) negotiate marginalized identities? How are marginalized identities empowered/self-empowered? As a teacher-scholar, Nicole has developed and taught two dozen courses across the communications discipline and delivered numerous lectures and conference presentations. As a teacher-scholar, she most values her work in undergraduate research, study abroad, and pathways to graduate school for students of color. She holds leadership positions in the National Communication Association (NCA) and the Eastern Communication Association (ECA). Her most recent publications can be found in the journals of *Critical Studies in Media Communication* and *Women & Language*. She is a 2019/2020 Fulbright U.S. Core Scholar conducting her participatory action teaching and research project: "Race, Culture, Sustainability and New Media: Implications for Applied Digital Communication and the Informal and Sharing Tourism Economies in Jamaica" in Jamaica, West Indies.

Karima A. Haynes (EdD, Bowie State University) is an assistant professor of journalism in the Department of Communications at Bowie State University where she serves as coordinator of the print journalism concentration and advisor to *The Spectrum* student newspaper. She is a former adjunct professor of journalism at Biola University, Regent University, University of Maryland at College Park, and Bowie State University. Before transitioning into the classroom, Haynes was a staff writer for the *Los Angeles Times*, *Ebony,* and the *Providence Journal-Bulletin*. She has two decades of experience as a newspaper reporter, magazine writer, essayist, book reviewer, copy editor, news editor, photo editor, and page designer. She holds a bachelor's degree in mass communication with a concentration in print journalism from Clark Atlanta University and a master's degree in journalism from the Medill School of Journalism at Northwestern University. She earned a doctorate in education from Bowie State University.

John W. Howard, III (PhD, Bowling Green State University) is a professor in the School of Communication at East Carolina University. His research has examined the intersections among gender, soldiering, and nationalism and is transitioning into studies of gender and leadership. His publications have appeared in *Women's Studies in Communication, Human Communication Research, Women & Language* and *International and Intercultural Communication Annual*.

Pavitra Kavya (MS, The University of Texas at Arlington) is a graduate instructor and doctoral student in the Department of Communication at the University of Oklahoma. Her research focuses on organizational and leadership communication with an emphasis on understanding how people can derive more energy and joy at their workplace.

Sheryl Kennedy Haydel (PhD, APR, University of Southern Mississippi) earned her doctorate in mass communication and holds an MBA from the University of Wisconsin–Madison, with a focus on marketing and an MA in journalism from the University of Maryland, College Park. She is an assistant professor of public relations at Louisiana State University's Manship School of Mass Communication. She has worked as a journalist and a public relations executive and serves as a media expert on the use of social media in political and social movements and campaigns. She was awarded the Individual Award of Excellence by the Public Relations Society of America's New Orleans chapter. She also serves as the director of the National Association of Black Journalist's high school program J-SHOP. She has held both academic and administrative positions at several institutions. Her research examines the role of the Black collegiate press in the Civil Rights era and the use of social media today for both branding and activism.

Michael W. Kramer (PhD, University of Texas) is professor and chair in the Department of Communication at the University of Oklahoma. His research focuses on the socialization/assimilation process of people joining and leaving organizations, along with leadership and decision-making. His work examines both employees and volunteers.

Stephanie Norander (PhD, Ohio University) joined the University of North Carolina at Charlotte in 2015 as the executive director of Communication Across the Curriculum program and as associate professor in the Department of Communication Studies. Her work with CxC focuses on enhancing college curriculum and student learning through emphasis on communication. In this role, she consults with administration faculty to create, implement, and assess innovative curricular changes that are integrated within the broader goals unique to each discipline. Her scholarship, teaching, and mentorship focus on organizational communication, communication pedagogy, and professional development in higher education. She has published in the *Journal of Applied Communication Research*, *Management Communication Quarterly*, *Health Communication*, and *Communication Studies* in addition to numerous book chapters.

Laura C. Prividera (PhD, Bowling Green State University) is a professor of communication, East Carolina University. She is also the associate dean of graduate studies for the College of Fine Arts and Communication and the associate director of the School of Communication. Her research examines the social constructions of gender, race, and/or power in military, health, and pedagogical contexts. Her research has appeared in *Women's Studies in Communication, Health Communication, Women & Language, International and Intercultural Communication Annual,* and *The Howard Journal of Communications.*

Shearon D. Roberts (PhD, Tulane University) earned her doctorate in Latin American studies with a focus on Caribbean media. She also earned her master's in mass communication from Louisiana State University. Roberts is an assistant professor of mass communication and affiliate faculty member in African American and Diaspora studies at Xavier University of Louisiana. Her research examines media representation and media discourse of race and gender. She worked as a reporter covering Latin America and the Caribbean, and now studies Caribbean media systems in addition to working with journalists and media professionals in the region. She coauthored two books on the role of the media in post-disaster recovery and has published in leading mass communication and interdisciplinary studies journals. She was awarded for her excellence in teaching by the Association for Journalism in Education and Mass Communication's International Communication Division and History Division and served as president of the Southwest Education Council for Journalism and Mass Communication.

Jeanetta D. Sims (PhD, APR, University of Oklahoma) is dean of the Jackson College of Graduate Studies and professor in the Marketing Department of the College of Business at the University of Central Oklahoma (UCO), where she has taught undergraduate and graduate courses in marketing and communication. At UCO, she oversees admissions, recruitment, and degree programs for graduate students as well as manages the education and learning lab for undergraduate students. She is the first woman to serve as the dean of the Graduate College in the university's more than 125-year history. She has received university and national awards for her teaching and scholarship and has made more than 100 conference and professional presentations, many of which have included undergraduate students as coauthors. Her scholarship is in the areas of strategic communication, social influence and persuasion, and workforce diversity, and her research appears in multiple book chapters as well as in the *Journal of Communication, Journal of Public Relations Research, Human Communication Research, Atlantic Marketing Journal, Corporate Reputation Review, Communication Research, Communication Monographs, Western Journal of Communication,* and *Council on Undergraduate Research Quarterly.* Sims has been elected or appointed to national leadership positions in all disciplines associated with her research including the National Communication Association, North American Management

Society, Marketing Management Association, MBAA International, and the Council on Undergraduate Research.

Sarah Stone Watt (PhD, The Pennsylvania State University) is an associate professor of communication at Pepperdine University. She served as chair of the Ad Hoc Committee on Women Faculty at Pepperdine's Seaver College helping it gain recognition as a standing faculty committee. She is currently serving as the first female divisional dean of communication at Pepperdine University and president of the Association for Communication Administration. She would like to thank Maire Mullins for her work in creating the Committee on Women Faculty and for sharing resources for the chapter. She would also like to thank Kendra Killpatrick and Lauren Amaro for their work on the committee and their feedback on earlier drafts of her chapter.

Mary E. Wildner-Bassett (PhD, University of Bochum, Germany) earned her BA at Eastern Illinois University, her MA (with distinction) at the University of Wisconsin—Madison, and her PhD at the University of Bochum, Germany. After teaching at the *Zentrales Fremdspracheninstitut* at the University of Hamburg for two years, she joined the faculty of the University of Arizona in 1986. Her publications include *Improving Pragmatic Aspects of Learners' Interlanguage* (Tübingen, 1984), *Zielpunkt Deutsch* (New York, 1992), and many contributions to anthologies and journals on foreign language pedagogy and second language acquisition, applied linguistics, and computer-mediated second language communication, and leadership theory and practice. She served as the Dean of the College of Humanities from 2008 to 2016. She is also a faculty member of the Inter-disciplinary PhD Program in Second Language Acquisition and Teaching (SLAT), and a member of the faculty of the newly formed Department of Public and Applied Humanities. She enjoys teaching culture and language courses on the under-graduate level, as well as leadership and professional development, pedagogy, and applied linguistics theory and application courses on the graduate level.